For ...
ing ...
par ...
the ...
fea...   ...therapy proved a
wel...   ...d quickly achieved an established
position on the lists of many counselling and psychotherapy courses.

This revised and expanded edition takes into account further
developments in the profession over the last decade, and its bibliographical material has been brought completely up to date. It is an
invaluable reference book for any professional working in the mental
health field and a first-class introduction for anyone interested in
psychotherapy.

'The authors have succeeded in providing an up-to-date and integrated account of the many different forms of psychotherapy without
taking sides in some of the controversies which still exist in this
field. They describe the different forms of psychoanalysis, analytical
psychotherapy, group therapy, family and marital therapy,
behavioural psychotherapy, social therapy, transactional analysis,
action techniques like encounter groups, bio-energetics and psychodrama. [Each] is discussed in its historical, theoretical and practical
context. . . . Medical students, general practitioners, psychiatrists,
students of psychotherapy, both medical and non-medical, and also
experienced psychotherapists will all find it a pleasure to read and a
useful and practical guide to modern psychotherapeutic concepts and
practice.'
                Dr Heinz Wolff, *Group Analysis*, review of the first edition

'In a way that no large textbook does, *Introduction to Psychotherapy*
provides an invaluable sorting out of any confusion, concentrating
on the therapy end of psychotherapy.'
                Louis Appleby, *British Journal of Psychiatry*, review of the
                                                                first edition

The authors are both psychoanalysts, and the first edition arose from
their experience of working and teaching together as consultant
psychotherapists at St Mary's Hospital and Medical School, London.
Dennis Brown is now associated with the Institute of Group Analysis
and Jonathan Pedder is Consultant Psychotherapist at the Maudsley
Hospital, London.

INTRODUCTION TO PSYCHOTHERAPY

An Outline of Psychodynamic
Principles and Practice

Second Edition

Dennis Brown

and

Jonathan Pedder

TAVISTOCK/ROUTLEDGE
London and New York

First published in 1979 by Tavistock Publications
Reprinted twice
Reprinted 1987

Second edition published in 1991
by Routledge
11 New Fetter Lane, London EC4P 4EE

Simultaneously published in the USA and Canada
by Routledge
a division of Routledge, Chapman and Hall, Inc.
29 West 35th Street, New York, NY 10001

Phototypeset by Intype, London
Printed in Great Britain by Mackays of Chatham PLC, Kent

British Library Cataloguing in Publication Data
Brown, Dennis 1928–
Introduction to psychotherapy : an outline of
psychodynamic principles and practice. – 2nd edn.
1. Psychotherapy
I. Title
616.8914

Library of Congress Cataloging in Publication Data
Brown, Dennis.
Introduction to psychotherapy : an outline of psychodynamic
principles and practice / Dennis Brown and Jonathan Pedder.—2nd
edn.
p.   cm.
Includes bibliographical references.
Includes indexes.
1. Psychodynamic psychotherapy. I. Pedder, Jonathan. II. Title.
[DNLM: 1. Psychoanalytic Theory. 2. Psychotherapy. WM 420
B8772i]
RC489.P72B76 1991
616.89′14—dc20
DNLM/DLC   91–419
for Library of Congress   CIP

ISBN 0–415–06443–0
0–415–06444–9 (pbk)

CONTENTS

CONTENTS

FOREWORD TO THE FIRST EDITION

We have often been asked to recommend some introductory text in psychotherapy, and felt at a loss. Freud's (1911–15) papers on technique or Bion's (1961) *Experiences in Groups* make fascinating if not essential reading for those embarking as therapists on formal individual or group psychotherapy. Yet we were not aware of any one book – certainly none written by psychotherapists in this country – which answered basic questions such as 'what is psychotherapy about?'. This book was born out of our attempts to answer that question and to convey something about dynamic psychotherapy to medical students and newcomers to psychiatry from various disciplines. We have been unashamedly simple in trying to delineate basic psychodynamic principles in Part I. We have described something of the range of methods based on these principles in Part II. We do not say very much about the practice of psychotherapy – that is 'how to do it' – for we believe that this can only really be learnt by embarking on the journey of exploration, either as patient or as therapist under regular supervision.

We are both psychoanalysts working part-time as consultant psychotherapists in a teaching hospital psychiatric unit where all current opinions and treatments in psychiatry are represented. In our view Freud's work and psychoanalysis have provided the spring which has nourished all later forms of dynamic psychotherapy, be they individual or group psychotherapy, marital or family therapy. With the proliferation of new forms of psychotherapy, both within and beyond the fringe of psychiatry, we felt some simple statement of basic aims and principles would help to orientate ourselves and, we hope, others.

The psychoanalytic view is, among other things, essentially a developmental one. It sees man against the evolutionary background of his long pre-human and especially more recent primate past; it sees man in his historical and social setting; and lastly, it sees each individual in his own unique cultural and developmental context, which is our particular concern in psychotherapy. The present can only be understood in terms of the past. The past is ever-present.

Dennis Brown
Jonathan Pedder
St Mary's Hospital, London
1979

FOREWORD TO THE SECOND EDITION

The Foreword to the original edition began by explaining that there was a gap in the literature. Before 1979 there were no simple, comprehensive, introductory texts to which we could direct newcomers to psychotherapy. Clearly others were thinking along similar lines. In the same year Bloch (1979) edited a multi-author book describing a range of psychotherapies, and Malan (1979) produced *Individual Psychotherapy and the Science of Psychodynamics* which sums up in vivid everyday language years of working in this field at the Tavistock Clinic. In 1979 Whiteley and Gordon published a comprehensive survey of group methods in psychiatry, and Storr an account of his own approach to individual psychotherapy. Six years later came Casement's (1985) lively description of the interactional process in psychoanalytic work. This was followed by Symington's (1986) Tavistock Clinic lectures on key contributors to modern psychoanalysis; and Frosh's (1987) exposition of different developments within the psychoanalytic tradition, and their implications for culture. All of these we would recommend to students of psychotherapy at different points in their professional development. Two other books have appeared which are of particular use to lay-people and potential patients: Knight's *Talking to a Stranger* (1986) and *Families and How to Survive Them* by Skynner and Cleese (1983).

Nevertheless, the steady interest in our book leads us to believe that it is of continuing value. It is regularly included in the reading lists for trainee psychotherapists, psychiatrists, and other professionals, and it is often recommended to interested lay-people and prospective patients.

It was meant as a brief and simple introductory overview to

the many forms of dynamic psychotherapy and their origins in and links with psychoanalysis. It traces the similarities and differences between individual, group, family, and social therapy and some of the 'newer' therapies. In updating we have continued the original aim, taking into account developments since 1979, including valuable new additions to the literature for those who want to read further, with an expansion of the sections on selection and research. We have touched on shifts in the social climate and impending changes in the organization of psychotherapy practice and training in the United Kingdom.

We wish to thank Dr Robin Skynner and Dr Don Montgomery for their comments on family therapy and gender assignment respectively; and Mrs June Ansell for her ready and efficient help with the manuscript.

Dennis Brown, Institute of Group Analysis, London
Jonathan Pedder, Maudsley Hospital, London
1991

PROLOGUE

What is psychotherapy? It is essentially a conversation which
involves listening to and talking with those in trouble with the
aim of helping them understand and resolve their predicament.

Mrs A. went to her family doctor complaining of bouts of
tearfulness and acute attacks of panic and anxiety. She considered herself to be happily married and could not account
for her symptoms. Her doctor regarded them as the manifestations of a depressive illness, that is to say of some physical
disease process of presumed, but as yet undiscovered, bio-
chemical origin. He prescribed various anti-depressants in
turn, but these had little effect; rather Mrs A. began to feel
that something dreadful was happening to her which nobody
understood and that perhaps she was even going mad.

Are there other ways of trying to understand such problems?

When an alternative point of view of her predicament was
sought, the following aspects of her life and its history
emerged. Her symptoms had begun when her only child (a
daughter) was six years old. At that time Mr and Mrs A. had
been discussing the possible need for their daughter to go
away to a boarding school because of their remote situation in
the country. It seemed likely that Mrs A. was far more
depressed over this projected separation than she herself had
acknowledged. Moreover when Mrs A. herself had been six,
her parents had separated and she was sent to live with an
aunt, so that the possibility of separation from her daughter
in the present had re-awakened the heartache of her own
separation from her parents at the same age long ago. When
Mrs A. reviewed her recent experiences in relation to the past
within this suggested framework, her tearfulness and anxiety

began to make sense to her and to resolve. She no longer felt prey to some mysterious and frightening disease process beyond her control, but began to recognize herself as a dis-eased person, discomforted by a situation that only too painfully reminded her of the past.

Symptoms that patients bring to doctors may often be the expression of unacknowledged feelings in the present, which remain hidden because of painful associations with the past. One of the central aims of this book will be to try and provide a framework within which to understand such problems and begin to approach them psychotherapeutically.

Part I

PSYCHODYNAMIC PRINCIPLES

Part I

PSYCHODYNAMIC PRINCIPLES

INTRODUCTION TO PSYCHODYNAMIC PRINCIPLES

It is widely agreed that about a third of all patients who go to their family doctor have primarily emotional problems. About half of these will have a recognizable psychiatric condition, but only one in twenty is referred to a psychiatrist (Shepherd *et al.* 1966). A still smaller proportion will be referred on for formal psychotherapy in the National Health Service. However, psychotherapy at varying levels will be appropriate for some patients at each of these stages. We will discuss these different levels and types of psychotherapy in further detail in Part II. The term 'psychotherapy' is used in both *general* and *special* ways; it includes forms of treatment for emotional and psychiatric disorders that rely on talking and the relationship with the therapist, by contrast to physical methods of treatment (such as drugs and electroconvulsive treatment (ECT)).

Most psychotherapy in the *general* sense is carried out informally in 'heart-to-heart' conversations with friends and confidants. 'Everyone who tries to encourage a despondent friend or to reassure a panicky child practices psychotherapy' (Alexander 1957:148). Well-worn sayings such as 'a trouble shared is a trouble halved' make sense to everyone. Such help is more likely to be sought in the first instance from the most readily available help-giver, such as a friend, family doctor, priest, or social worker, rather than from a psychiatrist or psychotherapist. In the medical field, the art of sympathetic listening has always been the basis of good doctoring. There has been a risk that this might be overshadowed by the enormous advances in the physical sciences and their application to medicine, which have resulted in an increasing attention to *diseased* organs, to the relative neglect of the whole *dis-eased* person. In the last generation, interest has shifted back again to the individual as the focus of stress in the family and community, and psychodynamic principles have helped to illuminate this interest. While many acute and major forms of psychiatric disturbance are best treated by physical methods, many less acute forms of neurotic and interpersonal problem are helped more by psychotherapeutic methods. We shall take up this issue further in Part II, particularly in discussing Levels of Psychotherapy (p.87) and Selection (p.180).

There have been two major approaches to psychotherapy in the *special* sense, competing with varying mixtures of rivalry and cooperation. These are *Psychodynamic Psychotherapy* which has its historical origins in Freud's work and psychoanalysis; and *Behavioural Psychotherapy* which involves an application of learning theory and stems from the work of Pavlov on conditioning principles. Here we are principally concerned with psychodynamic rather than with behavioural psychotherapy (though see p.90 and p.187). Basically the approach of the behaviourist is that of a physiologist or psychologist studying the patient from the *outside*. He* is interested in externally observable, and preferably scientifically measurable, behaviour and in manipulating (by suitable rewards and punishments) deviant or mal-adaptive behaviour towards some agreed goal or norm. Behaviour therapy and, more recently, cognitive therapy have been studied and pursued mostly by non-medically qualified psychologists with a background in experimental psychology.

The dynamic psychotherapist is more concerned to approach the patient empathetically from the *inside* in order to help him to identify and understand what is happening in his inner world, in relation to his background, upbringing, and development; in other words, to fulfil the ancient Delphic injunction 'Know Thyself'. Dynamic psychotherapy has been the major influence in the field of mental health, and has appealed more

---

* Where the sex of therapist or patient is not defined by the particular circumstance described, he or she is referred to, for convenience, in the masculine gender throughout this book; such references should be taken to imply male or female.

to doctors, social workers, and those psychologists immersed in the complexities of relationships with patients or clients; and to patients wishing to understand themselves and their problems rather than to seek symptomatic relief alone. Sutherland (1968:509) wrote, 'By *psychotherapy* I refer to a personal relationship with a professional person in which those in distress can share and explore the underlying nature of their troubles, and possibly change some of the determinants of these through experiencing unrecognized forces in themselves'. (Those unclear about the respective training and role of psychiatrists, psychologists, psychoanalysts and psychotherapists, will find them briefly described in Appendix 1 (p.202).)

It will be our contention that all forms of dynamic psychotherapy stem from the work of Freud and psychoanalysis, which has produced many offshoots. Jung and Adler broke away before the First World War to found respectively their own schools of Analytical Psychology and Individual Psychology. Between the wars Melanie Klein and Anna Freud, applying analytic ideas to the treatment of disturbed children, developed Child Analysis. During the Second World War, Foulkes and others explored the use of analytic ideas in groups and developed Group Psychotherapy. Since the last war further developments have included Family, Marital, and Social Therapy. Rogers in the Encounter Movement, developments such as Bioenergetics and other forms of Humanistic and Integrative Therapy have been seeking new ways of encouraging direct interpersonal contact to help free people from a sense of isolation and alienation from themselves and others. (Some of the links between these developments are traced in the 'family tree' of *Figure 10* on p.176.)

However, despite their apparent diversity and different theoretical formulations, we believe that all schools of dynamic psychotherapy hold in common certain key concepts. These basic concepts are briefly introduced now and each expanded in later sections of Part I.

People become troubled and may seek help with symptoms or problems when they are in *Conflict* over unacceptable aspects of themselves or their relationships. This is contrasted with the traditional medical model where symptoms are viewed solely as an expression of disordered anatomy and physiology.

Aspects of ourselves which so disturb us that they give rise to *Anxiety* or *Psychic Pain*, may be consciously rejected, and become more or less *Unconscious*. We all employ a number of *Defence Mechanisms* to help us deny, suppress, or disown what is unacceptable to consciousness; these may be helpful or harmful.

Unacceptable wishes, feelings, or memories may arise in connection with basic *Motivational Drives*. The different psycho-dynamic schools may disagree over how to categorize human drives or as to which are the more important and troublesome, for example, those associated with eating, attachment, sexual, or aggressive behaviour. The central importance of conflict over drives and their derivatives remains.

Again, although *Phases of Development* have been conceptualized in a number of different ways, it is widely agreed that how we handle our basic drives begins to be determined in infancy by the response of others to our basic needs and urges, at first mother and subsequently others of emotional significance (father, siblings, teachers etc.)

It is in *Models of the Mind*, or theorizing about the structure of the psyche, that greatest disagreement has arisen. Freud revised his theories several times. At first he saw the psyche simply in terms of Conscious and Unconscious levels; later he introduced the concepts of Super-ego, Ego, and Id. In more anthropomorphic terms Berne (1961) has written of the Parent, Adult, and Child parts of each one of us. Yet running throughout is the idea of different psychic levels, with the potentiality of conflict between them.

Aspects of the *Therapeutic Relationship* will be the last of the theoretical principles dealt with, and it naturally leads us on to the area of practice. We will distinguish between the therapeutic or working alliance, transference, and counter-transference.

HISTORICAL BACKGROUND TO DYNAMIC PSYCHOTHERAPY

Before developing each of these concepts further, let us take a brief look at the historical background, where we are much indebted to Whyte (1962) and Ellenberger (1970). Although it might be broadly true to say that all modern forms of dynamic psychotherapy – whether psychoanalysis, individual or group psychotherapy, family or marital therapy – stem from the work of Freud and others at the turn of the century, it would not be true to say that Freud 'invented' psychotherapy.

The idea of a talking cure through catharsis of feelings is at least as old as the Catholic confessional, and current idioms such as 'getting it off your chest' testify to the widespread belief in its value. A work on Aristotle's concept of catharsis was being much talked of in Vienna in the 1880s and may have influenced Breuer and Freud.

Nor is there anything revolutionary in the idea that we are often in conflict with our feelings, wishes, and memories. In 1872, a year before Freud entered university, Samuel Butler wrote in *Erewhon*, 'there are few of us who are not protected from the keenest pain by our inability to see what it is that we have done, what we are suffering, and what we truly are. Let us be grateful to the mirror for revealing to us our appearance only' (p.30).

Writers down the ages, who have attempted to penetrate the complexities of human motivation, have known this intuitively. Shakespeare, for example, recognized unconscious conflicting wishes in *King Henry IV Part II*:

Prince: I never thought to hear you speak again.
King: Thy wish was father, Harry, to that thought.

Pascal (1623–62) in his *Pensées*, knew that 'The heart has its reasons, which reason knows not.' Rousseau (1712–78) wrote: 'There is no automatic movement of ours of which we cannot find the cause in our hearts, if we know well how to look for it there.' Writing in the 1880s Nietzsche anticipated Freud: ' "I did that" says my memory. "I could not have done that" says my pride, and remains inexorable. Eventually the memory yields.' (Whyte 1962).

Freud's achievement, combining the gifts of a great writer and scientist, was to address these ideas to a medical context, in such a way that they have since been given continuing and increasing, if at times faltering, attention. Yet as we have said, Freud did not invent psychotherapy any more than Darwin invented evolution. Darwin too had his forerunners; yet it was the added impetus of the evidence he collected for his new

7

causal explanations of natural selection that gave a fresh weight to already current ideas on evolution.

Ellenberger (1970) has traced the ancestry of dynamic psychiatry from its origins in exorcism, and its evolution through magnetism and hypnotism. In primitive times, disease, both psychic and somatic, was commonly thought to be due to possession by evil spirits. Healing was expected to follow exorcism and such treatment was naturally in the hands of religious leaders or traditional healers, such as shaman, witchdoctor, or priest.

Alternatively, it was thought that disease might arise from infringement of taboos. Then again cure was expected to follow confession and expiation. Healing by exorcism and confession have both played a part in the Christian tradition. However, with the rise of Protestantism, the Catholic monopoly on confession weakened. There was an increased interest among laymen and some doctors in the idea of the 'pathogenic secret' formerly disclosed only to priests at confession. Thus, by around 1775, the time of the last executions for witchcraft in Europe, exorcism as practised by priests such as Gassner (1727–79) gave way to new techniques (which we would now call hypnotism) stemming from the work of the physician Mesmer (1734–1815). We might now find Mesmer and his disciples fanciful in their theories about magnetic fluid as an explanation for what they called magnetic sleep, but increasing attention was being paid to such phenomena. The similarity between magnetic sleep and natural somnambulism (or sleepwalking) led to its being first re-named artificial somnambulism, and later hypnotism.

Towards the end of the nineteenth century there was further acceleration of interest in all sorts of psychic phenomena (which we would now see as different examples of dissociation within the psyche) such as hypnotism, spiritism, mediumistic trances, automatic writing, and states of multiple personality, all of which suggested split-off unconscious psychic processes. Phenomena that were formerly thought to be caused by possession and therefore to be cast out by exorcism, were now attributed to unconscious agencies to be reached and revealed by hypnosis. Accounts of possession were replaced by clinical accounts of multiple personality. In 1882 the Society for Psychical Research was founded in London to examine such phenomena. In the same year Charcot gave an important lecture to the Academy of Sciences in Paris, which brought a fresh respectability to hypnosis in medical circles, and helped to dispel some of the scepticism psychiatrists had felt towards it.

Throughout the century there was an increasing interest among writers in such phenomena, particularly that of dual or multiple personality, a well-known example being Stevenson's 'The Strange Case of Dr Jekyll and Mr Hyde', published in 1886. By the 1880s there was also considerable interest in the importance of repression of emotional and instinctual life in determining human conduct. For example, Schopenhauer (1788–1860) had already anticipated psychoanalysis; in Freud's own words, 'not only did he assert the dominance of the emotions and the supreme importance of sexuality but he was even aware of the mechanism of repression' (Freud 1925:59). Benedikt (1835–1920), a Viennese physician known to Freud and Breuer, was among the first medical men to show that the origin of neuroses, and especially hysteria, often lay in a painful pathogenic secret involving sexual life. Nietzsche (1844–1900) emphasized the importance of instincts and their sublimation, of self-deception, and of guilt feelings arising from the turning inwards of impulses which could not be discharged outwardly. In literature and drama, Dostoevsky and Ibsen were exploring the theme of passions that lurk below the surface and dictate the actions of men who may deceive themselves that they are rational beings. Ellenberger (1970) refers to this as the 'unmasking trend' that was prevalent in the 1880s. Ibsen's father had been a miner and his tomb bears a miner's hammer put there by his son to emphasize how he had continued the mining tradition of digging away at what lies below the surface – similar to the archaeological metaphor that Freud was fond of using.

Sigmund Freud (1856–1939) was born at Freiberg in Moravia (now part of Czechoslovakia); when he was a child of four, his family moved to Vienna. At school Freud had some leanings towards the law, but as he wrote in his autobiography, 'the theories of Darwin, which were then of topical interest, strongly attracted me, for they held out hopes of an extraordinary advance in our understanding of the world' (Freud 1925:8). He was later to consider that, following Copernicus and Darwin, he had himself delivered the next major blow to man's self-esteem and view of his central position in the universe. It was on hearing Goethe's essay on Nature read aloud just before he left school that he decided to become a medical student.

He entered medical school in Vienna in 1873 but did not qualify until 1881 because he spent some time working in Brucke's physiology laboratory while considering an academic career. This was a time when the rational hope was high that the ills of mankind would yield to discoveries in the basic physical sciences. Brucke had pledged, 'No other forces than the common physical and chemical ones are active within the organism' (Jones 1953:45). Freud shared that hope early on and to some extent never quite abandoned it since he later predicted the more recent vogue for drug treatments in psychiatry.

The name of Freud is so closely identified with psychoanalysis that it is often not appreciated that he had an established reputation in several other fields before he ever came to his psychoanalytical discoveries in his forties. As a medical student he had already done original work in neuro-histology; as a neurologist he had made important contributions and written on aphasia and on cerebral palsies in children; and he had been associated with the introduction of cocaine, as a local anaesthetic, into ophthalmology.

Freud felt that he encountered some anti-semitic prejudice in his ambition to achieve a University post. He had been engaged for some time and, impatient to get married, determined to set up in private practice in Vienna as a neurologist. Before doing so he obtained a grant to visit Charcot in Paris in 1885.

Charcot at that time was giving grand theatrical demonstrations of neurological cases, amongst which there were hysterical patients with paralysis, anaesthesia, or bizarre gait. Freud noted that Charcot could create by hypnosis conditions identical to those arising spontaneously in hysterical patients; and that furthermore the pattern of the disorder followed the idea in the patient's mind rather than any anatomical pathway (as seen in true neurological lesions). He therefore concluded that if hysterical disorders could be created by hypnosis, perhaps they arose spontaneously by auto-suggestion – in response to any idea in the patient's mind of which he was *unconscious*.

Freud returned to Vienna and married in 1886. In his private neurological practice he found the usual proportion of hysterical cases. At first he used hypnosis as a treatment in an attempt to dispel the symptoms by suggestion. Through his association with Breuer, with whom he wrote the *Studies on Hysteria* (Breuer and Freud 1895), he found that by putting patients into a light hypnotic trance and encouraging them to talk freely, memories or ideas might be revived that had become repressed and unconscious because unacceptable to conscious ideals. Hence the 'talking cure', as one of Breuer's patients called it, was born. Freud soon abandoned hypnosis as a direct method of intervention and not long after gave up using it even as a lubricant to talking, relying entirely on *free association* (p.110). The couch remained in psychoanalysis because of its original use by Freud the neurologist, and its convenience to Freud the hypnotist. He himself slowly withdrew from the position of active examining doctor seated beside the patient, to that of the accompanying ally on a voyage of self-examination sitting behind him. He thereby rescued the neurotic patient from the public theatre of Charcot's demonstrations, where only external appearances counted, and created the private space of the analytic consulting room where hitherto unmentionable and unacknowledged aspects of man's inner world could be faced. Symptoms that had been taken for meaningless by-products of as-yet-undiscovered somatic processes could be viewed afresh as meaningful communications about inner states of conflict.

THE CONCEPT OF CONFLICT

The idea of conflict over unacceptable aspects of the self is central to the psychodynamic point of view. Indeed, the very expression 'dynamic' itself was borrowed by Freud from nineteenth century physics to convey the idea of two conflicting forces producing a resultant third force acting in another direction.

So long as medical students were only taught anatomy and physiology (or their subdivisions, such as histology and biochemistry) it was natural that doctors should try to understand their patients' complaints as symptoms of disordered anatomy and physiology and, therefore, treat them physically. But there is widespread agreement that about one-third of all patients presenting to doctors have primarily emotional problems which cannot be understood in this way, with much resulting frustration to both patient and doctor. It is a romantic view to think that this is some new phenomenon due to the pressures of modern life; Cheyne, a London physician, writing in 1723, estimated that one-third of his patients had no organic disease.

If we bear in mind (as in the case of Mrs A., p.xi), that patients' complaints may not be symptoms of a discrete disease caused by an external agency alien to the person, but indicative of a conflict in someone who is dis-eased or alienated from a part of himself, we may be better equipped to understand the puzzling complaints of some people in distress. The discovery of micro-organisms in the last century was a vast advance in the understanding of disease, but also satisfied man's need to blame forces *outside* himself (an updating of devil theories of disease) rather than accept responsibility *within* himself.

The importance of conflict in human distress is not only relevant to psychiatry, but to the whole field of medicine. If a child complains of abdominal pain, this might well be symptomatic of a physical disorder such as appendicitis; or alternatively might be the child's way of saying that he does not want to go to school for some reason that he cannot acknowledge or admit for fear of adult reactions. A woman who complains of dysparunia (pain on intercourse) may have a painful somatic lesion such as a cervical erosion; or not want intercourse, but feel unable to say so. The problem may lie in her relationships rather than in her body. The level at which the conflict operates may be relatively conscious or deeply unconscious.

A young single woman went to her family doctor complaining that she was disgusted with her nose. He took this in a literal and anatomical sense and sent her to a plastic surgeon, who felt there was little abnormal with her nose and referred her for a psychiatric opinion. She herself then said that when she had first gone to the doctor she had felt that she was merely disgusted with her nose (the underlying conflict was still deeply unconscious). Now she had begun to realize she was really

disgusted with herself (the conflict was reaching consciousness) and particularly because of what she called
her lesbian feelings. One might go further and say that
some distaste for her own sexuality and genitalia had
undergone displacement upwards and become focused
on her nose.

This idea of conflict is not just a fanciful one dreamt up by
man to understand himself. Ethologists now well recognize its
importance in understanding animal behaviour. A bird exhibit-
ing territorial behaviour may approach another aggressively at
the edge of its territory, then become afraid, retreat and go on
to repeat the pattern of approach-avoidance conflict several
times; or it may turn aside and begin pecking at the ground
as an indirect outlet for the aggression. This behaviour, which
ethologists term re-direction, psychoanalysts call displacement
(p.29).

Which aspects of the self give rise to such conflict? We shall
discuss this at greater length in the section on motivation; but
a common misrepresentation of Freud is to assume that he
attributed all problems to sex, and thereby to dismiss psychoanalysis as culture-bound to bourgeois Vienna of the 1880s,
and not of general relevance. Indeed Freud found that many
of his female hysterical patients were suffering from sexual
conflicts, but it is instructive to quote his actual words about
this (1894:52): 'In all the cases I have analysed it was the
subject's sexual life that had given rise to a distressing affect
. . . Theoretically, it is not impossible that this affect should
sometimes arise in other fields; I can only report that so far I
have not come across any other origin.' Since then we have
indeed come to recognize the immense importance of conflict
'in other fields', for example, aggressive feelings, which may
be turned against the self (in depression and suicidal attempts)
or converted into psychosomatic symptoms (such as migraine
or hypertension) (see p.27–8).

Depression itself, or the grief that follows bereavement, or
some other loss vital to self-esteem, may not be consciously
acknowledged but find outlet instead in physical symptoms.
This commonly occurs when a patient presents symptoms at
the anniversary (possibly unacknowledged) of a bereavement.

It should not be thought that all forms of psychiatric disturbance can be explained as the result of conflict. There is almost certainly a considerable genetic predisposition to functional psychoses such as schizophrenia and manic-depression. There are also some rare forms of organic psychosis caused by physical cerebral dysfunction, i.e., by brain tumour or vitamin deficiency. In conditions such as borderline psychoses and profound character disorders, we are dealing with early 'harm inflicted on the ego by endowment, environment and vagaries of internal maturation, i.e., by influences beyond its control' (Anna Freud 1976) which impair the ego's strength and therefore its capacity to contain and manage primitive anxieties and impulses. Many forms of *trauma*, including early separation and loss (Bowlby 1973, 1980) and the many forms of *child abuse* (Bentovim *et al*. 1988), are increasingly recognized today. Early traumas have been shown to influence development and the effect of later trauma in studies of survivors of the Holocaust and other disasters (Pines 1986; Kestenberg and Brenner 1986; Menzies Lyth 1989; Garland 1991).

The concept of conflict is of more especial importance in understanding neurotic disorders, where we are dealing with the internal damage which the Ego in the later course of development has inflicted on itself by repression and other defences. Neurotic conflicts ultimately orginate in personal relationships during a person's formative years, which become internalized and determine the sort of relationships formed with others thereafter; though the outcome may depend on what is happening in current close relationships, as will be discussed especially in considering Family and Marital Therapy (p.136).

UNCONSCIOUS PROCESSES

Aspects of ourselves which conflict with consciously held ideals may be denied, suppressed or disowned and become more or less unconscious. It is preferable to think in terms of *different levels* of consciousness and use the word unconscious as an adjective rather than as a noun. We then avoid implying that there is a mysterious realm 'the unconscious' which is quite separate from the rest of the mind.

Something may be unconscious merely because we are not aware of it at a particular time, for example, the colour of our front door at the moment of reading these lines; or because we find it easier to function by suppressing disagreeable feelings or painful memories, though we might easily be reminded of them. These levels Freud called *preconscious*. Alternatively an idea may be unconscious because it is actively *repressed* owing to its unthinkable nature – a memory, fantasy, thought, or feeling which conflicts with our view of ourselves and of what is acceptable, and which would cause too much anxiety, guilt, or psychic pain if it were acknowledged. This level Freud called *dynamically unconscious*. Repression may weaken at times so that previously unconscious mental contents become manifest, usually modified by defensive elements, for example, during sleep in the form of dreams, at times of stress in the form of symptoms, or in the emergence of apparently alien impulses under the influence of drugs or alcohol.

The idea of different psychic levels parallels that of different neurological levels, with higher centres controlling and inhibiting more primitive ones which, in turn, might find expression if higher controls were relaxed. Freud, with his own neurological background, had always been impressed by the saying of the neurologist Hughlings Jackson (1835–1911): 'Find out all about dreams and you will have found out all about insanity.' In dreams and insanity we get the most direct insight into deeper levels of the psyche. Our idiom 'I wouldn't dream of it' seems to imply the idea of several levels, i.e., there are things we would dream of but not do; then more deeply, things we would not even let ourselves dream of.

Some philosophers have objected to Freud's ideas about the unconscious on the grounds that only conscious phenomena should be considered as mental events. Yet the idea of the Unconscious had been increasingly discussed throughout the nineteenth century. Psychologists such as Herbart (1776–1841) emphasized the conflict between conscious and unconscious ideas; and the philosopher Schopenhauer (1788–1860), anticipating Freud, wrote: 'The Will's opposition to let what is repellent to it come to the knowledge of the intellect is the spot through which insanity can break through into the spirit' (Ellenberger 1970:209).

As the authority invested in man's idea of God declined in Europe from the Middle Ages onwards, there was a corresponding increase in human self-awareness which reached a particular intensity around 1600. The word 'Conscious' first appeared in European languages in the seventeenth century. The dualism of Descartes (1596–1650), separating mind from body and thought from feeling, marked the high tide of this movement with its assertion that mental processes are limited to conscious awareness. This emphasis on rational thinking was one of the forces that led to the Enlightenment of the eighteenth century and many positive achievements in the spread of education and political freedom; but it devalued imaginative and emotional life so that a natural reaction was the Romantic movement of the early nineteenth century typified by poets such as Wordsworth, Keats, and Shelley. The idea of unconscious mental processes was 'conceivable around 1700, topical around 1800, and became effective around 1900' (Whyte 1962:63). By 1870 'Europe was ready to discard the Cartesian view of mind as awareness' (ibid.:165). If anything, Freud made the idea of the unconscious temporarily less popular by his early emphasis on its sexuality.

Perhaps the idea is now so much part of our thinking that no further argument is needed, but evidence in support of the notion of unconscious psychic activity comes from the following sources.

Dreams

Freud always regarded dreams as 'the royal road to the unconscious' and *The Interpretation of Dreams* (1900) as his greatest work, of which he wrote: 'Insight such as this falls to one's lot but once in a lifetime' (Freud 1900:xxxii). He drew a distinction between the often apparently absurd *manifest content* of a dream and the *latent content* hidden behind it by a censorship which could be by-passed by free association. Dreams were the 'disguised fulfilment of a repressed wish'. This wish-fulfilling function of dreams is a commonplace. Children dream of feasts or treats, adults of forbidden pleasures, or of lost persons or places they long to see again. Dreams may also be attempts to master unpleasant experiences or to solve problems. Rycroft (1979) emphasizes the creative and imaginative aspects of dreaming, rather than just the conflictual and neurotic, and regards dreaming as the non-discursive mode of communication of the non-dominant cerebral hemisphere.

Artistic and scientific creativity

Many writers, artists, and composers, in describing their own creative processes, have told of how they feel taken over by some inner force, not entirely within their conscious control. Often the creative process actually takes place during sleep or dreaming. Kekulé, wrestling with the problem of the structure of benzene, dreamt of a snake eating its tail and then immediately saw that the benzene molecule must have a ring structure (Findlay 1948). Coleridge is said to have conceived his poem 'Kubla Khan' while dozing under the influence of opium (Koestler 1964). The playwright Eugene O'Neill claimed to have dreamt several complete scenes and even two entire plays; he urged himself as he fell asleep by saying, 'Little subconscious mind, bring home the bacon' (Hamilton 1976). Mozart described in a letter the vivid experience of his own creative genius when his ideas seemed to flow into him at a rush: 'Whence and how they come, I know not – nor can I force them . . . Nor do I hear in my imagination the parts successively, but I hear them, as it were, all at once . . . All this inventing, this producing, takes place in a pleasing lively dream' (Quoted by Vernon 1970:55).

By contrast to the flash of inspiration experienced by Mozart, Bertrand Russell writes of a slower process of 'subconscious incubation' preceding the final sense of revelation:

> 'It appeared that after first contemplating a book on some subject, and after giving serious preliminary attention to it, I needed a period of subconscious incubation which could not be hurried and was if anything impeded by deliberate thinking . . . Having, by a time of very intense concentration, planted the problem in my subconsciousness, it would germinate underground until, suddenly, the solution emerged with blinding clarity, so that it only remained to write down what had appeared as if in a revelation.'
>
> (Quoted by Storr 1976:65)

Apart from the creative activity actually occurring in dreams, dramatists and writers have described how in a waking life too their characters emerge from within them with a life of their own. Pirandello, whose play *Six Characters in Search of an*

Author illustrates this process, wrote in his journal: 'There is someone who is living my life. And I know nothing about him' (see foreword to Pirandello 1954).

Hysterical symptoms

We have already seen how, on his visit to Paris, Freud developed the idea that hysterical conditions – paralysis, anaesthesia, ataxia – could be caused by an idea of which the patient was not conscious. This could arise from the suggestion of an outsider (by hypnosis) or from inside (by auto-suggestion). Such hysterical symptoms, Freud proposed, are constructed like dreams as 'compromises between the demands of a repressed impulse and the resistance of a censoring force in the Ego' (Freud 1925:45).

A young woman walked into the casualty department of a hospital complaining of weakness of her left arm. It transpired that she had just come from a psychotherapy group at the same hospital, where she had felt extremely angry with the male therapist sitting on her immediate *left*, but too frightened to say so. The weakness of the arm was a compromise between her wish to hit him and her fear of doing so, though she was then able to complain about him indirectly to the casualty doctor. It was necessary to know her story to explain this fully. She was angry with the therapist because he had just announced he was leaving the group. She had been abandoned as an infant and adopted from an orphanage by an elderly couple. They could not tolerate any 'bad behaviour', and if she were 'naughty' would threaten to send her back there.

Post-hypnotic phenomena

A subject may be hypnotized and given the suggestion that when he awakens he will forget consciously what the hypnotist has said, but that after an interval, when the hypnotist snaps his fingers, the subject will cross over to the window and open it. The subject awakes and, on being given the signal, opens the window. When asked why he did so, he looks briefly confused and then says that it was too warm in the room.

This illustrates how a complicated sequence of behaviour (opening the window) can be under the control of an idea (implanted by the hypnotist) of which the subject is not conscious and furthermore that when a conscious explanation is demanded, a rationalization follows (that it was too warm).

Parapraxes

When we make a slip of the tongue or forget something, it could be due to a simple mistake in the machine of the brain, but often, on further examination, as first suggested by Freud in the *Psychopathology of Everyday Life* (1901), it turns out to be emotionally motivated. For example, we may forget an appointment or the name of somebody we are annoyed with and wish to forget, but all this happens outside consciousness.

> A young woman had not been able to come to a meeting. Later she met the chairman and apologized, saying that, 'Dr X raped . . . I mean roped . . . me into doing something else'. Was this a simple mistake, or the expression of a wish, or most probably the expression of a resentful feeling of having been coerced into doing something against her will?

Beyond the 'psychopathology of everyday life' many everyday phenomena indicate the co-existence of different levels of consciousness. Drivers often find they are 'miles away' in their thoughts, especially on motorways, and 'come back' to find they have been negotiating traffic without conscious awareness. People commonly find themselves singing a popular song for no apparent reason, until they discern an associated link triggered by a preceding mood, impulse, word, or preconscious perception.

Subliminal perception, selective attention, and perceptual defence

Below a certain threshold, light or sound stimuli can lead to psycho-physiological responses without consciously being noticed. Thirty years ago there was a furore in the USA about the use of subliminal advertising; messages like 'Eat Popcorn' were flashed onto cinema screens for a fraction of a second,

19

an exposure too short for recognition by the public, but long enough for sales of popcorn to be dramatically increased. There is a great deal of experimental evidence (Dixon 1971) that the threshold of perception is influenced by motivation; below a certain level of stimulation we can see what we want to see, but be blind to what we do not want to see (for example, words giving rise to fear or embarrassment flashed momentarily onto a screen). It would seem that there is a selective and discriminating filter mechanism at work, which operates below the level of awareness in much the same way as Freud suggested that the censor operates in dreams.

Sometimes those fresh to the psychodynamic way of thinking question how remote events remain unconscious and dormant for years before causing any effects for good or ill, in the way that streams flow underground before suddenly breaking to the surface. This seems less of a mystery to writers such as Thomas Hardy who wrote 'I have a faculty for burying an emotion in my heart and brain for 40 years, and exhuming it at the end of that time as fresh as when interred' (Quoted by Gittings 1975:5).

ANXIETY AND PSYCHIC PAIN

Aspects of ourselves and our experience sometimes cannot be readily assimilated into our conscious view of ourselves and our world, because of the anxiety or psychic pain they arouse. The notion of psychic pain may at first seem strange to those used to thinking of any pain as physical. They may believe that pain is either real (physical) or imagined (psychological). However, any experience of pain is ultimately a psychic experience, whether the origin of the pain is somatic or psychological. Furthermore the experience of pain of physical origin depends on our mood and attention at the time; in the heat of battle severe wounds may pass unnoticed. The older English expression 'sore' unites the two realms of psyche and soma, since we talk of 'feeling sore' in both areas. We also speak of being injured in both body and feelings; and our idioms describing a problem as a 'headache' or a person as 'a pain in the neck' acknowledge that seemingly physical pain may reflect a relationship between psychic and somatic pain.

For brief periods we may be able to tolerate considerable

anxiety, for example, coping with an emergency, or to bear considerable psychic pain and depression, for example, following bereavement. Alternatively we may try to ward off such emotional discomfort by employing a number of defence mechanisms. Yet again, the stress may prove too great and defences fail; a state of decompensation follows and we may fall ill either psychically or somatically.

The experiencing of anxiety is not of course necessarily abnormal. Anxiety accompanies autonomic arousal, which is the normal response of an individual to threatening situations and prepares him for fight or flight. This has obvious original evolutionary survival value in the wild and we all still experience anxiety in competitive situations such as athletic competition, examinations, or interviews. This helps key up the individual for optimal performance; only if the anxiety is excessive or out of proportion is it mal-adaptive and abnormal. The anxiety aroused in a situation such as public speaking may be disturbing for the very reason that there is no motor outlet for its discharge.

The problem of anxiety and how we deal with it in ourselves is seen as central in most formulations of the origin of neurosis. Freud offered different formulations of the origin of anxiety in the early and later phases of his career. At first he thought defence caused anxiety, later that defence was provoked by anxiety.

His earlier model (1894) was a more physiological/hydraulic one; he suggested that anxiety was the expression of undischarged sexual energy or libido. A classic example would be an individual practising coitus interruptus (withdrawal during intercourse to avoid conception), whose undischarged sexual tensions were then thought to be expressed in the form of anxiety symptoms. Although the model has now generally been discarded, there are still situations in which it has application. For example in a situation of danger, where autonomic arousal is appropriate and has obvious survival value, we may be unaware of anxiety so long as we are occupied in taking avoiding action. When action is blocked or ended we may become more aware of anxiety. However, Freud (1926) later revised this view of anxiety (as undischarged libido) and came to see anxiety as the response of the ego to the threat of internal sexual or aggressive drives. Although the earlier model

21

of anxiety has largely been given up in relation to sexual drives, the idea of 'actual neurosis', the result of undischarged aggressive drives, is still useful in relation to psychosomatic disorders (McDougall 1974).

Bowlby has offered some very interesting comments on the connection between anxiety, mourning, and defence. A young child, who has developed an attachment to a mother-figure, when separated from her, shows distress in three recognizable phases of *protest*, *despair*, and *detachment*. Bowlby (1973:27) writes: 'the phase of *protest* is found to raise the problem of separation anxiety; *despair* that of grief and mourning; *detachment* that of defence. The thesis that was then advanced (Bowlby 1960) was that the three types of response – separation anxiety, grief and mourning, and defence – are phases of a single process and that only when they are treated as such is their true significance grasped.' Yet these three processes of separation anxiety, mourning, and defence were encountered in the reverse order by Freud. He first became aware of the significance of defence (Freud 1894); later of mourning (Freud 1917); and lastly came to the revised view of the significance of anxiety (Freud 1926).

Initially Freud was preoccupied with the problem of anxiety and the defences used against it as he observed them in the neurotic conditions he saw, such as hysterical, obsessional, and phobic states. Only later did he turn his attention to depression, which is a much larger clinical problem; in psychiatric practice about half of all patients seen are depressed. A simple way of stating the relationship between anxiety and depression is to say that whereas anxiety is the reaction to the threat of loss, depression is a consequence of actual loss.

It was not until 1917 in 'Mourning and Melancholia' that Freud drew attention to the similarities between bereavement and depression, such as sadness, despair, loss of interest in the outside world, and inhibition of activity. Whereas

'mourning is regularly the reaction to the loss of a loved person, or to the loss of some abstraction which has taken the place of one, such as one's country, liberty, an ideal and so on' (p.243); 'in melancholia, the occasions which give rise to the illness extend for the most part beyond the clear case of a loss by death, and include all those situations of being slighted, neglected or disappointed, which can import opposed feelings of love and hate into the relationship or reinforce an already existing ambivalence' (p.251).

In other words, in melancholia or depression the loss may not be an obvious external one, but more of an internal one involving a loss of self-esteem. Depression, for example, may follow failure to achieve some longed for ambition or position vital to self-esteem (Pedder 1982).

Another way of expressing this is to say that a painful discrepancy has arisen between the subject's ideal self or ego-ideal (myself as I would like to be) and his actual self (myself as I am). This discrepancy gives rise to a state of psychic pain (Joffe and Sandler 1965), to which there may be one of several responses. A normal response might be to protest, 'fight' rather than 'flight', to direct aggression against the source of pain. The subject may attempt to master the pain in an adaptive way, or in the case of a mature, robust individual, may be able to bear the pain and work through the ensuing disappointment and loss of self-esteem. Alternatively there may be one of several less healthy responses to this central state of unbearable psychic pain. If the wished-for state cannot be restored there may ensue a state of helplessness which Joffe and Sandler suggest (1965:395) may 'represent a fundamental psychobiological response which could be conceived of as being as basic as anxiety. It has its roots in a primary psychophysiological state which is an ultimate reaction to the experiencing of helplessness in the face of physical or psychological pain in one form or another.'

One response to this state of helplessness might be to give up and relapse into physical illness, described by Engel (1967) as the 'giving-up, given-up complex' which often precedes somatic disease. Another would be for the psychic pain to become converted into psychogenic bodily pain (Merskey and Spear 1967). A third is to relapse into depression itself.

Alternatively, defence mechanisms such as denial of a loss, may prove sufficient to cope with the pain – at any rate for a while.

A middle-aged woman presented with depression. She knew that her father had died when she was 10; she thought she believed what she had been told as a child that he had been reported missing, presumed dead, on active service during the war. This allowed her to go on hoping that perhaps after all he was not dead and might one day turn up, so that for 30 years she had hoped every knock on the door might be her father. During psychotherapy she one day recalled with horror a memory of her brother coming into the kitchen when she was 10 and saying, 'There's a man in the garage with blood all over him'. At that moment she knew that her father had killed himself but simultaneously denied the knowledge; the memory remained, though buried, for years. Only by painfully accepting the fact of his death and its horrifying circumstances could she begin to work through the process of mourning and to move forward again.

In the following section we consider further mechanisms of defence.

DEFENCE MECHANISMS

One way of dealing with aspects of the self, which, if consciously experienced, might give rise to unbearable anxiety or psychic pain, is by using a variety of defence mechanisms.

Everyone needs and uses defences at some time – the question is, 'to what extent and when?'. Sometimes, over-enthusiastic workers in psychiatry or its fringes appear to feel that no one should have any defences, regarding them as a modern form of sin; but an uninvited attack on someone's defences is as unjustified as any other form of assault. Another link with religious attitudes is the neurotic person's belief that it is as bad to sin in thought as in deed, so that there seems no alternative to either completely repressing a sexual or murderous feeling or acting on it. Maturity includes a capacity to acknowledge and tolerate such feelings within ourselves without acting on them except when appropriate.

Freud (1894) first introduced the term 'defence' to describe the specific defence mechanism operating in the cases of hysteria which he was then studying; he later termed this particular defence 'repression' and went on to describe others. By

1936 Anna Freud, his daughter, was able to list nine mechanisms of defence (regression, repression, reaction-formation, isolation, undoing, projection, introjection, turning against the self, and reversal). She added a tenth normal mechanism (sublimation) and one or two more (such as idealization and identification with the aggressor). Melanie Klein emphasized the defences of splitting and projective identification (Segal 1964) occurring in both normal and abnormal development. Our list of defences which follows is not exhaustive but made up of those which we find ourselves thinking of most commonly in everyday clinical work.

Repression

As described at the beginning of the previous section, we all at different times *suppress* inconvenient or disagreeable inner feelings, or totally *repress* what is unacceptable to consciousness. There is nothing abnormal or pathological about this, unless carried to extremes. Before the days of anaesthetics, a sensitive surgeon had to ignore or suppress feelings about the screams of patients in order to be effective. In extreme cases though, people who declare they have never felt angry or sexually aroused may be severely repressed.

Denial

We may deny or forget unpleasant external events; for example, an unhappy affair or an examination failure. It has been reported that following bereavement, up to 40 per cent of widowed people experience the illusion of the presence of their lost spouse and 14 per cent actually imagine they have heard or seen the lost spouse (Parkes 1972). This could be seen as a form of denial of a painful loss which is fairly normal, i.e., common in exceptional circumstances. The experience of a phantom limb following amputation (sensations suggesting the limb is still there) may have neurological origins, but may also be understood in the same way as a denial of the loss. This view is supported by reports that phantom limb is experienced more commonly after sudden and unexpected amputation (for example, following a road accident) than when there has been time to prepare for it psychologically. A more extreme form of denial occurs in cases of hysterical fugue or amnesia. In war-time, a soldier might come wandering back from the front line in a fugue state having had to obliterate the intolerable memory of seeing all his comrades killed by a shell. In peace-time, a person may appear in a casualty department declaring that he does not know his name, address, or anything about his past life. This may have followed some imbroglio or misde-meanour, such as knocking down his wife in a row or being discovered committing a fraud, the emotional consequences of which cannot be faced because of the shame and blow to self-esteem involved.

Projection

We commonly externalize unacceptable feelings and then attri-bute them to others: 'The pot calling the kettle black.' Christ knew this well: 'Why beholdest thou the mote that is in thy brother's eye, but considerest not the beam that is in thine own eye?' It must be as old as time to blame our neighbours, or neighbouring village, tribe, country, etc. for our own short-comings. This is a normal though tragic and dangerous human trait. In extreme forms it amounts to paranoia, for example, when individuals disavow their own hostile or sexual feelings but declare that others have hostile or sexual designs upon them.

Sometimes people behave as though not only feelings but important aspects of their own selves are contained in others; for example, the mother who unconsciously deals with the deprived-child part of herself in caring for her baby, may spoil it and prevent it growing towards greater independence. This helps mother to cope with the pain of her own frustrated longing for closeness and dependence, but the baby's develop-ing needs may be thwarted by mother seeing in the child an aspect of herself and provoking the child to enact it. In the technical language of Kleinian psychoanalysis this is an exam-ple of *projective identification* (Segal 1964; Ogden 1982).

Closely associated is the phenomenon of *splitting*, which involves the complete separation of good and bad aspects of the self and others, as illustrated by the perennial interest of children in heroes and monsters, good fairies and witches (Bettelheim 1975). Clinically we see it in splitting between good and bad feelings, between idealization and contempt of self and others.

Reaction formation

We may go to the opposite extreme to obscure unacceptable feelings, for example, excessive tidiness to hide a temptation to be messy. Extreme cleanliness may have its usefulness, for example, 'scrubbing up' in an operating theatre. Out of context it can be crippling, for example, in obsessional neurosis where many hours a day may be spent in washing rituals. The psychodynamic view of such obsessional states is that hostile feelings are usually being concealed. The person who carefully checks some magic number of times (three or seven) to make sure the gas taps are switched off may be terrified of giving way to unrecognized impulses to harm others. Instead he justifies his behaviour by saying that he is saving gas; this would be an example of rationalization.

Rationalization

Another example of this has already been given in discussing post-hypnotic phenomena (p.18) when the subject justifies an unconscious impulse and is unaware of its source. Our idiom 'sour grapes' is a third example deriving from Aesop's fable of the fox who could not reach the grapes and consoled himself with the rationalization that they were sour anyway.

Conversion and psychosomatic reactions

Unacceptable feelings or affects may be converted into physical symptoms as in hysterical conversion or psychosomatic disorders. We have already given a classical example of hysterical conversion above (p.18). Such hysterical disorders are becoming increasingly uncommon in developed societies, almost as if people now know that the deeper meaning would be rumbled. On the other hand, psychosomatic disorders have gained increasing attention in recent years. Bottling up of rage may, for example, contribute to an attack of migraine or to high blood pressure.

A conscientious but inhibited nursing sister could never

express her exasperation with her junior nurses whenever they made a silly mistake, for fear she would be too destructive. On such an occasion she would bottle up her rage and typically have an attack of migraine later that evening. During the course of psychotherapy she became more in touch with her anger and more able to express it. One day she reported that she had been able to tell off a nurse at fault and was surprised but delighted to find that no migraine had then followed.

In hysterical conditions there may be a symbolic element to the symptoms, which hints at an underlying fantasy, as in the example of the girl whose paralysed arm represented a defence against her wish to hit her therapist (p.18). Psychosomatic disorders are now less often thought to have this symbolic significance, but to occur in those restricted in their fantasy life, whose emotions are expressed physically and whose thinking tends to be concrete and conversation circumstantial. The word 'alexithymic' has been introduced to describe such people who have no words for their feelings (Nemiah and Sifneos 1970). These qualities are now recognized as occurring in post-traumatic states and in some people with addictive problems and sexual perversions as well as those prone to psychosomatic disorders and reactions (Taylor 1987).

Phobic avoidance

To a greater or lesser extent, we all avoid situations which arouse unpleasant affects, for example, the sight of accidents, heights, public speaking, and so on. Some circumscribed mono-symptomatic phobias, such as of spiders or thunderstorms, which often date from early childhood, may be well understood in terms of learning theory as arising from some traumatic situation in childhood. So-called agoraphobia (fear of the market place) cannot be so easily understood. This usually starts in adolescence and rather than being a fear of open places is more a social phobia or fear of encountering people in crowded places, such as tubes, lifts, and cinemas, because of the feelings that might be aroused.

A young woman with high conscious ideals of marital and pre-marital chastity, married a man who had had several pre-marital affairs. After a few years he got an evening job which left her free to go out to evening classes and shortly after this her 'agoraphobia' developed until she was unable to go anywhere unless (chaperoned) with her husband. During psychotherapy it became clear that if she went out on her own she was terrified of giving way to previously repressed impulses to flirt with other men and to level the score with her husband's pre-marital affairs. When one evening a married male friend, to whom she had given supper, kissed her goodnight, in a socially acceptable way, to thank her for supper, she slapped his face and called him a 'lascivious beast', i.e., *projecting* into him her own unrecognized lascivious feelings.

Displacement

When we are too afraid to express our feelings or affects directly to the person who provoked them, we may deflect them elsewhere. A cartoon example is the office hierarchy; the boss is angry with his next-in-command, who in turn takes it out on the one beneath him, and so on till the office boy is left kicking the office cat. The phenomenon of displacement is widespread in other animals and known to ethologists as re-direction (p.13). A common type of displacement is the *turning on the self* of affects such as anger, as seen in self-destructive behaviour and masochism; it is particularly prominent in de-pressive conditions and suicide attempts.

Regression

It is perfectly normal and indeed desirable on holiday to aban-don our more usual adult responsibilities and go back (regress) to the less mature joys of childhood, such as swimming, games, etc. In the face of disasters with which we feel unable to cope – such as severe illness or accidents – we may also regress to more childlike and dependent ways of behaving. Then we look for adults or leaders in whom we can repose our trust (see Transference p.54ff) though this may also leave us vulnerable to domination by demagogues.

Sleep might be seen as a normal daily form of regression

from the challenges and responsibilities of waking life. A child who has achieved bladder control may, following the birth of a younger sibling, regress to bed-wetting again. The condition of anorexia nervosa (severe weight loss and amenorrhoea in teenage girls caused by dieting) can be understood as a retreat from the difficulties of coping with adolescent sexuality (Crisp 1967).

Depersonalization and confusion

These are both terms with a well-recognized meaning in general psychiatric phenomenology. Depersonalization is the name given to a state in which someone feels himself to be unreal, as if separated from his feelings and from others by a glass screen; this may occur in any psychiatric state. Confusion is the term given to a state of disorientation in time and place, in which the subject may not know the date or where he is; this is the hallmark of an organic psychiatric state due to underlying somatic cerebral dysfunction.

However, though these are both well-accepted terms in general psychiatry, which we do not wish to challenge, patients much more often complain of feeling confused when they have no such organic state. They are usually in intense conflict between opposing feelings, say of love and hate, and confusion has descended like a sort of defensive fog to deal with the unbearable conflict. This mechanism operates in many cases of depersonalization. Like confusion (in our sense), depersonalization occurs during intense emotional arousal and the subject may notice quite a sudden moment of 'switching off' of feelings within himself. There is evidence from psychophysiological studies in line with this; measures of autonomic arousal suddenly change at the moment that the subject experiences depersonalization (Lader 1975).

Sublimation

This was defined by Anna Freud (1936:56) as, 'the displacement of the instinctual aim in conformity with higher social values'. It is the most advanced and mature defence mechanism, allowing partial expression of unconscious drives in a modified, socially acceptable, and even desirable way; for example, murderousness may be given a partial outlet in work in abbattoirs or in field sports. The drives (pp.31–7) are diverted from their original primitive and obviously aggressive and sexual aims, and are channelled into a 'higher order' of manifestation; or in other words, 'to direct, hallow and channel the unruly wills and affections of mankind'.

An intellectual young man of 18, brought up in an emotionally confusing family, was outwardly very inhibited and unassertive. His pleasure in self-display, competition, and sexual curiosity were so stunted by conflicts that he avoided girls and was shocked to read a biological account of reproduction at 16. However, from an early age he had built up a remarkable collection of tin soldiers, and was fascinated by the flamboyant costumes of historic times. They seemed to give expression to the otherwise repressed but healthy parts of himself. Until he worked through his neurotic inhibitions, his curiosity and his exhibitionistic and competitive impulses were dealt with as though intolerable except in this indirect and sublimated form.

Beyond neurosis, sublimations enrich both individual and society. Freud saw culture as a sublimation of our deepest and darkest urges as well as an embodiment of our highest aspirations, as in sport or drama. The writer Kafka (1920) said something similar in an aphorism: 'All virtues are individual, all vices social; the things that pass for social virtues, such as love, disinterestedness, justice, self-sacrifice, are only "astonishingly" enfeebled social vices.'

Vital parts of an individual may only be expressed in dreams or pastimes. Through cultural activities we can participate indirectly and vicariously in propensities otherwise unexpressed; Carnival is a time-honoured example. A society's culture is the outcome of its life at all levels, from instinctual roots to highest ethical ideals; unconscious drives press for expression.

MOTIVATIONAL DRIVES

Any attempt to understand the springs of human behaviour in all its complexities in both health and disease must, sooner or later, confront the problem of human motivation. Dramatists, novelists, and poets were exploring the fields of human love and hate, heroism and destructiveness, long before scientists began to turn their attention to such concerns.

Clearly there are many types of innate behaviour, from simple in-built reflexes to complicated patterns which depend more on learning, such as maternal caring behaviour. There are also basic physiological needs for air, food, and water, which, if not satisfied, lead to powerfully motivated behaviour. But ordinarily, in contemporary Western society, we are not deprived of such needs and they do not give rise to conflict. We are concerned more with those areas of motivation where conflict does arise.

In talking about motivational drives we come immediately to a central problem for the language of psychotherapy (Pedder 1989a), which is the same whenever we try to grapple with the mysterious relationship between psyche and soma (or mind and body). From the side of the psyche we can use the language of human experience and speak of urges or wishes; from the side of the soma we can talk like biologists or scientists about instincts or drives. Sandler and Joffe (1969) distinguished between the *experiential* and *non-experiential* realms. In the experiential realm lie all our sensations, wishes, and memories; all that we 'know' through subjective experience, whether conscious or unconscious, at any given moment. By contrast, the non-experiential realm of instinct and drive remains intrinsically 'unknowable'.

Instinct has been defined as 'an innate biologically determined drive to action' (Rycroft 1972). The term has been in use since the sixteenth century and derives from the Latin for impulse (*Shorter Oxford English Dictionary*). In the nineteenth century the notion of an instinct or drive was coloured by the language of the physical sciences and seemed to convey the over-simplified idea of hydraulic pistons pushing an animal forward. Nowadays biologists prefer to speak of innate patterns of potential behaviour, acknowledging their greater complexity. Such patterns, or 'motivational systems' (Rosenblatt and Thickstun 1977), require particular external triggers or releasers for their activation. Yet at times we do still subjectively experience our drives or impulses as welling up from inside us, perhaps against our will. We have chosen to use the expression 'motivational drives' to try to convey elements of both the psychic experiential side and the somatic biological side.

We have already said in the Introduction that different psychodynamic schools may disagree over how to categorize motivational drives and about which are the more important or troublesome, but all agree about the central importance of conflict over drives and most give prominence to sexual and aggressive drives. Other drives considered important are those associated with eating, attachment, parental, and social behaviour. A brief historical sketch seems the best way of reviewing the problem.

As we have seen (p.13) Freud was at first impressed by the frequency of conflict over sexual feelings, particularly in his female hysterical patients. Jung (1875–1961) reacted against what he considered to be Freud's excessive emphasis on sexuality, and thought more in terms of some general life force or libido (p.102). Adler (1870–1937) gave more importance to aggressive strivings and the drive to power (p.103). Initially Freud believed the stories his patients told him of sexual seduction by adults in infancy and felt that it was the repression of such traumatic memories that gave rise to neurotic conflict. Before long, however, prompted by his self-analysis (from 1897) and thinking that child seduction could not be as common as his theory required, he felt he must be mistaken. He believed that what he was hearing from his patients, if not true historical accounts, were the expression of childhood fantasies of wished-for occurrences. Now he thought that *psychic reality* was often far more important than actual historical reality. However, more recently the pendulum has swung back with the increasing recognition of the reality of child sexual abuse (Bentovim *et al.* 1988).

The ensuing discovery of the importance of *infantile sexuality* led to the publication of *Three Essays on the Theory of Sexuality* (Freud 1905). Up until this time the accepted view of the development of normal heterosexuality was that it arose *de novo* at puberty (the myth illustrated by Botticelli's painting of the birth of Venus arising from the waves as a fully formed woman). Freud saw that this account took no notice of the phenomena of homosexuality and sexual perversions nor of infantile masturbation and sexual curiosity. He came to see the sexual drive as present from birth and developing through a number of different stages (oral, anal, phallic, etc.), pleasure being derived from different erotogenic zones at different stages (p.38). The best known of all these must be the Oedipal phase (around 3–5) named after the myth of Oedipus who unknowingly killed his father, married his mother, and then blinded (symbolically castrated) himself on discovering his crime.

In his later years, perhaps following the influence of Adler and the destructiveness of the First World War, Freud paid more attention to man's aggressiveness. The debate continues as to whether aggression is innate in man or a response to frustration and deprivation. Both views are valid; on the one hand there is a healthy assertiveness which man needs for survival and competition (for example, in work or sport); on the other hand a more pathological destructiveness (for example, football hooliganism) born of frustration.

The theme of aggression between members of the same species has been taken up and explored by ethologists (for example, Lorenz 1966). One example of such aggression is territorial behaviour. In circumstances where food supplies are not abundant, individuals or separate groups need to be spread out widely to ensure their food supply. Intraspecific aggression may have developed to achieve this. The bright colours of some coral fish or the song of birds has evolved, Lorenz suggests, as a warning signal to others of the same species to 'get off my patch' as it were. These assertive signals serve to delineate the territory of an individual; only if a rival does not heed them does fighting arise and the owner of the territory react aggressively to drive the intruder away. Another function of intra-specific aggression, especially between males, is to ensure the sexual selection of the best and strongest animals for reproduction. This is more common in animals living in nomadic herds (antelope, bison, etc.) where there is less need for territorial jealousy, as food supplies are abundant, but selective pressure operates to produce strong males to ensure the defence of the herd against predators. In social animals, particularly the higher primates and man, another important function of aggression is in status-seeking and the maintenance of dominance hierarchies; it contributes to the social stability of a group if everyone 'knows their place' and is afraid of their superior. While this is valuable in facing and meeting acute dangers, as in the discipline of the military hierarchy in wartime, or the operating theatre team in surgery, at other times hierarchical behaviour can be stultifying to individual growth and initiative.

The early psychoanalytic view of sexuality as a pleasure-seeking drive present from birth has had considerable explanatory value. However, to some it appeared to be too much centred on the individual and his gratifications. 'Object relations' theorists (Fairbairn 1952; Guntrip 1961; Winnicott 1965; Balint 1968; Greenberg and Mitchell 1983) have suggested that the primary motivational drive in man is to seek relationship with others. Rather than the individual finding satisfaction through different means at different stages (beginning with the oral stage), the individual seeks *relationship* with the other (at first, mother) through different means at different stages. This search would necessarily be carried out through the means appropriate to the stage of development (at first via the feeding relationship). Rather than an infant seeking gratification of an oral impulse, we have a couple finding satisfaction through a feeding relationship.

Harlow's (1958) well-known work on infant chimpanzees dramatically illustrates this drive for attachment to objects. When taken away from their mothers and provided with 'surrogates' composed of metal frames representing heads and bodies, either covered with simulated fur or incorporating milk-filled bottles and teats, the infants clung to the soft furry ones or returned to them when startled; they only turned to those with bottles when hungry. In other words holding had primacy over feeding. It was the tactile substitute 'mothering experiences' that were crucial in providing a sense of security. It formed a base from which to develop relatively normally, though without the company of other young chimpanzees, normal sexual and social behaviour did not develop in later life.

Bowlby (1969), following his work on maternal deprivation (1952) and the effects of separation of mother and infant, came to view attachment as an important primary drive in higher primates, including man, and considers that attachment behaviour should be 'conceived as a class of behaviour that is distinct from feeding behaviour and sexual behaviour and of at least as equal significance in human life' (Bowlby 1975). Attachment behaviour reaches a peak between 9 months and 3 years, and probably evolved in 'man's environment of evolutionary adaptedness' (for example, the savannah plains in Africa) to ensure the protection of the helpless infant from predators.

Yet still this list of biological drives or relationship-seeking behaviours does not exhaust the range of human activity. There is the curiosity and exploratory drive of the human infant which Piaget (1953) has emphasized. Should this be seen merely as a derivative of sexual curiosity, later to be 'sublimated' in scientific and artistic exploration; or is it a drive in its own right which leads to some of our more unique human creative achievements? Storr (1976) argues that the retention of the capacity for childhood playfulness into adult life is one of the mainsprings of creative activity.

Exploratory and attachment behaviour have a reciprocal relationship. An infant or growing child, for example a toddler playing on the beach, will explore further and further away from mother (or home base) until he becomes anxious about separation from her. He then returns to base for security and reassurance, to recharge his batteries, as it were, before setting off to explore once more.

We need a base throughout life; man is a social animal. Of another, the bee, Maeterlinck (1901:31) wrote: 'Isolate her, and however abundant the food or favourable the temperature, she will expire in a few days not of hunger or cold but of loneliness. From the crowd, from the city, she derives an invisible aliment that is as necessary to her as honey.' There seems little doubt that man has a natural tendency to seek out others, and that in so doing he finds and fulfils himself. How much this can be called a primary social instinct, in the sense of a biologically determined drive to action, is debatable. In more developed societies social behaviour transcends biological necessity; it is more of a psychological necessity. Social networks provide the setting in which individuals struggle to find significance for themselves through relating with others. At first the network is the mother-child attachment, then the family, then developing networks of school, work, sexual relationships, the new family, and the wider community. Man's sense of self and of his own value depend on the presence of others and his interaction with them throughout his life.

The group known as Neo-Freudians that arose in the USA in the 1930s (Fromm, Horney, Sullivan, and Erikson) particularly emphasized this *interpersonal* dimension in contrast to the *intrapsychic* dimension stressed earlier by Freud (J.A.C. Brown 1961). Conflict and breakdown in these supportive and self-defining relationships cause distress and even illness. We are now increasingly aware of the need to combat isolation and to find substitutes for disintegrated family and social groupings; in other words to promote and channel a drive towards cooperation and cohesion in both individuals and societies.

Whatever formulation of motivation is preferred, the central dynamic concept of conflict over primitive impulses remains. Freud himself revised his own theories of instinct several times, though throughout his work the idea of an opposing duality persisted. At first he saw the struggle to be between self-preservative and reproductive instincts; later between self-love (narcissism) and love of others; finally, he spoke more poetically of a clash between life and death instincts. His first formulation is not unlike that of the poet Schiller who said that till the influence of the spirit governed the world, it was held together by 'hunger and love'.

Science and literature will continue their attempts to fathom the complexities of human motivation. Perhaps it is premature at this stage in our knowledge, and unnecessary for the purpose of this book, to be more precise in classifying motivational drives. Psychotherapy is more concerned with the impulses, urges, and fantasies which cause people distress and conflict. The force behind them comes from deep within us, with a driving quality which justifies the term 'unconscious peremptory urge', coined by Sandler (1974). Failure to come to terms with these vital parts of our nature can be the basis of overt mental illness or lesser degrees of neurotic suffering and inhibition.

DEVELOPMENTAL PHASES

'So was it when my life began;
So is it now I am a man;
So be it when I shall grow old,

Or let me die!
The Child is father of the Man;'
(Wordsworth)

The way in which we handle our basic drives begins to be determined in infancy by the response of mother, or mother substitutes, and subsequently by significant others (father, siblings, teachers, etc.). Stages in development have been conceptualized in many different ways, but the concept of successive phases, each needing to be negotiated at the appropriate and critical time to allow satisfactory progression to later phases, is widely held. Shakespeare wrote of the seven ages of man long before anyone in a more scientific field of psychology attempted their own classifications. The very existence within psychiatry of different areas of specialization dealing with childhood, adolescence, adulthood, and old age, testifies to the existence of different problems at different ages. The idea of different phases proceeding from simple to more complex as maturation and learning progress, is somewhat analogous to the idea of different neurological levels building up from simple to complex. As earlier stages or levels are negotiated, they may be left behind or incorporated into later patterns, but there remains the potentiality of reversal or regression to more primitive levels in psychology, as in neurology, especially when difficulties of an earlier phase were not fully resolved.

Freud's (1905) classical psychoanalytic theory of libidinal or psychosexual development is one such theory of phases. He viewed adult sexuality as the outcome of a libidinal drive present from birth and developing through a number of pre-genital phases, pleasure being derived from different erotogenic zones at each stage. First, he proposed an oral phase (0–1) where satisfaction is derived by the infant via the mouth from sucking, for example, nipple or thumb, which appears to be independent of, and to go beyond, nutritional needs. Second, an anal stage (1–3), where gratification is derived from gaining control over withholding or eliminating faeces. Third, a phallic-oedipal phase (3–5) when the child begins to be more aware of his or her own genitalia, with consequent curiosity and anxiety about sexual differences. He or she may develop a passionate attachment to the parent of the opposite sex, with rivalrous and hostile feelings to those who stand in the way.

This is followed by latency, a period of relative quiescence of sexual interest, perhaps even prudishness, while interests are turned more to the outside world and to intellectual development at school. Latency ends with puberty, when hormonal changes re-fire the sexual drive and the genital phase begins. Nowadays, we would add that although an individual may be physically capable of reproduction from puberty, a further period of adolescence follows before a person's final sexual identity is established and sexual adulthood reached at around 20–21 (Laufer 1975). Erikson has referred to the 'psychosocial moratorium' of adolescence, following the 'psychosexual moratorium' of latency, before more adult responsibilities are expected.

Another important theory of stages in development is that of the psychologist Piaget (1953), who focused more on cognitive and intellectual (rather than emotional) development. He has described intellectual development as proceeding from an early sensorimotor stage (0–2) before the development of language, through the stage of pre-operational thought (2–7) to concrete thinking (7–11) and not arriving at a capacity for formal abstract thinking till around 11 or so. Piaget's ideas have particularly influenced educationalists, who now recognize that a child's readiness to learn depends upon the stage of development he has reached. A child can only be taught what he is ready for; the effect of any experience depends upon the individual's developmental phase.

Erikson's (1965) eight stages of psychosocial development are somewhat reminiscent of Shakespeare's seven ages of man. They are summarized alongside other phase theories in *Table 1*. It will be seen that each stage may be resolved for good or for ill; for example in the first stage towards the establishment of trust or of mistrust.

It may be noted that the first five of Erikson's stages correspond roughly to the stages of Freud's classical theory of libidinal development. The last three of Erikson's stages correspond more to those of Jung (p.102) who was particularly interested in man's later development and his individuation as maturity and old age approach, with all the problems of success and achievement or disappointment and resignation.

Can we find common ground between these developmental theories – the classical Freudian theory with its possible over-

Table 1 Developmental phases

Ages	Shakespeare's Seven Ages of Man	Freud's classical libido theory	Erikson's eight stages of psychosocial development	This book
0–1	At first the infant mewling and puking in the nurse's arms	oral	trust vs. mistrust	dependent (two-person)
1–3		anal	autonomy vs. shame and doubt	separation–individuation
3–5		phallic–Oedipal	initiative vs. guilt	rivalry (Oedipal three-person)
6–puberty	The whining schoolboy unwillingly to school	latency	industry vs. inferiority	psycho-sexual moratorium
adolescence	The lover sighing like a furnace	puberty	identity vs. identity diffusion	psycho-social moratorium
early adulthood	A soldier full of strange oaths	genitality and later stages of individuation emphasized by Jung	intimacy vs. isolation	marriage
middle adulthood	The justice full of wise saws		generativity vs. self-absorption	parenthood
later adulthood	Lean and slipper'd pantaloon Sans everything		integrity vs. despair	involution

emphasis on the individual and his gratifications, Erikson's more socially orientated viewpoint and others, such as object-relations theory (p.35)? Let us consider the newborn infant and his developing relationships through the early years of childhood. Broadly speaking three stages can be delineated: (1) a phase of more or less total dependence on mother from

0–1; (2) a phase of growing separateness and individuation from 1–3; (3) a phase of increasing differentiation and rivalry from 3–5.

1. In the first year of life the infant gains a growing awareness of the outside world and of self as distinct from others, within the context of a feeding and nursing relationship. At first he has only to cry when hungry, cold, wet, or uncomfortable and, provided 'good-enough mothering' (Winnicott 1965:145) is available, his wishes will appear to be satisfied magically; the infant may even be encouraged to believe in the omnipotence of his wishes. With the beginnings of awareness that mother's breast, smile, comforting arms, smell, and warmth are not his own but belong to another, the infant begins to be anxious that she might go away; especially if he feels he has been too greedy or demanding and, as teeth develop, that he may have bitten and hurt mother and caused her withdrawal. How mother responds to the infant's basic needs is bound to affect how he feels thereafter about them. This first phase has been called the oral phase in classical psychoanalysis. Certainly the infant begins to explore the world by putting things into his mouth, but to subscribe all that happens under the label 'oral' is too narrow. This is the stage when (as Erikson has indicated) basic trust in other people is established; trust that others will continue to provide support and comfort. Gross failures (by the environment) at this early stage can lead to the most severe forms of psychiatric disturbance later. Psychosis has even been called an 'environmental deficiency disease' (Winnicott 1965:256).

2. Towards the end of the first year, the infant begins to be more aware of himself as separate from mother and those who supply his needs; Margaret Mahler has called this the Separation/Individuation phase (Mahler et al. 1975). Stern (1985) argues that this process of differentiation even begins soon after birth. The sense of self is developing; ego boundaries are being established between self and others, between 'me' and 'not-me'. Classical psychoanalysis called this the anal phase, but it is too restricting to focus solely on the pleasure derived from withholding or releasing faeces. Certainly, as this is a phase of establishing independence from mother, there may be battles over toilet training, but so there are over eating, dressing, or other activities as the child begins to exert his

own will, often to the point of considerable negativism or contrariness. The story of banishment from the Garden of Eden might be seen as the story of loss of a state of bliss (mother's breast) when man first learnt to say no to God (the father) and discovered sexuality. However, to reduce all these strivings to the concept of anality seems too narrow. Indeed, an excessive preoccupation with elimination or soiling in the child is more likely to be the consequence of deprivation in other areas. Moreover, in normal development there are other important things happening. There is the development of speech and cognitive functions, exploration and locomotor development, with increasing mastery of the environment.

This is Erikson's second stage, when autonomy is established. The infant begins to separate from mother but is still largely dependent on her, not only for food and locomotion but above all for protection from danger. The period from 9 months to 3 years is the time of maximal attachment behaviour (Bowlby 1969). It is Bowlby's contention that this type of behaviour evolved largely to furnish protection from predators (p.35). Any premature or imposed disruption of attachment at this stage, such as might be caused by prolonged separation or hospitalization of mother or infant, may lead to later anxieties about the reliability of attachment figures, such as difficulty in trusting people in relationships both personal and professional.

3. By the age of about three, the infant is well aware of himself as a separate person, of his parents as separate and different people and of his siblings (if any) as rivals in his environment. He is aware of sexual differences in a broad sense and more specifically becoming curious about actual genital differences. A vast amount has been written about the development of psychosexual identity and gender role, as distinct from genetic sex, and the extent to which this is determined by inbuilt genetic or hormonal differences in contrast to post-natal social and cultural factors. In brief, as we ascend the animal kingdom, biological factors such as hormones have less influence, and psychological and environmental factors a much greater one. The work of the Harlows (1962), for example, has shown that monkeys separated from their parents at birth and reared in isolation, so that they have no opportunity

to learn by observing sexual behaviour in adults, may later be sexually incompetent themselves as adults.

Money *et al.* (1957) and the Hampsons (1961) have studied the effects of re-assigning the sex of a human child when it has been wrongly assigned at birth in intermediate sex types. Normally, humans have either male (XY) or female (XX) sex chromosomes and corresponding external genitalia to match. In some intermediate types there may be male genetic constitution with apparent female external genitalia or vice versa. At birth, sex is always assigned on the basis of external genitalia, although in these hermaphrodite and pseudohermaphrodite cases the apparent genitalia may be incongruent with the chromosomal sex and the gonadal sex. Money and the Hampsons demonstrated that it is comparatively easy to re-assign the sex correctly before one year, but almost impossible after about five. They suggested that somewhere between one and five, gender role is established by cultural expectation whatever the actual genetic sex, and that this process can be likened to a permanent 'imprinting'. However, although all researchers in this field acknowledge the importance of sex of assignment in determining gender identity, a number of writers have produced evidence that in some cases genetic and hormonal factors can overcome the sex of rearing long after the age of five (Hoenig 1985). This gender interchangeability is in accord with Plato's and Freud's view of man's inherent bisexuality or Jung's view that the opposite is concealed by appearances, the anima by the animus (or vice versa).

The strength of sex drive may be determined by both biological and psychological factors, and indeed to some extent follows androgen levels in both male and female. However, gender role, like gender identity and sexual object choice, is determined by a combination of psychological and cultural factors acting on a biological substrate.

This phase (3–5) of increasing sexual differentiation, as we have already said, was called by Freud the Oedipal phase after the myth of Oedipus who unknowingly killed his father and married his mother. The 'Oedipal complex' has, unfortunately, tended to become one of those frozen clichés of psychoanalysis which can easily be ridiculed if taken too literally and concretely to mean that every child wishes to murder the same-sexed parent and have intercourse with the opposite-sexed parent. Children do not have exactly an adult's concept of either death or intercourse, but certainly they may wish their rivals (parent or siblings) out of the way so as to enjoy greater intimacy with mother or father. This period of childhood is undoubtedly a time of passionate love and hate, rivalry and jealousy, the outcome of which can have a decisive effect on later character formation. It would be a Utopian dream to imagine children could be protected from conflicts at this (or earlier) stages. If all goes well, conflicts may be weathered; but if a rival parent or sibling, whose presence is resented at that time, becomes ill, dies, or is absent through hospitalization, divorce, or war, the child may fear that hostile wishes have magically come true and grow up fearful of the intensity of his jealousy. The neurotic, like the child, fails to distinguish between fantasy and reality, between thought and deed, between the wish and its realization. This phase corresponds to Erikson's third stage, when the crucial issue is whether initiative prevails over guilt.

An advantange of thinking in terms of these three broad stages of childhood development, although of course each merges into the other, is that they can be roughly related to different kinds of clinical problem. Neurotic disorders, such as hysterical and phobic states, are classically thought to derive from problems at the Oedipal phase of development (3–5). Some severe psychiatric disorders, such as borderline psychoses and gross character disorders, are thought to result from disturbances in the earliest phase (0–1) of the mother-child relationship. Disturbances in the intermediate phase (1–3) may later contribute to problems of self-determination, such as resentful compliance, or problems over separation and loss, such as anxiety and depression. The earlier the stage in development at which the problem arose, the more difficult it will be to reach psychotherapeutically, particularly when it arose at a pre-verbal stage (before the development of speech). Then it may only be reached, if at all, by considerable regression and re-enactment in the transference (p.54) before verbalization is possible.

By the time of entering latency the child has come to adopt his own ways of integrating internal and external pressures and the conflicts they engender. He has begun to deploy a characteristic range of coping strategies and defences, as described in a previous section (pp.24–31). Development does not stop here; but whether early crises have been resolved for good or for ill, towards or away from the establishment of sufficient trust, autonomy, and initiative, will determine an individual's attitude and response to subsequent challenges. One of the first of these is starting school, when separation from mother, new disciplines, and exposure to rivalry with peers test earlier solutions. In adolescence, pressure comes from the internal upsurge in strength and sexuality, fired by hormonal changes which give new impetus to primitive drives (pp.31–7). At the same time, the young person is having to face detaching himself from the family, both for social reasons and because sexuality in the family runs counter to the universal taboo on incest. The adolescent has to work out a new psychosocial identity for himself; the task of separating from the family and establishing one's own individual identity repeats the task of separating from mother in the earlier separation-individuation phase. Earlier problems of dependency, autonomy, rivalry, and sexual differentiation are reactivated in a way that accentuates the crisis, and may lead to disturbances of feeling or of behaviour such as delinquency, promiscuity, or experimentation with drugs. However, adolescence provides a second chance for the solution of these problems, as Anna Freud (1958) has pointed out.

The table of developmental phases shows what everyone learns from experience; that each phase of life involves fresh opportunities and challenges. Marriage and parenthood will appear desirable and possible, and be achieved more or less easily, according to our resolution of earlier crises. Attitudes to them will be influenced by our experience of our own parents in these roles. Success at a later stage can help to correct earlier imbalances. For example, attainment of a successful marriage, through learning to trust oneself and the other in an intimate relationship, can modify the effect of mistrust learned in the earliest dependent stage. In other words, the past shapes the present, but the present can also re-shape the influence of the past. This is the basis of development and change in life and in psychotherapy.

Many people experience more or less of a 'mid-life crisis' (Jaques 1965) when the fires of enthusiasm and optimism begin to abate and when the discrepancies between aims and achievements dawn on them. Some change their career, or their sexual partner, in an attempt to regain their sense of youth and purpose, sometimes successfully, at least for a time. Contacting the yet unexpressed aspects of themselves, or going back to those parts they have lost touch with because of the demands of career and parenthood, can lead to enrichment and completion, as Jung (1933) has emphasized.

Eventually, however, everyone has to face the death of their parents, the involution or running down of physical and mental powers, the relinquishing of children, the loss of career at retirement and the death of friends and eventually of themselves. At this final stage the balance is between despair and a sense of completion or fitting into a scheme in which death and birth are part of the same cycle of renewal. How the scale tips depends not only on our current circumstances, but on attitudes which represent the summation of solutions to every earlier crisis.

MODELS OF THE MIND

We need some sort of working model of the mind as a framework within which to organize our experience, much as we need a map when embarking on a journey in unfamiliar territory. It is probably in this area of the theories of psychic structure, or metapsychology, that most disagreement has arisen among the different psychodynamic schools. It must be remembered that these are theories or models of how the mind works; we should expect constant revision of such theories in the light of advances in our understanding of man, comparable to the revisions in other scientific fields such as in the theories of the structure of matter or of the nature of gravitation.

Freud revised his own theories several times, though fundamental to his thinking and that of other psychodynamic schools is the idea of different psychic levels. Here there is more than a hint of Freud's neurological background and the influence upon him of the neurologist, Hughlings Jackson. At first (in the 1890s) he described the psychic apparatus simply in terms of *Conscious* and *Unconscious* levels. Next (in *The Interpretation of Dreams*, 1900) came his topographical theory with the idea of Conscious, Preconscious, and Unconscious realms. Consciousness would correspond to what we are immediately aware of at any given moment. The Preconscious would include all those memories or sense impressions, of which we are not immediately aware, but which can fairly easily be brought to full consciousness. The Unconscious would include repressed memories and sensations, which are not so readily available, as well as more primitive impulses and fantasies (p.14).

In 1923 (in *The Ego and The Id*) Freud introduced his structural theory with the now familiar concepts of *Super-ego, Ego, and Id* (Ego and Id corresponding roughly to Conscious and Unconscious respectively, and Super-ego approximating to Conscience). This is a much more complex theory than the previous one. The Conscious, Preconscious, and Unconscious labels of the topographical theory describe different levels or areas of experience. The structural theory is a hybrid that attempts to combine biological, experiential, and interpersonal dimensions. For example, by Id is meant the basic biological aspect of the psyche, the inherited instinctual and constitutional aspects which we share to a large extent with other higher primates. It recalls Darwin's closing words in *The Descent of Man* (1871): 'Man with all his noble qualities . . . still bears in his bodily frame the indelible stamp of his lowly origin.'

The Ego (corresponding roughly to Consciousness) is concerned with rational thinking, external perception, and voluntary motor function (movement). It may be noted that there is some correspondence between such Ego functions and cortical functions (in neuro-physiological terms). These Ego functions are mostly waking functions, concerned with external reality, and are largely suspended in sleep. Other functions such as defence mechanisms (p.24) operate at a more unconscious level, but are also relaxed during sleep and fatigue or under the influence of drugs and alcohol. The Ego is at the centre of object relations, both as they are represented in our inner world and met in the outer world. The Ego is the mediator between the needs and demands of the inside world and the realities and opportunities of the outside world. In performing this refereeing task it has to heed the Super-ego, which is roughly equivalent to conscience, both in its conscious and unconscious aspects.

The Super-ego is built up from the internalized representations and standards of parental figures from infancy onwards, with contributions from later relationships with teachers and other admired or feared figures. We can distinguish further between the more primitive and punitive aspects of the Super-ego ('Thou shalt not . . .') and the more positive Ego-ideal or those precepts we may try to follow. The primitive Super-ego and the Ego-ideal are somewhat like the Gods of the Old and New Testaments respectively. It must be remembered that not all the operations of the Super-ego are conscious. We may think out for ourselves, as adults, our attitudes to major issues of the day such as abortion, euthanasia, etc., but more frequently in many (often trivial) ways, such as queuing in shops, we operate according to the less conscious dictates of conscience. Indeed, society could hardly survive without them. Difficulty arises when the unconscious Super-ego (unnecessarily) represses feelings and impulses which may then give rise to symptoms, as in the case of the paralyzed left arm of the young woman who wanted to hit her therapist (p.18).

We have already said that the structural theory is a hybrid. The Id is more of a biological concept that refers to the instinctual processes within a single person. The Super-ego is an entirely different sort of concept, which moves away from one-person psychology towards family and social psychology. It is a concept which implies an interpersonal dimension including others in the external world who become internalized and set up as internal representations or images. These internal images people our dreams, but may be externalized and experienced in our ready response to myths, fairy stories, and drama. Such images are not exact representations of real past external figures, but, coloured by our feelings towards them, may become exaggeratedly good or bad objects. This process has been particularly emphasized by the followers of Melanie Klein (Segal 1964). These idealized and denigrated figures become the heroes and demons of our dreams and mythology.

From the 1920s onwards there was a movement in theory building away from models involving physical notions of psychic energy, towards more interpersonal models involving relationships between people. The Object Relations Theorists (Balint, Fairbairn, Guntrip, Winnicott) whom we have already mentioned (p.35) were an example of this movement.

Eric Berne, in *Games People Play* (1966), has given a popular account of a serious psychodynamic school in the USA known as Transactional Analysis (see also Berne 1961). His use of the concept of 'Ego states' representing the Adult, Parent, and Child parts in each one of us is a particularly graphic way of expressing psychic structure in terms which will also be helpful when considering the phenomenon of Transference in the next section. If we consider the different levels of the psyche (*Figure 1*) as described by psychoanalytic and transactional analytic theory, we can discern a rough correspondence between the primitive child part of us and the Id; a closer correspondence between the Ego and the Adult, rational, reality-orientated part of us; and the closest correspondence of all between the Super-ego and the Parent within ourselves. Among the advantages of using these terms is that they have immediate meaning to most people. To speak of conflicts between Super-ego and Id may be thought to give a scientific ring to discussions amongst professionals but would make little sense to most patients; to talk of conflicts between the parent and child parts within us makes sense to most people.

We have emphasized repeatedly the notion of different psychic levels and, in particular, the frequent dualities which ran throughout Freud's thinking and appear also in other psychodynamic formulations (*Table 2*). For example, Freud contrasted Conscious and Unconscious; Ego and Id; Secondary Process thinking (rational and logical), as characteristic of Consciousness, and Primary Process (illogical and irrational) as character-

Figure 1

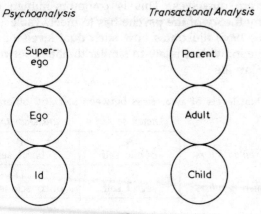

Psychoanalysis	Transactional Analysis
Super-ego	Parent
Ego	Adult
Id	Child

Table 2 Dual levels of psychic structure

conscious	unconscious
Ego	Id
defence	impulse
secondary process	primary process
thinking	thinking
reality principle	pleasure principle
outer world	inner world
external reality	psychic reality
present	past
culture	instinct
false self	true self
persona	shadow
adult	child

istic of the Unconscious; the Reality Principle which dictates the workings of the Ego, and the Pleasure Principle dictating the Id. There may be conflict between the Present and the Past and between Culture and Instinct. There is a conflict between the Outer World or External Reality and our Inner World or Psychic Reality. Jung wrote of the contrast between the Persona or mask which we present to the world and the Shadow or darker side of our nature which we wish to hide. Winnicott (1960) and Laing (1960) have written similarly of the False Self which hides the inner True Self. In Berne's terms the Adult obscures the Child.

We have specially emphasized how this way of thinking in terms of different psychic layers or levels is common to all psychodynamic schools. Sometimes there are things we admit to ourselves but hide from others; sometimes we also hide things from ourselves. This is common human experience which any theory of the psyche has to meet. Table 3 (modified from Luft 1966) illustrates how such dual levels of awareness within the individual relate to similar dualities between people in everyday life.

Table 3 Dual levels of awareness between self and others

	known to self	unknown to self
known to others	A public self	B blind self
unknown to others	C secret self	D unconscious self

As will be discussed in Part II, psychotherapy involves information being communicated from C to A (self-disclosure), from B to A (contributions from others), and from D to A (in more intensive treatments).

So far we have tended to speak of personality dynamics as self-contained, the Ego working to integrate the diverse pressures from Id, Super-ego, and external reality as perceived by the sensory apparatus of the individual. This model portrays the individual as essentially isolated, with the external world represented by images and memories based upon interpretations of his experiences. Although this model is extremely useful in explaining *intrapsychic* phenomena, it has limitations when we come to more complex *interpersonal* phenomena. This is not surprising; scientists have long been discovering that events cannot be fully understood without taking into account the environment or setting in which they occur. Just as the malfunctioning of an organ may be part of the distress of the whole person, so a malfunctioning individual may be part of a whole family in trouble, or a family disturbance may be part of a social malaise. A disturbance may permeate all three levels; for example a child may develop abdominal cramp which keeps him off school so that he can remain reassuringly close to mother, who is depressed and talking of suicide because of her husband's inability to get employment.

The model of the individual mind can be seen as a system inside a wider system, that of the family, inside another, that of society. These systems are not enclosed in watertight boundaries; they inevitably influence each other. In talking of one person and his impulses, the concept of psychic 'energy' may be useful. When considering the effect of early relationships on the interaction between two individuals, object relations theory (p.35) is more helpful, with its emphasis on the role of internal images or representations of people in the outer world. In discussing more complex interpersonal and social phenomena, notions of communication and information (Watzlawick, Beavin, and Jackson 1968) are more relevant. The contrasts between these three levels of interaction are more spurious than real. People function on all three levels at once; the isolated individual is an abstraction.

General Systems Theory (von Bertalanffy 1968) has been developed over the last few decades to study and explain interactions in a wide range of fields from cybernetics to sociology, and more recently psychiatry. A system is a set of interacting elements within a hypothetical boundary which makes it more or less open to mutual influence with the environment; in sociology and psychology this influence is largely effected by informational communication. Systems theory allows us to think more clearly about the well-known fact that a setting determines what happens inside that setting, and that parts cannot be understood without considering the whole, as expressed in John Donne's view that 'No man is an *island*, intire of itself – every man is a peece of the *Continent*, a part of the *maine*'. It helps us to understand self-regulating processes, which depend on control and feedback, and the interaction of cause and effect.

Traditionally, in the physical sciences, and therefore in medical thinking derived from them, effect was always thought to follow cause and it was considered illegitimate to suggest that the effect might be the cause. The cause of a symptom had to be sought in the physical lesion which resulted in the symptom; for example, abdominal pain caused by appendicitis. However, where there is no physical lesion the effect of the symptom may itself be the cause. This way of thinking – to consider the effect of the symptom in seeking its cause – has often been dismissed as shoddy teleological reasoning. However, as Bowlby (1969) has shown, it is now perfectly legitimate in many complex scientific spheres to think in this way. The trajectory of an old-fashioned cannon ball or bullet will be described by its velocity, aim, and so on when fired. The end is determined by the start. This is the 'billiard ball' universe of Newtonian mechanics. However, in more complex systems, such as a guided missile, the trajectory will be constantly adjusted according to whether or not the desired end point is being achieved. Similarly, in living organisms, complex behaviour is often 'goal-corrected'; abdominal pain, the effect of which is to miss school, may be caused by unwillingness to go to school.

Human beings exist in a series of systems. From the start they are part of a system (the mother–child pair) which is part of a larger one (the family) which in turn is part of further overlapping and concentric systems (the extended family, school, the neighbourhood, the wider community, etc.). These are termed 'open systems', in that their boundaries are permeable to influences from the smaller sub-systems they comprise and the larger supra-system of which they are a part. We can discern hierarchies of systems in which smaller ones are subject to the rules and expectations of larger ones; for example the individual to the rules of the family, the family to those of society. Furthermore, each system contains a 'decider sub-system' with functions of communication, control, and coordination; such as the central nervous system or Ego in the individual, the parents in the family, or government in society. In trying to understand phenomena at any level, we have to decide where to focus attention. Can we understand someone's headache or high blood pressure in terms of an isolated physical system, or do we have to include the whole person (body plus mind)? Can we adequately explain an underlying anxiety or rage without taking into account the family network or relationships at work? Finally, can we explain a person's condition fully without taking social phenomena into account, for example, whether his social conditions, such as poor housing or unemployment, are contributing to the poor family relationships and thus to his emotional disturbance?

'Observe how system into system runs,
What other planets circle other suns.'
(Alexander Pope, *An Essay on Man*, 1733)

A systems theory approach allows us to conceptualize the organization of such interacting levels and to clarify where we can usefully concentrate therapeutic intervention. For example, we might not accept a family's view as to who the sick person is. A child brought with bed-wetting or school-refusal may be best helped by looking at the whole family; the arrival of a new baby, mother's depression, or parental discord may need to be considered in order to help the child. Until we look at the wider system we cannot see the meanings and messages, overt and covert, which the patient is conveying or to which he is responding. Unless we look at the whole family, we might be unable to explain why, following treatment, beneficial change in one member leads to a detrimental change in another, for example the husband of an agoraphobic housebound wife becoming depressed when she gives up her help-less role.

Similarly, we may not understand what is happening between the patient and doctor until we recognize that the patient is treating the doctor as though he were somebody from the past, from the earlier family system, as will be dis-cussed in the following section in considering transference.

THERAPEUTIC RELATIONSHIPS

In considering the total doctor-patient or therapist-client relationship, we feel it is helpful to distinguish three elements. These are the *therapeutic* or *working alliance, transference,* and *countertransference.*

The *therapeutic* or *working alliance* refers to the ordinarily good relationship that any two people need to have in cooperating over some joint task. In medicine it has often been known as establishing a good rapport with a patient. It is an everyday affair, fostered by friendliness, courtesy, and reliability, as any good tradesman or professional person unselfconsciously dem-onstrates. Greenson (1967:46) has defined it as 'the relatively non-neurotic, rational relationship between the patient and the analyst which makes it possible for the patient to work purposefully in the analytic situation'.

The concept of *transference,* like psychotherapy itself, has both general and special meanings, though some would use the term only in the restricted sense to refer to a special phenomenon which arises in psychotherapy. In a general sense we respond to every new relationship according to pat-terns from the past. We *transfer* feelings and attitudes developed in earlier similar experiences, especially where there are no particular clues available as to how we should react; this is what psychologists call 'set'. For example, in a new job, we may find ourselves reacting inexplicably strongly to a male or female supervisor, until it becomes apparent that the super-visor reminds us of, and reawakens feelings about, an authori-tarian father or domineering mother.

This phenomenon is intensified when we are anxious due to illness or disaster. All mothers know that a child, when ill or frightened, reverts to behaviour characteristic of an earlier age and needs more cuddling and attention. As adults, too, when severely ill we tend to regress emotionally to earlier, more childlike, levels of functioning and react to doctors or nurses as if they were parents or figures from the past. This usually causes few problems in medicine, because it is reversible as the acute phase of illness passes. After all, in traditional medicine much of nursing is a mothering function – feeding, dressing, washing, comforting; and much of doctoring, from a patient's emotional viewpoint, is more of a paternal function – visiting the ward to see how nurse/mother is coping. This holds true psychologically whether the nurse or doctor is actually male or female.

More particularly, in any developing psychotherapeutic relationship, patients may begin to experience feelings towards the therapist as if he were a significant figure from the past. Transference then becomes a tool for investigating the forgotten and repressed past. Greenson (1967:155) has defined transference as:

> 'the experiencing of feelings, drives, attitudes, fantasies and defences toward a person in the present, which do not befit that person but are a repetition of reactions originating in regard to significant persons of early childhood, unconsciously displaced onto figures in the present. The two outstanding characteristics of a transference reaction are: it is a repetition and it is inappropriate.'

Let us go back to using the terms of Berne and Transactional Analysis (p.49) and consider various situations where any person seeking help (on the left) may consult any help-giver (on the right). Parent, Adult, and Child parts of each are represented by P, A, and C (*Figure 2*).

Figure 2

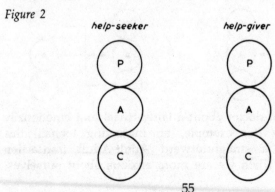

help-seeker   help-giver

If, for example, we take our car to the garage for a service, this should remain an emotionally neutral and therefore purely Adult-Adult transaction or working alliance (A ↔ A, *Figure 3*). However if, for example, we go to our bank manager

Figure 3

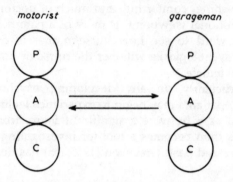

motorist   garageman

to ask permission for an overdraft, we might think we have perfectly good grounds and that this will be a purely Adult-Adult transaction (A → A) and then be taken aback to find the bank manager behaving like a heavy handed and lecturing parent, as if we were a demanding child (C ← P, *Figure 4a*). On the other hand, we might go along feeling like a guilty child asking for more pocket money and expecting a stern parental refusal (C → P); we may then be pleasantly surprised to find that the manager treats us straightforwardly as another Adult (A ← A) (*Figure 4b*).

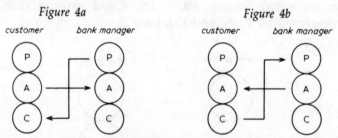

Figure 4a   *Figure 4b*

customer   bank manager   customer   bank manager

If we consult a doctor about a fairly trivial and emotionally neutral problem (for example, an ingrowing toenail) this should remain a straightforward Adult-Adult transaction (*Figure 5a*). But when we are more anxious about ourselves,

56

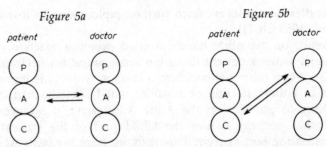

Figure 5a   Figure 5b

or when acutely ill, we tend to regress to more childlike levels of functioning and invest doctors or nurses with whatever good or ill we may have felt towards parental figures in the past (*Figure 5b*). As we have already said, this matters little in acute illness as it is readily reversible. How, indeed, could a patient requiring emergency surgery permit a stranger to cut into his flesh unless the child part of him were capable of considerable basic trust and of investing the surgeon with goodwill as a benevolent parent figure?

However, the same regressive phenomena may cause problems in less acute medicine and not be so easily reversible. For example, in the past the admission of patients to remote mental hospitals for long periods robbed them of their adult responsibilities for feeding, clothing, and supporting themselves. Treating them as children, and thereby infantilizing them, exposed patients to the risks of institutionalization and added to whatever underlying disease process there may have been.

We now move on to the occurrence of Transference in the special field of psychotherapy. One of Breuer's famous cases, described in the *Studies on Hysteria* (Breuer and Freud 1895), was that of Anna O, who had numerous hysterical symptoms, including paralyses and disturbances of vision and speech. Breuer found that these could be relieved by putting her into a light hypnotic trance and inviting her to express in words the repressed feelings and unacceptable thoughts that she had experienced at the time of nursing her sick and dying father. Anna herself called this her 'talking cure' or 'chimney-sweeping'. Towards the end of treatment, erotic feelings emerged towards Breuer which alarmed him as he took it for an Adult-Adult (or frankly adulterous) reaction. He is said to have taken his wife for a second honeymoon to reassure them both; and thereafter he withdrew from further explorations in this field (Jones 1953:Ch.11).

Freud, on the other hand, puzzled over this reaction, particularly when a patient flung her arms round his neck (Jones 1953). When other patients began to express towards him feelings of either affection or hostility that he felt he had done nothing to provoke on the Adult-Adult level, it occurred to him that perhaps it was the Child part of the patient re-experiencing him as some Parent figure from the past. At first he thought such feelings were an obstacle to the treatment and to the smooth flow of free associations. Soon he realized that this was an invaluable new tool for investigating the forgotten and repressed past. As inner representations of figures from the past become superimposed on to the image of the therapist, feelings are expressed towards him that belong to the past. The consciously forgotten past becomes re-enacted in the present of the transference. This re-enactment has been called the 'private theatre' of transference (Pontalis 1974).

In analytic psychotherapy (*Figure 6*) the therapist sets up a therapeutic or working alliance (Greenson 1965) between the Adult part of the patient and the Adult part of himself (A ↔ A) in order to investigate the way this relationship is distorted by the Child part of the patient, which colours his feelings towards the therapist with residues of feelings about important people from the past (C → P or the Transference). Sometimes the working alliance itself has been called the positive transference, but this is confusing and it is useful to distinguish

Figure 6

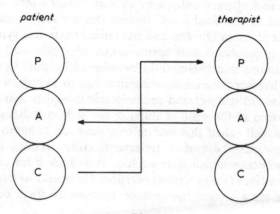

patient   therapist

between the working alliance and positive and negative aspects of the transference (Sandler, Dare, and Holder 1973).

It follows that analytic psychotherapy can only really work satisfactorily when the patient has sufficient Adult capacity or 'Ego strength' to recognize, tolerate, and sustain the paradox that, though he may have intense feelings towards the therapist 'as if' the latter were a parent, yet in reality this is not the case. This capacity to appreciate the paradox is similar to that needed by the audience in the theatre (Pedder 1977) or to the 'conscious acceptance of the as-ifness' (Milner 1971) needed to enjoy any form of art. There may be insufficient Ego strength for this in the immature or in those of markedly low intelligence; and in the psychotic the 'as if' quality may be lost, and the transference become psychotic, so that the therapist really is confused with the parent (p.183).

In individual psychotherapy or analysis, the most likely manifestation of transference will be when the patient begins to experience the therapist as if he were mother or father, even regardless of the sex of the therapist. However, feelings about other family members from the past may also be transferred into the present, as for example when a patient begins to experience the therapist's other patients as siblings to whom he may feel intensely rivalrous. The re-enactment of forgotten feelings about siblings may become even more obvious in a psychotherapy group.

A young adult woman started in a group because she was chronically depressed. She was the elder of two children brought up in an old-fashioned family who (it was presumed) had longed for a son as the first-born child. The second child, born 3 years after her, was a boy and his arrival probably much feted, so that she may well have felt intensely jealous or even frankly murderous towards him. Perhaps to a certain extent she overcame these feelings and as they grew up came to appreciate him as a companion. But when she was about 20 he was killed in a road accident and it was then that she became chronically depressed. A psychodynamic formulation would be that her brother's actual death in the recent past had awakened guilt about her childhood feelings of hostility in the remoter past, as if her earlier murderous feelings had somehow come magically true, leaving her feeling weighed down by guilt and so depressed. However, when at first any suggestion was made to her along these lines in the group, she dismissed it contemptuously. Then after a few months a new male patient, slightly younger than herself, joined the group. She attacked and criticized him mercilessly in a way which, to everyone else in the group, was evidently out of proportion to any real characteristics the unfortunate newcomer may have had. Then she began to see that she was reacting to this new arrival in the family of the group with all the repressed and forgotten hostility she had felt towards the arrival of her brother in her original family. But it was only re-experiencing these buried feelings in the transference here and now that enabled her to get in touch with them.

Transference phenomena are directed towards the therapist and towards others in the therapeutic situation, e.g. fellow group members as in the example just cited, where the transference was to the group as family and to a new group member as an unwelcome new-born brother. The setting – the couch, the consulting room, the continuity of sessions, the group as a whole, the therapeutic community, the hospital – can become charged with powerful feelings and fantasies that we need to consider if otherwise incomprehensible actions are to be understood (see example on p.90). For many patients the hospital or other institution is experienced as an extension of the therapist (Main 1989:Ch.3), so feelings and actions directed towards one or the other are similar. In contrast, they may be very different, as when disturbed, often 'borderline' patients split staff into good and bad aspects of themselves and their 'internal objects' (ibid.:Ch.2). This causes rifts and disagreements in the staff that need to be recognized if they are to be healed.

The development of positive transference to an institution and its staff can make it difficult for patients to leave, but for chronically dependent and damaged patients it can ensure that they are sufficiently sustained. The diffusion and generalization of transference enables them to feel secure in the availability of help if they should need it, despite the inevitable change of staff over the years; the six-monthly rotation of junior psychiatrists can otherwise be devastatingly disruptive to the chronically disturbed patients who are relegated to their care.

So far, in discussing transference, we have largely been considering the patient's feelings and attitudes towards the therapist. What about the latter's feelings towards the patient, which in the field of psychotherapy are generally referred to as *countertransference*? Sometimes doctors and nurses seem to feel guilty that they have any feelings towards patients or that they have failed to rise above them. Yet if young people were not moved by the sufferings and plight of others, the helping professions would be seriously denuded. Certainly there are times – such as in attending bad accidents or acute emergencies – when professional people need the help of their training in disciplining themselves to face the situation, without fainting or running away. Yet we need not be ashamed of our feelings and in less acute situations can learn a lot from them.

For example, a medical student who had been interviewing a very withdrawn schizoid patient said, 'I'm very sorry but I could get nothing out of the patient'. Now this might have been a reflection on the student's poor interviewing technique, as he feared; or it could have been the response any human being would have experienced with this particular uncommunicative patient. The interviewer's inability to feel with and understand the patient has long been recognized as a clue to the diagnosis of schizophrenia in general psychiatric practice (Mayer-Gross *et al.* 1977). Provided we can be sure that we are in a reasonably good humour, not too distracted by our own problems or too pressurized by badly organized work load, then our feelings about a patient can be most instructive. Hill (1956) even said that a feeling of irritation in the doctor suggests a presumptive diagnosis of hysteria. Clearly such a concept can easily be abused since people react differently, and if the doctor got out of bed on the wrong side, all patients that day might be dismissed as hysterics. But by acknowledging such feelings in ourselves and reflecting on them – rather than by immediately acting on them and showing the patient the door – we can begin to wonder what it is in the patient that is making us feel this way.

Within the special field of psychotherapy, the concept of countertransference has had various meanings; we find it helpful broadly to distinguish two uses. As in the development of the concept of transference, countertransference was at first thought of as an obstacle. Any strong feelings the therapist might have had about the patient were thought to represent his own unresolved conflicts and problems, from his own past or present life, transferred on to the patient. For this reason, among others, it was thought desirable that anyone specializing as a psychotherapist should first undergo a personal psychotherapeutic experience himself. This then is one meaning of countertransference, when the therapist contaminates the field with his own problems from elsewhere.

However, assuming that the therapist comes to the patient not unduly ruffled by his own problems and is able to maintain an attitude of 'free-floating attention' or 'listening with the third ear' in order to hear the message behind the patient's surface communication, then the therapist's own spontaneous feelings and emotions, as his unconscious 'tunes in' to that of the patient, may provide the key to understanding what is at first incomprehensible. Heimann (1950) was among the first to begin turning attention to this second aspect of countertransference, which, far from being an obstacle, becomes an important tool in psychotherapy. She assumed that the analyst's unconscious understands that of the patient, and that rapport at this deep level stirs feelings which it is the analyst's task to sustain and use as a source of insight into the patient's conflicts and defences.

About the same time Little (1951) was developing similar ideas in her work with severely disturbed patients, whom she recognized were often as exquisitely sensitive to the analyst's unconscious countertransference as to his intentional communications. Such patients test out the analyst's capacity to sustain the consequent tensions (Little 1957). Winnicott (1947) described patients' capacity to evoke feelings of hatred in their helpers which are in some measure 'appropriate'. He usefully distinguished between such 'objective' countertransference, and 'subjective' aspects which stem more from situational or unresolved personal issues in the therapist. Since those early papers much has been written about the usefulness of analysing our countertransference reactions to our patients (e.g. Sandler 1976; Brown 1977; Epstein and Feiner 1979; Searles 1979). As Michael and Enid Balint (1961) put it, what the doctor feels is part of his patient's illness. In other words, what the therapist feels may be part of the patient's communication, conscious or unconscious. The patient may feel more threatened, and therefore cut off from his feelings, than the therapist, whose capacity to tolerate conflict and anxiety should be less restricted. By putting himself empathically in the other's shoes, the therapist allows himself to feel what the patient has been unable to acknowledge in himself, such as anxiety or grief; or the therapist may experience feelings appropriate to the person the patient is treating him as in the transference, for example a protective or rejecting parent. In short, the therapist's countertransference feelings may be either a reflection of what the patient feels about, or is doing to, the therapist, consciously or unconsciously.

In the treatment of a young woman struggling to free herself from a destructively critical and possessive elderly mother, the therapist found herself being drawn into feeling critical and controlling towards the patient. Recognition of this by the therapist enabled her to comment upon it and led to the patient herself recognizing how she repeatedly drew women into relationships of this sort.

This is an example of what Racker (1968) calls 'complementary countertransference'; the therapist reacted in the way the patient expected her to behave, as a critical mother, drawn into it by the patient's unconscious provocation. The latter doubtless felt the aggrieved and hurt child. Indeed it was the therapist's ability to detach herself from the complementary countertransference sufficiently not to act on it, but instead to reflect about it, and her capacity to tune in empathically to how the hurt child felt – which Racker calls 'concordant counter-transference' – that got them both beyond re-enacting the pathogenic early relationship.

In discussing transference we have tried to relate the phenomenon to other areas of experience in order to emphasize that this was not just something peculiar to psychoanalysis and psychotherapy. Can we do the same for countertransference? At times it may seem to imply something rather mysterious to suggest that the therapist is able to pick up feelings of which the patient is unaware, or disowns. But as Darwin (1872) argued in *The Expression of the Emotions in Man and Animals*, this is a basic mammalian capacity to pick up non-verbal cues about the emotional state of fellow beings so as to be able to know whether they are friend or foe. And the everyday proto-type of what the analyst does in sensing the patient's feelings is surely what the mother does for her infant, who is literally 'in-fans' or without speech and cannot yet put feelings into words.

At first the infant is entirely dependent on mother for ident-ifying states of distress and doing something about them, with-out words being exchanged. A little later mother begins to name the baby's feelings for him so that he can begin to think about them for himself. All infants must pre-verbally pass through a developmental phase of alexithymia, or having no words for feelings, which we see perpetuated so strikingly in psychosomatic patients. Just as mother helps her baby become acquainted with his feelings, and eventually able to symbolize and talk about them, so does the analyst/therapist help his patient achieve the same via the use of the countertransfer-ence.

Distinguishing between the working alliance, transference and countertransference will help in clarifying the different therapeutic methods described in Part II.

Part II

PSYCHODYNAMIC PRACTICE

Part II

PSYCHODYNAMIC PRACTICE

INTRODUCTION TO PSYCHODYNAMIC PRACTICE

In Part I we argued that people may become ill and present problems to a potential helper, such as a doctor, when in unbearable conflict with unacceptable and often unconscious aspects of themselves and their relationships or struggling with the effects of harmful early experiences. The basis of dynamic psychotherapy is the provision of a setting in which a person may begin to reconcile himself with these disowned aspects of himself and his experience. Essentially, the setting for this process is *the relationship with the therapist*; without it psychotherapy cannot begin.

From the time of Hippocrates it has been recognized that the doctor-patient relationship must involve trust and confidentiality if the physician is to be permitted to examine a patient and do what is needed to heal effectively. In this century, following Freud, psychoanalysts and other psychotherapists have developed the potential of trust and confidentiality in the consulting room, which has become their theatre of operations; not an operating theatre where an active doctor works on an inert patient, but a *shared space* in which patient and therapist engage together in exploring and resolving pathogenic conflicts and mitigating the effects of early failure and trauma.

Although this special kind of relationship has been formalized in psychoanalysis and psychotherapy, the role of attentive listener has always been played by the good doctor. In 1850 the American novelist, Nathaniel Hawthorne, described it vividly:

'If the latter (the doctor) possess native sagacity, and a

67

nameless something more, – let us call it intuition; if he show no intrusive egotism, nor disagreeably prominent characteristics of his own; if he have the power, which must be born with him, to bring his mind into such affinity with his patient's, that this last shall unawares have spoken what he imagines himself only to have thought; if such revelations be received without tumult, and acknowledged not so often by an uttered sympathy, as by silence, an inarticulate breath, and here and there a word, to indicate that all is understood; if, to these qualifications of a confidant be joined the advantages afforded by his recognized character as a physician; – then, at some inevitable moment, will the soul of the sufferer be dissolved, and flow forth in a dark, but transparent stream, bringing all its mysteries into the daylight.'

(*The Scarlet Letter*, 1850)

The capacity for empathy, or putting oneself intuitively in another's shoes and identifying emotionally with him in his predicament, is clearly not restricted to psychotherapists, doctors, or other professionals. It is doubtful that this capacity is wholly inborn, as Hawthorne suggests, rather than learnt from early experiences of parents and others, and from its later encouragement in professional training. Moreover, it is essential that the capacity to relate intuitively is balanced by the ability to view both the sufferer and our response to him objectively. With these qualifications, the passage from Hawthorne describes well the *facilitating* role of the therapist. The experience of someone trying to understand, rather than judge or control, provides the sense of safety and space in which to begin to be oneself. Then the person in distress can feel secure enough to share his problems and to explore what he dared not think or speak of before.

Therapeutic listening is not passive, 'but involves alert and sympathetic participation in what troubles the patient' (Bruch 1974). It is in this sense that psychotherapy is a conversation; it is not a superficial chat and does not seek quick, temporary relief by reassurance and suggestion. It involves talking honestly and with increasing familiarity and intimacy, between people who are equally committed to understanding the sufferer and his problems, with the aim of bringing about change.

In Part II we will deal in turn with the main therapeutic *elements of psychotherapy*, the different *levels of psychotherapy*, and then the different types of dynamic psychotherapy practised at present. Several distinctive forms of treatment have emerged during this century. We have traced their evolution in the 'family tree' in *Figure 10* (p.176). *Psychoanalysis* developed in the private consulting rooms of a few pioneers early in the century, but continues to be the major form of intensive treatment and study, though for a relatively small number of patients and trainees. In the Twenties and Thirties, child analysis developed in child guidance clinics, using play material to engage the child's imagination and promote communication. Following the social upheavals of World War One, briefer face-to-face methods of *analytic psychotherapy* emerged in general hospital out-patient departments and clinics, to help the mass of non-psychotic patients who could no longer be ignored. These clinics were named Departments of Psychological Medicine so that patients could avoid the stigma of madness. With more liberal legislation, psychiatry was moving out of the mental hospital. One no longer had to be labelled insane to get help with emotionaal problems. In the Forties and Fifties, partly under the impact of World War Two, psychoanalytic principles were applied in the development of *group psychotherapy* for the treatment of neurotic and personality problems, so releasing new therapeutic potential, and making help available to more people. More recently, as the interaction between people in groups, such as families and institutions, was seen to cause as well as to reflect individual disturbance, group psychotherapy was joined by *family and marital therapy* and by *social therapy*. Now, new methods such as *Encounter* claim to free 'normal' people from social alienation, and forms of counselling (p.94) and self-help (p.87) are developing for many sorts of human problem and predicament. One no longer has to be labelled a psychiatric patient in order to be helped. Finally, we shall finish this outline of the practice of psychotherapy by considering some of the issues of suiting the therapy to the patient in discussing *selection and outcome*.

Historians could get some idea of the time sequence in which the main types of analytic psychotherapy emerged in the UK from the dates when the principal journals dealing with them were founded. The *International Journal of Psycho-Analysis* was

founded by Ernest Jones at the same time as the British Psycho-
Analytical Society in 1919. The *British Journal of Medical Psy-
chology*, the journal of the Medical Section of the British
Psychological Society, which was a meeting-place for psycho-
therapists between the two world wars, was founded in 1920.
Human Relations, the journal of the Tavistock Institute of
Human Relations, was founded in 1947; the *Journal of Child
Psychotherapy* was first published by the Association of Child
Psychotherapists in 1963; *Group Analysis*, the journal of the
Group Analytic Society (London) which set up the Institute of
Group Analysis, appeared in 1969; the *Journal of Family Therapy*,
journal of the Association of Family Therapists, started in 1979;
and the *International Journal of Therapeutic Communities* in 1980.
More recently, in the mid-1980s, three journals in our field
appeared, at roughly the same time in 1984–5: *Psychoanalytic
Psychotherapy*, journal of the Association for Psychoanalytic
Psychotherapy in the NHS; the *British Journal of Psychotherapy*;
and *Free Associations*.

ELEMENTS OF PSYCHOTHERAPY

The personality, like the body, has a natural tendency towards
healing and growth; the fundamental task of psychotherapy,
like that of medicine and surgery, is to create conditions which
facilitate these processes. It is because they are threatening or
painful that aspects of the self and relationships are treated as
unacceptable and therefore disowned, whether by individuals
or groups such as families; for example, an individual may
repress unwanted feelings, or a family may project them into
the 'black sheep' of the family or into the 'big bad world
outside'. The process of psychotherapy involves discovering
the unreality of the fears of calamity if they are allowed into
awareness, expressed, and owned. It also involves finding new
ways of integrating such feelings in order to function and
develop more freely and effectively.

Figure 7 illustrates the way in which conditions provided by
the treatment setting initiate and interact with dynamic processes in the patient. A *relationship of trust*, allowing *communication in words*, promotes the *understanding and integration* of
previously unacknowledged aspects of self and relationships.

Figure 7

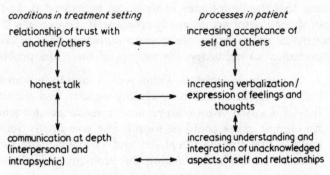

conditions in treatment setting | processes in patient

relationship of trust with another/others ↔ increasing acceptance of self and others

↕ ↕

honest talk ↔ increasing verbalization/ expression of feelings and thoughts

↕ ↕

communication at depth (interpersonal and intrapsychic) ↔ increasing understanding and integration of unacknowledged aspects of self and relationships

Relationship of trust

Seeking help from a stranger is bound to arouse anxieties and provoke conflicts additional to any already underlying a patient's symptoms. What is this person like? Will he understand? Will he be able to help? Will he want to help me? Will he think I'm wasting his time? Will he judge me harshly as too bad or too mad to be helped? The patient's wish to protect himself from the dangers implicit in questions such as these can conflict with his intention to be honest. Reticence and mistrust at interview exist over and above unconscious defence mechanisms (p.24). How the therapist meets the patient and responds to his tentative approaches helps to determine whether the patient feels the necessary initial trust.

To foster such a relationship the doctor/therapist needs to be respectful and non-judgmental. By conveying his recognition of a patient's anxieties, particularly those stirred up by the consultation, the therapist can help the patient to relax and speak more openly. Aware that the patient may be communicating *indirectly* about his real concerns, the doctor/therapist is ready to broaden the inquiry with a few questions such as 'how are things at home?' or 'are you worrying about anything else?'. If and when the patient finds that the doctor can be trusted with his confidences, and is on his side, the foundation is laid for a *working alliance* (p.54). This does not always come easily. For a while a patient might feel it safer to remain detached from the problems presented, for example joining in a collusive assumption that they are physical, rather than human problems of living with himself and others. Some-

71

times it is only after such a contact has been established and tested that the boundaries of trust can be extended, and then only if the doctor seems ready to allow it. Sometimes it takes months or years for people to learn sufficient trust to take the opportunity to unburden themselves of their real problem.

A woman in her thirties, living with a man by whom she had two children, and now again pregnant, had attended her GP for two years with recurrent headaches for which no organic cause could be found. She was finally able to confide that the man beat her and virtually made her a prisoner in the house. Airing the problem and releasing her suppressed rage brought her some relief, and opened up the possibility that something could be done for the disturbed family.

It so happened that this family was West Indian. We cannot be sure whether this affected the delay in getting at the psychological truth behind the patient's physical symptom. But there is increasing recognition that anxiety and mistrust are widespread between clients and professionals on different sides of a gender or ethnic divide, as well as one based on social class. So deep are these attitudes, often justified by ignorance or at least unconscious prejudices embedded in our society (Ashurst and Hall 1989; Littlewood and Lipsedge 1989), that they have led to some radical innovations in the provision of psychotherapy for women and for minority ethnic groups. In London there is now a Women's Therapy Centre (Ernst and Maguire 1987) and an Intercultural Psychotherapy Centre: NAFSIYAT (Acharyya et al. 1989) which provide therapy for those who want help from someone of their own sex or ethnic background, or from someone sensitive to its implications.

For the doctor/therapist, meeting a stranger who seeks help, can also create anxiety, more so perhaps in the novice wanting to prove his efficacy to himself and the patient. It is important for the therapist to recognize this in order to understand the patient's communications and his own responses to them (see Countertransference, p.61). Beyond this, however, the development of therapeutic ease and skill involves the ability to trust one's own responses and intuitions; and it is because most of us grow up with some blind-spots, distortions, or inhibitions that supervision and a personal therapeutic experience are so valuable a part of training in psychotherapy, and mandatory in further specialist training in dynamic psychotherapy.

If the initial barriers to trust are overcome, then therapy can begin. It will be recalled that in individual development as viewed by Erikson (p.39), basic trust should be attained in the first phase of the mother-child relationship. Of course many were not so fortunate in their earliest experiences, so distrust may infiltrate any relationship with a potential helper; rejecting help may be an ultimate defence against a world seen as treacherous. But the discovery that the doctor/therapist does not fail him can be an important corrective experience for a patient. Bowlby (1977) has spoken of this as the provision of a secure base (a temporary attachment figure) from which the patient can explore himself and his relationships.

It is noteworthy that the earliest, seventeenth century, meaning of the word *conscious* was *knowing together with another* (*Shorter Oxford English Dictionary*). Discoveries about oneself are difficult to establish unless they are shared with another person. Freud's self-analysis was an heroic enterprise since he ventured alone into the dark, with no one present to accompany him and affirm his often disturbing discoveries. Nevertheless it is questionable whether he could have managed without the sounding board of his friendship and correspondence with Fliess (Jones 1953:Ch.13). The difficult task of accepting and coming to terms with previously unacknowledged aspects of the self is eased by the experience that they are being accepted and understood by another person. The therapeutic relationship provides the safe space in which confidence can be tested, and confidences entrusted. What has been private or unknowable becomes known together with another. It can be explored and evaluated within the counterpoint of subjective and objective experiences; the therapist provides, as it were, a mirror through which the patient is enabled to see himself and the way he sees others. The experience of mutual reflection within the therapeutic relationship reinforces the patient's own capacities for reflective thinking.

Communications in words

Putting things into words makes them explicit. It involves a commitment to communication, which a patient may be reluctant to make until he has found out more about the doctor's response to his problems, especially those he feels bad about. The doctor/therapist tries to 'read between the lines', and to judge whether or when to indicate that he realizes that there is more to talk about. A tactful question may then open up a difficult topic by providing the right words.

However, the initial communications between patient and doctor, which are crucial in determining whether a relationship of trust develops, may very well be non-verbal, conveyed by manner, facial expression, gesture, or posture (Argyle 1972; Fraser 1976) in the same way that infant and mother communicate and establish a relationship before attaining a common verbal language. Interest, respect, and reliability are not conveyed by words alone. Yet the attainment of a common language in therapy can initiate changes comparable to those brought about by the development of language in the child. Speech makes communication immeasurably richer, subtler, and more accurate. Words develop as symbols representing such things as ideas, shades of feeling, and moral attitudes. The fact that words can also be used to conceal the truth is a sign of their power; this is why we use the more primitive and sometimes more truthful non-verbal signs to check on the validity of communications. The lack of marked discrepancy between what is said and how it is said is a sign of genuineness looked for by both parties in the developing patient-therapist relationship. The presence of discrepancies alerts us to things not yet spoken of, or being avoided, perhaps unconsciously.

Psychotherapy is a voyage of discovery. The patient tries to put his findings into words, and communicate them to his travelling companion, the therapist. One patient referred to her therapist as her Sancho Panza; she could not have embarked on the frightening inner journey without his comforting companionship. The patient's misperceptions of the therapist's attitudes and feelings, based on transference, are powerful aids in exploring aspects of the past which distort current relationships. When spoken of by the patient and 'received without tumult' by the therapist, as Hawthorne put it, isolating experiences and fears can be stripped of their power. The Grimm brothers' story of Rumpelstiltskin illustrates the relief that can be gained by naming a threat (Rowley 1951).

The move from unconscious, primitive, and often bodily experiences – based on primary process thinking, and located in the id (p.47) – to ideas about the self and relationships expressible in words – based on secondary process thinking located in the ego – is illustrated by the case described on p.12 of the young woman who was disgusted with her nose. In the consultation in which a relationship of sufficient trust developed, she was able to talk about her fear of homosexual feelings, and became aware of the link between this and her feeling about her nose. Usually, however, such awareness is not achieved so rapidly; the nature of the unspeakable conflict takes a long time to work out and resolve. The move from allusion and metaphor to usable and clear verbal communication may be slow.

A young woman had developed such a fear of her own developing independence and sexuality that she had starved herself for several years. Even when the clinical condition of anorexia nervosa had receded, she continued to purge herself daily with huge quantities of laxative. It was only when she had been in a psychotherapy group for over a year, gradually overcoming her distrust and her conviction that the therapist did not like her, that she was able to link her purging with her *guilt* feelings. These were about her adolescent use of sexuality to find a sense of being wanted and to take revenge on her mother. She had experienced mother as critical and rejecting, particularly after the birth of a brother whom she could not bear to see mother breast-feed; yet she still wanted her approval and love. As the patient's self-esteem grew through greater acceptance, understanding, and assertion of herself, she was finally ready to use the group's interpretation of the link between guilt and purging. She was able to forgive herself and renounce her childhood tie to her mother. Then she discovered to her own surprise that she no longer needed to purge herself, literally and metaphorically. Her conflicts had become the stuff of conversation.

Talking is not an end in itself; if it becomes so then it is being used as a defence against real communication and change, like the parliamentary filibuster (Langs 1979a). Used creatively, talking is the channel through which the patient's discoveries can be expressed and examined with the therapist and any other companions in the therapeutic enterprise, such as fellow members of a group or family.

This emphasis on talking by the patient stems from psychoanalysis, with its accent on finding meaning where there had been ignorance and confusion. Freud discovered that deep fears motivate the avoidance of disowned experiences and wishes, and that these have to be gradually faced and worked through. However, in recent years some schools of psychotherapy, notably Encounter, Psychodrama, Gestalt, Bioenergetics, and Primal Therapy (pp.163–75) have attempted to avoid the defensive use of rational talking by inducing direct confrontation between people and by encouraging the physical expression of feelings and relationships. Their methods, which involve active techniques of catharsis, re-enacting, touching, and bodily expression, often promote very intense experiences, and require a more obviously active and directive role of the therapist. They can sometimes reach people for whom talk is not an easy medium or who use it predominantly defensively. Such methods emphasize doing rather than thinking, in order to avoid the danger of defensive talk and rationality, but run the converse risk of defensive doing and feeling. Both feeling and talking are ultimately necessary for full expression; Shakespeare's Malcolm urges Macduff, who had been told of the slaughter of his wife and children (*Macbeth*; Act IV: Scene III) to 'Give sorrow words; the grief that does not speak/Whispers the o'er-fraught heart and bids it break.'

A young woman of thirty was extremely inhibited in a psychotherapy group, and characteristically became silent instead of expressing anger. This could be understood in terms of her parent's inability to understand or tolerate her rage at the arrival of a baby sister when she was eighteen months old; they had responded by taking her to see a child psychiatrist with whom she would not share even the few words she had at that time. She had stopped trying to talk in the family for a long while. One day in the group, members noticed she was withdrawing again and tried to help her to express her anger. She was so tongue-tied that the therapist handed her a cushion which, against intense internal resistance, she was eventually able to pummel. Only when she experienced the relief of giving vent to her feelings, within a supportive environment, was she able to put words to her destructive fantasies and to her fear of the group's shock and abandonment, as though the group were her early family. Then she could begin to understand her fears and to integrate her anger in a modified form.

Understanding and integration

Understanding a problem is usually the first step in its solution. However, the true nature of a problem may be deliberately hidden by a patient, because of fear or feelings of shame or guilt; or it may be outside his conscious awareness. Sometimes, a person wants to be *passively* 'understood' by someone else without wishing to understand himself; then, the 'understanding' expected of the doctor is likely to be a misnomer for benevolent sympathy. The dynamic forms of therapy seek to engage the patient in *actively* understanding himself and his problems. They involve exploration of the origin and meaning of his symptoms and the human problems they reflect. It has been suggested (Home 1966; Rycroft 1968) that this properly implies a semantic rather than a mechanistic view of behaviour; that is, one concerned with discovering meaning in phenomena rather than with the deterministic cause and effect linkages characteristic of the physical sciences. As he explores disowned aspects of himself and his relationships, the patient gains new clues for the deeper understanding of his problems. If authentic, this understanding is reinforced by the way it links and makes sense of many experiences, or leads to fresh discoveries. But what is to be done with this self-knowledge? To be therapeutic, discovery and understanding have to be paralleled by a process of integration and change.

For example, the young woman who purged herself (p.75) needed to see the meaning of her symptoms as an expression of conflict in her relationship with her family, and *re-experience* it in the transference with the therapist and 'sibling rivals' in the group, before she could understand it emotionally and at depth – that is with *emotional as well as intellectual insight*. Then, by reassessing her problems and the possibilities of change she was able to forgive herself and free herself from the hostile-dependent tie to her mother, and begin to use her self-assertive impulses in a more outgoing way. She was now more fully aware of what had previously been unconscious.

As in artistic and scientific creativity (p.17) understanding is arrived at in psychotherapy in all sorts of ways; sometimes in a seemingly spontaneous flash of realization, but often in slow stages and with a good deal of struggle against resistance. It is promoted by interaction with the therapist or others in the enterprise, and is mediated by both non-verbal and verbal communication. Three specific types of verbal communication contributing to therapeutic understanding have been delineated: confrontation, clarification, and interpretation (Greenson 1967). *Confrontation* draws the patient's attention to what he appears to be doing, often repeatedly and seemingly unawares; for example, coming late to sessions, showing hostility to a certain sort of person, or engaging in self-punishing behaviour. *Clarification* helps to sort out what is happening, by questioning or rephrasing. *Interpretation* offers new formulations of unconscious meaning and motivation.

Interpretation links the conscious and unconscious determinants of an experience, act or symptom, and thus extends the patient's understanding of himself and his relationships, including those in the therapeutic setting. Interpretations play an important part in psychoanalysis and the forms of dynamic psychotherapy deriving from it, which are sometimes called *interpretative* or *insight-orientated* psychotherapy. As Rycroft (1966:18) puts it, the analyst is someone 'who knows something of the way in which repudiated wishes, thoughts, feelings and memories can translate themselves into symptoms, gestures and dreams, and who knows, as it were, the grammar and syntax of such translations and is therefore in a position to interpret them back again into the communal language of consciousness'. An interpretation is not a dogmatic assertion delivered *de haut en bas*, but rather a suggestion or tentative hypothesis offered in the spirit 'could it be that . . . ?' or 'I get the feeling that . . .' This has been called 'framing speculations as an invitation to a mutual exploration' (Meares and Hobson

1977). Increasingly, as treatment progresses, patients become able to understand and interpret their own experience and behaviour.

The dynamic concept of insight supposes an awareness of the interaction between external and internal reality, that is between objective and subjective experience. Health involves awareness of both. The balance between the two can be disturbed either way: on the one side, extreme withdrawal, introversion, or even psychosis, cuts a person off from external reality; on the other side, excessively extraverted or constricted personalities may be cut off from subjective feelings or inner reality. The correction of such imbalances plays an important part in the analytical psychology of Jung (1946). All psychodynamic schools of thought agree that partial failures of insight result from the operation of defences: for example, denial of an external fact such as a painful bereavement, or the projection of an unwanted internal impulse.

Just as understanding between people can lead to reconciliation, so can self-understanding and insight lead to reconciliation with disowned aspects of oneself. In other words, understanding has an integrating function. Freud's (1933) dictum 'where id was, there ego shall be' implies the integration of external and internal realities. Less mature defences may be given up or superseded by sublimation. Repressed and split-off parts can be restored to the self in the new climate of experimentation and growth, if the therapeutic relationship provides the necessary security and flexibility. The person is enabled to discover the extent of his internal reality, perhaps even to discover for the first time that he has one. We know from studies of sleep that those who do not remember their dreams, or even claim never to have dreamt, spend a fifth or more of their sleep in dream activity; if woken during periods of rapid eye movement (REM) sleep, they are usually able to describe dreams (Berger 1969). Those who do not may show characteristics of alexithymia (Kalucy et al. 1976). It is striking how often people in therapy start remembering dreams for the first time.

It is arguable how necessary insight is for therapeutic change to take place, at least for limited change. Patients may recover and be none the wiser, knowing only that they were helped by medication or the psychiatrist. Even so, factors such as suggestion and satisfaction of the need to be helped by a reliable parent-figure are likely to be operating. These are part of the non-specific placebo effect of much medicine, including psychiatry and psychotherapy. When looking below the surface or becoming more deeply involved with the therapist are too threatening, some patients in psychotherapy get better quickly as a defensive *flight into health*; such an improvement may be short-lived, unless circumstances and important relationships change the whole balance of the individual's adjustment.

Many patients prefer to see their emotional disturbances as 'illnesses', unconnected with themselves or their relationships; they are only too glad to receive physical treatment with drugs or ECT, and to get relief as rapidly as possible. This is understandable and appropriate for many people, particularly in severe crisis or psychosis. It is probably right for others with less acute and severe disturbances, whose wish or capacity for introspection and verbalization is limited, though techniques such as psychodrama, and art and music therapy, may enable some people to enter gradually into the sphere of 'insight therapy'; so may massage, yoga, and other forms of body work (p.173), extension of relaxation techniques such as Autogenic Training and some forms of hypnotherapy (p.175). However, such methods can be used non-analytically and may be useful when deep exploration is best avoided; e.g. in those too threatened by the intimacy of a therapeutic relationship or the fear of opening a Pandora's Box inside themselves. The assessment of these criteria of motivation and 'Ego strength' will be considered in discussing Selection (pp.180ff).

Given the wish to explore and the capacity to bear what is discovered, understanding and integration still have to be achieved and maintained in the face of *resistances*. These can be very powerful, since they involve defences against anxiety and psychic pain. This is why by-passing resistances, by exploring people's problems under hypnosis or drugs, is so often of little use, because their need for defences has not been removed; they are not ready to use what has been discovered.

A young woman was admitted to a psychiatric department for the investigation of apparent encopresis (soiling the bed at night). On some mornings she would wake with her hands and sheets covered in faeces; on others they were stained with just mucus and blood. She had previously been under investigation in a department of gastro-enterology and treated for supposed ulcerative proctitis with steroid enemas and suppositories. She denied any other problems in her life. She had a happy family background, had done reasonably well at school and was now engaged to be married. If only we would clear up this embarrassing and messy problem she would get married and live happily ever after, or so she appeared to insist.

As there were no apparent problems to make a basis for exploration in dynamic psychotherapy, one suggestion was that she might be treated along behavioural lines, with a modification of the bell and pad method for enuresis, by the insertion of a rubber bulb in her rectum at night, which on pressure would ring a bell and awaken her. A dynamic psychotherapist, on the other hand, was struck by the discrepancy (or splitting) between her angelic daytime self, declaring she had no cares in the world, and the messy little girl who emerged in the night covered in faeces. It was suggested that this discrepancy might be worth exploring with an interview under sodium amytal (to loosen her tongue).

Quite soon after the injection of intravenous sodium amytal she surprised the interviewer by the following revelation. She had had a late start to her periods. Worried by this, and as her mother had given her no sexual information, she resorted to the public library. Having read details of the female anatomy for the first time, she went home and began exploring her own body, but found that putting her fingers in her rectum was as pleasurable as into her vagina. No doubt shocked at one level by this discovery, she nevertheless enjoyed it at another level and had continued the practice in her sleep. Her unconscious anal masturbation, therefore, explained why some mornings her fingers were covered in faeces and others in blood and mucus. The interview was terminated and the interviewer felt almost as delighted as the patient, who went home for the weekend and for the next few days remained euphoric. She remained clean at night and

said the staff were all wonderful and she would now fix
a date for the wedding.

However, three days later the soiling returned and she
was most upset and depressed about it. She was asked
what she remembered about the previous interview.
'Nothing,' she declared. 'I was given an injection which
cleared up the trouble'. Should the interviewer have told
her what she had revealed and risk being met with
incredulity, or worse, of putting into her head dirty ideas
which she clearly needed to disown? It was decided to
interview her once more under sodium amytal, when she
readily recalled the previous interview, and more time
was spent with her as she came round trying, as it were,
to anchor the idea in consciousness and then discuss it
with her. This time on waking, though, she was furious.
She declared that if that were her only problem she would
prevent it by sleeping with socks over her hands. She
discharged herself in angry mood and refused any further
contact or follow-up.

In this case psychotherapy did not begin. The story is a
warning that psychotherapy is much more than doing clever
detective work, fishing around in the unconscious and making
shocking revelations. It must involve the establishment of a
working alliance in which trust, talk, and understanding help
a person to accept the hitherto unacceptable. The patient needs
a fully conscious and cooperative ego, not one lulled off its
guard by drugs or hypnosis. For much the same reason the
beneficial effects of some of the more active techniques such
as Encounter (p.166), which stimulate the experience and discharge of very intense feelings, may be no more than transient
because they are not integrated and followed through. The
patient's need for symptoms and defences has to be explored,
understood, and *worked through* – repeatedly experienced and
resolved – before he can give up what has been called the
primary gain: that is the advantage in terms of immediate freedom from emotional discomfort.

If they are prolonged, as with any disability, the sufferer
may learn to make the best of his neurotic symptoms and
defences. They come to have a social function, maintaining
certain roles and relationships which might bring advantages:

for example, sympathetic consideration may be gained, along with covert revenge for its having been previously withheld. In some families it is difficult to gain attention, and illness may be the only means of being noticed as a person with special needs. People who have grown up in very large families are more inclined to complain of persistent physical pain (Gonda 1962), and, when reacting to stress with eczema, are less likely to complain of emotional distress at the same time (Brown 1967). Once gained, the advantages of receiving sympathetic consideration may need to be maintained by the same methods. A gross example of such *secondary gain* is the so-called Compensation Neurosis following an industrial injury, when a pension may depend on the perpetuation of a lifetime of suffering. The secondary as well as primary gain might have to be understood and relinquished before therapeutic change can take place. Finally, change in one person may depend on change in others in his family network, who may resist if they need the patient to be 'ill' in order to maintain their own adjustment. To allow the patient to change, other members of the family may need to be involved in family or marital therapy, or individual or group treatment in their own right.

A joint consultation with husband and wife showed that a recurrently depressed woman was subtly undermined by her husband, who seemed to need her to remain the weak incompetent one. This ensured him the role of strong trouble-free protector, without which he was thrown back on his own self-doubts and depression, related to the early loss of his mother. He needed to let his wife become more assertive and less dependent upon him, by facing his own problems in individual therapy.

In therapy, the relationship of trust and the realization that one can talk about what was thought to be unspeakable, and think about what was unthinkable, act as powerful antidotes to such resistances. Nevertheless understanding often has to be struggled for by both patient and therapist. The therapist needs to be able to tolerate uncertainty and ambiguity, sometimes for long periods of time, without jumping to premature conclusions. Of course there are human situations which demand quick decision and actions, such as surgical emergencies, when it is right to say, 'Don't just stand there, do something'; but in psychotherapy we need more often to remember the opposite, 'don't do something, just be there'. In other words we require what Keats (1817) called *Negative Capability*, 'that is, when a man is capable of being in uncertainties, mysteries, doubts, without any irritable reaching after fact and reason'. Even surgeons, when withholding an operation, sometimes speak of 'masterly inactivity'. In psychotherapy too, there are times when the most that the therapist can do is just be there, tolerating anxiety and uncertainty, surviving as a reliable concerned person (perhaps also surviving the patient's hostility and demands for immediate action and gratification) until such time as things become clearer and understanding is finally reached. Sometimes the therapist's survival is the crucial corrective experience for the patient as the parents' is for an adolescent; 'the best they can do is to *survive*, to survive intact, and without changing colour, without relinquishment of any important principle' (Winnicott 1971:145).

Although many people do not want to know the truth about themselves, because they fear what they avoid, quite a few patients referred for psychiatric treatment feel an urge to understand what has happened to them. A survey (Michaels and Sevitt 1978) revealed that almost one in three of a series of patients referred to a psychiatrist clearly hoped to gain insight into their problems, expressing this in such statements as, 'I want the psychiatrist to help me to see things I couldn't see myself', and, 'I want to understand why I feel this way so that I can do something about it'. Because dynamic psychotherapy seeks to understand a person in a developmental way – integrating what they were with what they are and what they are becoming – the insight gained fosters a sense of continuity of identity. It allows the work of psychotherapy to be continued and extended beyond the termination of therapy sessions; the patient learns his own way of understanding and working at problems.

Integration implies wholeness. A person becomes *at one* as he brings together and consolidates his previously divided parts, in keeping with the origin of the word *atonement*: at one in harmony (*Shorter Oxford English Dictionary*). Integration of previously unknown aspects of the self and relationships demands adjustment, as with any discovery, be it the earth's roundness or atomic power. Patients need to harness previously unexpressed impulses into their functioning. New facts and feelings have to be incorporated into a person's view of himself in relation to others, such as finding that enemies and parents are human, and can be at least partially forgiven, like himself. However modest, these changes amount to a reorganization of personality.

A married woman had for ten years been crippled by a fear of thunderstorms. She lived in dread that every weather forecast or rumbling lorry heralded a storm. When first seen, she described how, the eldest of a large family, she had married early to escape from being a skivvy to a strict and domineering mother. In childhood, despite her frustration and rage, she had been unable to stand up for herself. The phobia started soon after marriage, when unplanned pregnancy threatened an end to her briefly enjoyed freedom. She was able to admit that she had felt some dismay and resentment, but had had to disown any murderous feelings towards the baby inside her.

It could be postulated that this child, and the others who followed, provoked the patient's fury at being restricted and cheated, which revived her childhood conflicts, when the arrival of successive siblings evoked feelings which could not be expressed for fear of retaliation by mother; feelings and retaliation were therefore now symbolically externalized in the form of the phobia. The intensity of the patient's anxiety and her resistance to insight were contra-indications to dynamic psychotherapy at that time. Instead she was treated by a behavioural technique of reciprocal inhibition (exposing her to imagined thunderstorms while deeply relaxed). After some thirty-five sessions she was free of the phobia, and had come to trust the therapist towards whom she had developed a positive affectionate transference.

A few months later, when preparing a birthday party for her eldest child, she had a panic attack, with none of the previous precipitants (such as a thunderstorm, weather forecast or the sound of a lorry). The patient was dismayed when she arrived for a follow-up appointment a few days later, but was now able to trust herself enough in the therapeutic relationship to question her previous understanding of the phobia as a habit related to the occurrence of thunderstorms during her pregnancy with this child. The acceptance of intense disappointment and resentment towards the therapist, for whom she also felt warm affection, enabled her to admit to ambivalence too in her relationship with her child and the rest of her family, both past and present.

The truth, as it were, was out; but she was now able to think of owning her destructive feelings, and in five further sessions of more dynamic psychotherapy, made rapid changes in her view of herself and her relationships. She now understood herself and what had gone wrong over the last ten years much more fully. Instead of splitting off an important aspect of herself, she was able to integrate it and make changes in attitude which freed herself and her family from her role as resentful martyr, locked in a prison of dutiful devotion. She was able to demand more time for herself and her interests, and to expect more help from her family in carrying out domestic chores. Thus she was able to re-establish her relationships on a more honest and secure basis, which at follow-up fifteen years later had withstood the test of time.

This case illustrates three things. First, before the patient could change herself and her adjustment enough to outgrow her symptoms, she needed to integrate feelings previously disavowed because of neurotic conflicts based in early relationships.

Second, the case demonstrates that psychotherapy requires an optimum level of anxiety and tension, like many other sorts of learning. This is reminiscent of the Yerkes-Dodson law of experimental psychology, originally based on the effects of electric shocks in facilitating learning by mice (Yerkes and Dodson 1908). Moderate levels of anxiety facilitate learning, as everyone knows who has studied for examinations. Too much and performance falls off; too little and nothing gets started. The same is true in psychotherapy. Insufficient anxiety can reduce motivation for serious work; too much can prevent it, as in the early stages of this patient's therapy.

Finally, the case shows how the level of therapy is determined by the depth and extent of self-knowledge which the patient seeks and which the therapist fosters; and by the amount of simultaneous internal and external change sought in reaching a new adjustment. This question of the level of therapy will be pursued in the next section.

LEVELS OF PSYCHOTHERAPY

Broadly, psychotherapy is the use of personal relationships to help people in trouble. This can occur at many levels; the deliberate *formal* use of relationships occurs within a wider context which includes a lot of *informal* psychotherapy taking place between friends and confidants. Such relationships have neither the advantages nor disadvantages of the formality and relative distance of a professional relationship.

The value of airing problems, expressing feelings, and of receiving support, encouragement, and advice, is common knowledge, as witnessed by colloquial expressions such as 'getting it off your chest'. The friends who are sought out by distressed individuals are those who know intuitively the value of the principles described in the last section: they are trustworthy, willing to listen, and try to understand.

Informal groups, also, are widely recognized as having a prophylactic or therapeutic effect based on mutual encouragement and the provision of a sense of identity. The sharing of common interests or problems unites people; for example, in work or sport, in religious or political groups, and in self-help groups such as Alcoholics Anonymous, Gingerbread (for single parents), or Cruse (for the bereaved).

The *relief* and *support* offered by such informal relationships, with individuals or groups, are of great value in themselves, and are more acceptable to many who would be reluctant to seek professional help, even if it were available. While sympathetic support can be very helpful, a person can often be helped further if, at the same time, he is also offered some plain speaking. This may confront him with his own contribution to the creation and maintenance of his difficulties, and encourage him to take action to resolve them. Advice is often of less value than helping people to make up their own minds and be responsible for their own decisions. Principles such as these are known intuitively by many people, but it often requires the relative detachment and socially sanctioned authority of a professional relationship to make them acceptable to those seeking help. A fellow-traveller on the train may be entrusted with someone's life story and problems precisely because of the relative distance and anonymity provided by the lack of further personal contact.

At more formal levels of psychotherapy, many types of professional helper may nowadays be involved – though the personality, attitudes, and basic orientation of the therapist, are as important as his particular professional allegiance. Cawley (1977) provided a helpful classification in delineating four types of psychotherapy, based upon the professional background and training of practitioners, and the limitations imposed by their specialization. Types 1–3 involve increasing depth of exploration.

Psychotherapy 1 is what any good doctor (or other professional) does and is synonymous with the art of medicine. It involves an awareness of the person as well as the problem he presents, and requires an ability to communicate and empathize with people from different backgrounds. The doctor who decides to refer a patient to a psychiatrist or psychotherapist, recognizes the anxieties this may arouse, and helps the patient with them by explaining and dispelling unreasonable apprehensions.

Psychotherapy 2 is what a good psychiatrist, social worker or psychologist does. It encompasses Psychotherapy 1, but requires ability to understand and communicate with patients suffering from all types and degrees of psychological disturbance. It involves recognition that the individual's present state and attitude are influenced by previous experiences, often in ways which are outside his awareness and control; to this extent it incorporates some of the psychodynamic principles which underlie Psychotherapy 3. However, while the phenomena of transference may be recognized in Psychotherapy 2, and used to understand patients' behaviour, they tend not to be commented on and are usually used in the sense of allowing or encouraging a mildly positive transference – seeing the psychiatrist as a good and reliable parent – to reinforce the therapeutic alliance.

Psychotherapy 3 would be what many people mean by psychotherapy, especially in its formal or specialized sense, and is referred to here as *dynamic psychotherapy*. It includes the characteristics of Psychotherapies 1 and 2 which relate to the therapist's attitude to the patient – respect, understanding, and acceptance. It puts greater emphasis on helping patients to face the truth and to take responsibility for themselves and their relationships. Dynamic psychotherapy makes the doctor-patient relationship its focus, and uses the psychodynamic principles described in Part I to explore and understand patients' problems. Transference phenomena are encouraged and worked with in Psychotherapy 3, since they throw light on the continuing influence of past relationships, from which the patient can begin to free himself as he comes to recognize them. It is Psychotherapy 3 in its various forms which will concern us mostly in the rest of this book.

Psychotherapy 4 (in Cawley's classification) is *behavioural psychotherapy*. It uses techniques of behaviour modification based on learning theory (p.4). These methods have been developed largely by clinical psychologists, but psychiatrists and psychiatric nurses are also being trained in their use. Because its practitioners wish to be scientific, in the sense of measuring and validating, Psychotherapy 4 tends to concern itself with the patient's manifest behaviour, which can be more easily quantified than his inner experience. It avoids consideration of less conscious elements in motivation; instead of symptoms being seen as manifestations of underlying conflicts – rooted in the past, but still active – they are regarded as maladaptive patterns of behaviour or 'bad habits', learned as a result of past experience and not corrected. Behaviour therapy aims at correction of the overt mal-adapative behaviour; this is particularly effective in the treatment of monosymptomatic phobias (unreasonable fear of spiders, thunder etc.) It is said that the removal of one symptom does not usually result in its replacement by another (so-called symptom substitution). However, cases such as that described on p.85 do indicate that problems may not be solved merely by removal of their surface manifestations; after removal of her phobia of thunder, the patient still needed to come to terms with conflicts in relation to her daughter and her role in the family. Multiple phobias and agoraphobia (fear of crowds or open spaces) are more difficult to treat when they overlie more extensive disturbances of personality and relationships. Hafner (1977), a behavioural psychotherapist, has shown how successful behavioural treatment of agoraphobic women can sometimes lead to symptoms, such as depression, appearing in their husbands. This points to the complex family inter-relationships which lead a wife to take on the patient role; and to the need for a general readjustment in the family or marital 'system' when change takes place in one part.

We do not attempt to evaluate Psychotherapy 4 here; interested readers will find several books on the subject (for example, Hersen and Bellack 1985; Marks 1981). In its short life it has contributed a lot to the management of many difficult behavioural problems and offers help to patients who do not want to, or cannot yet, look into themselves. The Behavioural therapists play a more active and directive role than the dynamic psychotherapist, which suits some patients and some therapists. They seek to establish a friendly relationship as the basis for the therapeutic alliance, but in contrast to dynamic psychotherapists avoid the complexity of transference, and do not use it to explore the patient's problems. They may therefore be taken aback by its manifestations.

One behavioural therapist, who had successfully treated an inhibited, self-mutilating girl by assertion therapy, underestimated the intensity and ambivalence of what she felt for him. She had suffered several bereavements and abandonments in her childhood, but the therapist did not anticipate or prepare the patient for the upsurge of grief and rage she felt when he went away on holiday. He was surprised to find, on his return, that she had broken into his room and smashed it up.

Figure 8 (on p.91) illustrates how Cawley's Psychotherapies 1, 2, and 3 can be seen as deepening levels of dynamic psychotherapy, and how elements of both dynamic and behavioural psychotherapy (Psychotherapy 4) meet in the fields of family and marital therapy (p.136). These schematic links are elaborated further in considering the range of psychotherapeutic methods in *Figure 11* (p.192).

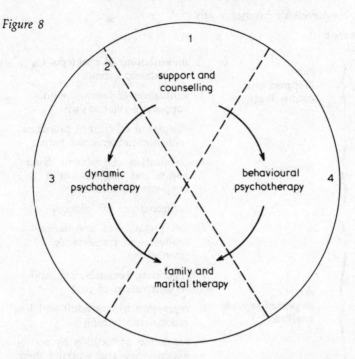

Figure 8

Psychotherapy can be aimed at any of the different levels of communication which may develop when patient and therapist meet, as depicted in Table 4.

Outer levels – relief, support and counselling

Unburdening of problems, ventilation of feelings, and discussion of current problems with a sympathetic and objective helper can enter into all levels of psychotherapy. They form the core of Psychotherapies 1 and 2 practised by any good doctor, psychiatrist, or social worker, as described above. They are the basis of less formal psychotherapy and of supportive psychotherapy and counselling. The psychotherapeutic aim can very properly be limited, at this outer level, to the relief of airing problems and coming to see them in clearer perspective when they are talked about with someone outside the immediate situation. In supportive psychotherapy the therapist will also make more obvious use of advice and judicious reassurance.

Table 4 Levels of psychotherapy

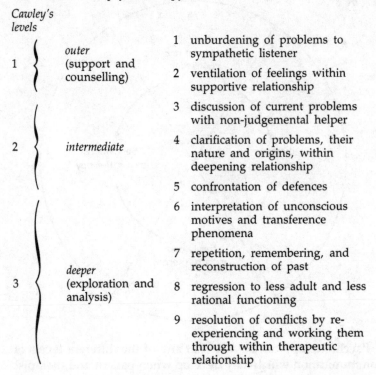

Cawley's levels		
1	outer (support and counselling)	1 unburdening of problems to sympathetic listener
		2 ventilation of feelings within supportive relationship
2	intermediate	3 discussion of current problems with non-judgemental helper
		4 clarification of problems, their nature and origins, within deepening relationship
		5 confrontation of defences
3	deeper (exploration and analysis)	6 interpretation of unconscious motives and transference phenomena
		7 repetition, remembering, and reconstruction of past
		8 regression to less adult and less rational functioning
		9 resolution of conflicts by re-experiencing and working them through within therapeutic relationship

Supportive psychotherapy is a term given to the commonest form of psychotherapy in medical and general psychiatric practice. As pointed out by Bloch (1977), its main aim is to restore or maintain the *status quo* in two groups of patients: the first contains those reacting to a crisis such as bereavement, divorce, loss of a job, or academic difficulties, when distress and tension impair their usual ways of coping. In the course of a few weeks of weekly or twice-weekly sessions, the therapist provides support while encouraging the patient in restoring his coping capacities.

The second group contains those severely handicapped, emotionally and interpersonally, by chronic schizophrenia, manic-depressive illness, or extreme personality disorder. While the therapist may see no prospect of fundamental improvement, he responds to the patient's need for continuing help to maintain the best possible adaptation. The therapist provides regular contact at say, monthly or three-monthly intervals, if necessary over years, and plays a fairly active and directive role in encouraging the patient to capitalize on his strengths, while avoiding pushing him too much. Bloch rightly points out the danger of inducing dependence in long-term supportive therapy. This can produce difficulties for patients and for therapists when they become burdened by the dependence and try to withdraw from it, or when they leave for another job. In psychiatric units it may be junior doctors who see most of the long-term patients, and their training posts are of limited duration. Hence the importance of team-work in supportive therapy, so that patients can look to a helping network, for example, the whole psychiatric unit or social services department, rather than to an individual.

Thus supportive psychotherapy is appropriate for relatively healthy people in a crisis, and for those whose defences are precarious or have broken down. In both groups, exploration at depth is usually neither necessary nor desirable. In the first group it can usually be avoided, in the second group it *should* be avoided; acutely psychotic patients are already overwhelmed by primitive feelings and unconscious fantasies – their need is to strengthen their defences, not to explore them (p.184).

This level of psychotherapy can be used very effectively by the general psychiatrist.

A young man from abroad, bitterly disappointed at failing to gain promotion in his country's Air Force, had to undergo an emergency operation. Post-operatively he complained of chest pain, and the foreign doctor looking after him, thinking the patient would not understand, joked to a colleague that he must have had a heart attack. On hearing this, the patient became acutely anxious and hypochrondriacal. He remained in this condition, despite examination and reassurance by several eminent physicians and surgeons, who, however, never spoke to him more than cursorily.

Eventually he was seen by a psychiatrist who recognized his depression and admitted him to hospital. He supported him in daily visits, and encouraged him to start moving about. He allowed the patient to talk to him about his feelings and the predicament of his life situation, so enabling him to translate symptoms into problems. The psychiatrist prescribed anti-depressant medication and, perhaps more importantly, saved his face by giving him *medical* grounds for leaving the Air Force, which he had wanted to do in order to make a new life for himself.

The psychiatrist provided him with a supportive relationship on the model of a good father with time to be interested, not aloof and disdainful as the patient imagined his own father would be. What the patient needed to get well, was not just reassurance that there was nothing physically wrong with him; he had had a lot of that to no avail. He needed someone to recognize and help him with the feelings and conflicts provoked by his life situation.

On this occasion there was no need to explore whether the patient's problems were more deep-seated; for example, whether they may have been perpetuated by unresolved Oedipal conflicts.

Counselling is another name for a form of psychotherapy at this outer level which is rapidly developing as a method of help offered by non-medical professionals (social workers, psychologists, teachers, and trained laymen) to specific groups of people or for specific problems. For example, Marriage Guidance Counsellors are consulted by those with marital problems; Student Counsellors at universities, colleges, and schools are seen by students with emotional and academic problems; Samaritans are contacted by people in states of suicidal despair. Counselling services have grown up for those with homosexual problems, HIV infection, or, in association with abortion services, for women with unwanted pregnancies. Recruitment, training, techniques, and standards are inevitably very varied, but are being studied and coordinated by the British Association for Counselling established in 1976. Counselling techniques vary from providing information, for example, about available sources of help in the community, to helping the client to understand his attitudes and feelings. The main psychotherapeutic component is usually at the outer level, where ventilation of feelings and discussion of current problems enable a client to make and carry out valid and appropriate decisions. Counsellors recognize that when clients are treated as responsible people, and helped to find their own solutions, opportunities for learning and growth are increased. The counsellor's non-directive role, leaving decisions to the client, and withholding direct advice or interpretations, discourages dependency, and so tends to ease termination (Newsome, Thorne, and Wyld 1973).

A major influence in non-directive counselling techniques has been the Client-Centred Psychotherapy of Carl Rogers (1961), later a pioneer of the Encounter movement (p.166). Having come to psychology from a theological background, he took a basically optimistic view of the individual's capacity for growth and self-realization when provided with an *enabling* relationship. He and his colleagues have demonstrated that effective therapists are those with three characteristics: *accurate empathy* (which they can communicate to the client), *non-possessive warmth* (which accepts whatever the client brings of himself), and *genuineness* (self-awareness and ability to be truly themselves in the relationship). The therapeutic process envisaged by Rogers is essentially an increasing frankness and extension of self-awareness within the therapeutic relationship. The therapist's activity is mainly reflecting what the client says, and paraphrasing his words. Rogers and Dymond (1954) have shown that these methods can lead to greater self-acceptance, expressed as a reduction of the discrepancy between the client's perceptions of himself as he is and how he would like to be. This is not surprising, as the therapist concentrates on accepting and affirming the client's awareness of himself as it unfolds; and he always helps the client to see himself in a favourable light. For example, a therapist might help a client plagued with guilt feelings to convert these into a sense of righteous bitterness at having been wronged, that is, to see badness outside rather than within himself.

Rogers's methods and the form of counselling based on them, are certainly psychotherapeutic in that they are based on a relationship of trust, verbal communication, and increase of understanding. However, Rogerian therapists do not confront defences or interpret unconscious processes such as transference phenomena. In other words, they do not explore at such depths as do more analytic therapists.

Before moving on to consider the deeper levels, it should be emphasized that support is a vital part of therapy at all levels, at least as much at the deeper ones as at the outer. It might therefore be more appropriate to talk, not of supportive psychotherapy, but of *non-exploratory* therapy. Often this would be more a non-exploratory *phase* of therapy, since later, when acute disturbance has passed, the time may be ripe for judicious exploration.

Intermediate levels

Many social workers, psychiatrists, and general practitioners work at this level, clarifying problems within a deepening relationship, and confronting defences and interpreting less conscious motives when appropriate. Whereas, in deeper levels of therapy, transference and other unconscious processes become the main focus of analytic exploration, they may be manifest even in a first interview and in the outer levels of more purely supportive therapy and counselling. At intermediate levels they are used to assist the psychodynamic understanding of the patient and the way he relates to the therapist. Even when the therapist encourages mildly positive feelings towards himself as a good reliable parent, and avoids the emergence of more intense positive or negative transference feelings, awareness of defence mechanisms and the complexities of transference and countertransference may enable him to engage with the patient more deeply and effectively. An example illustrates three successive levels of interview with one patient in general practice.

A middle-aged single woman had come to her doctor complaining of feeling tired and cold. He took a full history, examined her and had tests carried out to exclude physical causes such as anaemia ('traditional medical interview'). She still felt ill, so he asked her back for a longer interview, and inquired about her life and circumstances, discovering that she had been dominated by her mother and that her symptoms dated from a recent change in the office where she worked ('detective type of personal interview'); she agreed that this was relevant, thanked the doctor for his interest, but resisted further inquiry. He therefore prescribed anti-depressants and asked her to return in two weeks. When she did so she was even more depressed. The doctor apologetically said, 'Oh dear, we must try again', at which she burst into tears. He was shocked at his own reaction of thinking how ridiculous she looked crying while wearing such a formidable hat, but immediately realized that she might make other people unsympathetic to her in a similar way. This initiated what came to be called a 'flash type of interview' at depth, in which they *both* shared a new understanding of the way she longed for personal warmth, but hid it and kept people at bay with her stern manner. 'Before this could happen they both lowered the barriers, the doctor admitting his failure, and the patient letting herself cry. The interview was much warmer than the earlier ones and established a new relationship between doctor and patient, which should be useful in itself but also in helping her to react differently with other people' (Gill 1973:35).

A leading part in the promotion of psychotherapy at these levels has been played by the seminars for general practitioners started by Michael and Enid Balint at the Tavistock Clinic in London, and now spreading internationally (Balint 1957; Balint *et al*. 1972; Hopkins 1972; Sanders 1986). They have made clear how the doctor's attitude and response to patients, and his explicit and implicit expectations of them, shape what they bring to him. Patients learn the doctor's language. Balint (1957) called this the 'apostolic function' of the doctor, through which he develops in his practice a particular culture of complaining, diagnosis, and treatment. The complaints the patient offers, most often physical, can be accepted at face value or seen as overlying a more personal problem. Some doctors will accept the presenting complaint without question, like the general practitioner who sent the girl to a plastic surgeon when she said she was disgusted with her nose (p.12); others would have given her an opportunity to talk about any problems she might have in relation to herself and others. This is what Balint called 'patient-centred medicine', in contrast and in addition to 'disease-centred medicine'.

The experienced doctor is aware that some patients need to

go on indefinitely expressing their need for support, symbolized by visits for repeat prescriptions (Balint *et al*. 1970), and that he himself, or rather the doctor-patient relationship, is a powerful medicine, with its most active agent being the feeling of having a 'good reliable parent'. Social workers have parallel experiences. Whatever their professional background, therapists appreciate the opportunities offered by the special nature of the setting in which they work, and its influence on their relationship with patients. The general practitioner, for example, has opportunities to understand patients in the context of their families and to learn their various characteristic ways of reacting to difficulties. He can ask about other family members, visit them or ask them to come and see him. Because he is generally accessible he may choose to provide support over long periods of time. He may also propose deeper exploration of a problem if and when the patient is ready for it. He can offer longer interviews at the end of a 'surgery', a special appointment with himself or sometimes with a visiting psychiatrist or psychotherapist (Brook 1967; Temperley 1978). He may refer the patient to a psychiatric clinic; though some family doctors develop skill in working at depth in the five to ten minutes available in the average NHS surgery, as in the example above.

The therapist working at these intermediate levels has learnt to evaluate his countertransference (p.61), and discriminate between his personal feelings and those evoked in him by the patient. This understanding can assist his treatment of a patient and extend the help he may give. Furthermore, trial interpretation of transference phenomena and cautious confrontation of defences can be used to assess a patient's suitability and readiness for deeper analytic work, should referral be considered for more specialized psychotherapy (p.180).

Deeper levels – exploration and change

At all levels of therapy, the therapeutic relationship is the setting where therapy takes place, but, at the deeper more dynamic levels, it is also the main *focus* of therapeutic work, which concentrates on exploring transference and countertransference phenomena, unconscious motives, and anxieties and defences, especially as they emerge in the 'here and now'.

Many of the processes at this level have been described more fully in the section on Understanding and Integration (p.77). Briefly, as traced in *Table 4*, dynamic psychotherapy allows and encourages the re-experiencing, in the transference, of disturbing early experiences; such repetition fosters recollection of their origins (Freud 1912). They are then used to explore at greater depth the traumas and conflicts underlying symptoms, aided by conditions which permit regression to the child inside the adult: *reculer pour mieux sauter*. When understood, defences which are no longer necessary may be discarded or modified, so freeing the individual to function more flexibly.

The understanding sought is more emotional than intellectual: insight has to be an emotional experience to affect deeply a person's view of himself. Moreover, repetition or *working through* is required for a patient to resolve conflicts and establish a new way of experiencing himself and his relationships in the face of resistance from persistent anxieties and defences. The aim of treatment at this deeper level is therefore more than symptomatic relief; it is reintegration and change in personality functioning, both intrapsychic and interpersonal, towards greater wholeness, maturity, and fulfilment.

Table 5 outlines the similarities and chief differences between psychotherapy at the outer and deeper levels, that is, between so-called supportive psychotherapy and exploratory or analytic psychotherapy. It should be remembered that while support is an essential and fundamental part of all psychotherapy, exploration at depth is not; one can have support without exploration, but not exploration without support. Otherwise it may seem paradoxical that psychoanalysis, the form of psychotherapy which explores most intensively, provides the immense support of daily sessions. It is often desirable to plan supportive and exploratory phases in treatment; for example, support and management may be emphasized while acute emotional disturbance is contained and reduced, to be followed by exploration of underlying problems. It is important that the level is chosen and timed appropriately for each patient.

In the following sections which describe the distinguishing features of each of the main forms of dynamic psychotherapy, after a brief historical introduction we will consider in turn first, the therapeutic setting, second, the role of the patient, third, the role of the therapist, and fourth, the therapeutic

Table 5 Similarities and differences between supportive and
exploratory psychotherapy

similarities	unburdening of problems	
	ventilation of feelings	
	discussion of problems	
	support within 'working alliance'	
	reliability of time and place	
differences	*supportive (level 1)*	*exploratory (level 3)*
defences	supported and reinforced	confronted and modified
anxiety	kept to minimum	optimal level sought
transference	minimized and accepted	fostered, revealed, and analysed
regression	discouraged	allowed within sessions
reporting of dreams	not encouraged	welcomed
advice	offered as necessary	withheld
medication	offered as necessary	discouraged

processes most characteristic of that form of therapy. These
divisions made for the purpose of exposition are somewhat
artificial. They should not be taken too literally; the crux of
the therapeutic process is the interaction between patient and
therapist in the chosen setting.

PSYCHOANALYSIS AND ANALYTIC PSYCHOTHERAPY

Modern dynamic psychotherapy can be said to have begun
with Freud and psychoanalysis, the early development of
which has already been briefly outlined (p.6). To avoid confusion, it may be helpful to distinguish at this point between
at least three different meanings and uses of the word psychoanalysis (Main 1968). First, it is a technique for investigating
unconscious psychic life, by inviting a patient, lying on a
couch, to say whatever comes to mind. Second, it refers to a
theoretical body of knowledge built up on the basis of such
observations. Third, the term is used to describe an intensive

method of psychotherapeutic treatment. Although we prefer to see these three (the technique, the theory, and their application) as intimately connected, logically one does not entail the other. The theory might have explanatory value, but the treatment based on it be ineffective; or the treatment effective, but for reasons quite other than the theory supposes. It might avoid confusion if the term psychoanalysis were reserved for the theory of psychoanalytic *psychology* from which various methods of psychoanalytic *psychotherapy* derive. In the area of treatment we might then talk of intensive analytic psychotherapy rather than psychoanalysis.

Next we come to the much debated issue of similarities and differences between psychoanalysis (analytic psychotherapy three to five times a week), and less frequent psychotherapy. There is a considerable literature on this topic (Rangell 1954; Alexander 1957; Wallerstein 1969, 1989; and Adler 1970). We share the view of Alexander and others that the differences are blurred; that there is a continuous spectrum between the most intensive analytic psychotherapy (or psychoanalysis) through intermediate ranges of exploratory psychotherapy to the less intensive and more supportive psychotherapies. The ends of the spectrum may look sharply different. Analysts who only see patients five times a week will naturally consider what they do to be very different from what other psychotherapists do. Many others, however, prefer to find the right level and intensity for each individual patient to work at, rather than adjusting the patient to the method; for example, starting one to three times a week, before deciding with the patient what his further needs are.

Full psychoanalysis (or five times a week analytic psychotherapy) is appropriate and feasible as a treatment for only a minority of patients, though an intensive analytic experience remains the core of training for future psychoanalysts and specialist dynamic psychotherapists. In this section, psychoanalysis will be considered together with analytic psychotherapy of less frequency and intensity, since in our view their similarities outweigh their differences. But first let us take a further brief look at some of the developments and influences in psychoanalytic theory beyond the elementary principles set out in Part I.

The evolution of psychoanalytic theory is an immense subject. Many authors have reviewed its first half-century (E. Jones 1953, 1955, 1957; J.A.C. Brown 1961; Guntrip 1961; Ellenberger 1970; Sandler *et al*. 1972; and Gay 1988). In its earliest phase, psychoanalysis was based on a cathartic model. Most of Freud's early cases were young women with hysterical disorders, whose symptoms were traced to dammed up feelings associated with sexuality. Therapy, at first under hypnosis, aimed to uncover repressed memories and release the feelings held back because they were unacceptable to the patient's conscious view of herself. Freud wrote of 'releasing strangulated affects', and 'of making the unconscious conscious'. As his translator, James Strachey, wrote in the introduction to *Studies on Hysteria* (Breuer and Freud 1895:p.xviii):

'. . . Freud abandoned more and more of the machinery of deliberate suggestion and came to rely more and more on the patient's flow of 'free associations'. The way was opened up to the analysis of dreams. Dream-analysis enabled him, in the first place, to obtain an insight into the workings of the 'primary process' in the mind and the ways in which it influenced the products of our more accessible thoughts, and he was thus put in possession of a new technical device – that of 'interpretation'. But dream-analysis made possible, in the second place, his own self-analysis, and his consequent discoveries of infantile sexuality and the Oedipus complex.'

Freud's discovery of the importance of Oedipal conflicts may have emerged from his own family situation (Pedder 1987). He was the favoured eldest of eight children of his father's second wife, whom he also had to share with two half-brothers old enough to be his father. Many ill-informed critics of Freud think mistakenly that he stopped at the point where he emphasized sexuality, which led, by 1913, to his parting from both Jung and Adler.

Carl Gustav Jung (1875–1961) developed his own school of *analytical psychology* which moved away from man's biological roots to a study of the manifestation of his psychological nature in myths, dreams, and culture – in part products of the *Collective Unconscious* and its *Archetypes*. These are prototypes of figures to be found in many widely different cultures (Jung 1964). They include the Animus and the Anima (male and female elements found in members of the opposite gender), the Shadow (unacknowledged aspects of the Self), and the Great Mother, the Wise Old Man, and the Hero. He saw treatment as a process of *individuation*, the unifying of an individual through discovering the hidden or undeveloped aspects of his personality. Born in Switzerland, the son of a country pastor, Jung was an isolated child; his older brother died before he was born and his sister was nine years younger. He became very introverted, and for a time experienced fainting fits which kept him from school. Whereas Freud developed psychoanalysis from a background and private practice in neurology which brought him patients with hysterical *neuroses*, Jung started his psychiatric career working with *psychotic* patients in hospital. He was struck by the universal symbols (or archetypes) in their delusions and hallucinations. After his rupture with Freud, overtly because of disagreement about the importance of sexuality, but perhaps also over father-son rivalries, Jung again withdrew into what Ellenberger (1970) calls a 'creative illness' during which he too conducted a self-analysis. But instead of using free-association, as Freud had done, Jung provoked upsurges of unconscious imagery by writing down and drawing his dreams and telling himself stories which he forced himself to prolong. He subsequently became actively involved with others in developing analytical psychology, but he had to withdraw periodically to his lakeside retreat for long periods of replenishment, as though alternating between the outer and inner worlds. Jung's concepts of extraversion and introversion have become part of everyday language. His ideas of finding a fuller balance in the personality between its different trends (male and female, thinking and feeling, sensation and intuition), and his emphasis on creativity and imaginativeness, are of value in all psychotherapy. Fordham (1978) and Samuels (1985) provide useful introductions to Jung's ideas. Compared with some psychoanalysts, analytical psychologists tend to view the therapeutic relationship more as a direct encounter between two individuals. They often sit facing their patients and work less with transference, though in Britain, Jungian and Freudian analysts have much in common.

Alfred Adler (1870–1930), in contrast to Jung, moved away from preoccupation with intra-psychic life, particularly at deeper, unconscious levels, towards a more social view of man. Born in Vienna, the middle of three sons, he was acutely aware of sibling rivalry; as with Freud and Jung, his family experiences contributed to his particular insights (Pedder 1987). In his view, neurosis originated in attempts to deal with feelings of inferiority, sometimes based on relative physical handicaps ('organ inferiority'), which gave rise to a compensatory drive to power. Similarly, he saw 'masculine protest' in women as a reaction to their inferior position in society. Adler rejected Freud's earlier view that sexual drive (libido) was primary, and that aggression was merely a response to frustration. He postulated an aggressive drive before Freud did. Though he formed his own school of *individual psychology*, several of his ideas have become incorporated into the practice of many psychotherapists. These include the 'inferiority complex' and the recognition that 'striving for power' may reveal itself by its apparent opposite, i.e., retreat into manipulative weakness. His interest in the interaction of the individual with society, and between individuals in small groups, is taken up again in the section on group psychotherapy. Adler also influenced the development of the 'neo-Freudian' cultural school (Sullivan, Horney, Fromm etc.) (*Figure 10* p.176) and of Transactional Analysis (Berne). Ansbacher and Ansbacher (1957) have edited a useful anthology of Adler's writings.

Yet at the same time as Jung and Adler were leaving the psychoanalytic movement, Freud's ideas were also changing and developing. By the time he wrote 'Mourning and Melancholia' (Freud 1917), he was concerned less with instinctual drives as such, and more with internalized relationships with the people towards whom affectionate and hostile feelings are directed. He had recognized, for example, that depression could result from the loss, by death or otherwise, of a valued person or ideal (p.22). Hostile feelings provoked by the pain of loss may then be turned on to the self through the internalized image of the lost person, with whom the sufferer identifies. Clinically this is seen when a bereaved person, perhaps at an anniversary, develops the symptoms suffered by the deceased. These ideas led to Freud's (1923) final formulation of the personality structure into Ego, Super-Ego and Id (p.47).

Since then, two important developments in psychoanalysis could be said to have emphasized, respectively, the Ego and the Id. *Ego psychology* has concentrated on studying the ways in which the Ego organizes itself, adapts to both external and internal reality and deploys instinctual drives (Hartmann 1939). Anna Freud (1936) delineated many of the mechanisms by which the Ego defends itself from anxiety and psychic pain (p.24). However, even in severe neurosis, many Ego functions may be conflict-free; for example, someone may be functioning perfectly well at work, though handicapped in his personal life. The early development of Ego functions (p.41), as the infant becomes more aware of his boundaries and of the difference between me and not-me, has been studied by direct infant observation, notably by Mahler *et al.* (1975) and Stern (1985). In recent years Ego psychology has tended to move away from abstract disputation about types of psychic energy, to interest in the development of internal representations of the self in relation to others (Jacobson 1964) both in health and in severe character problems (Kernberg 1975). This development has brought Ego psychology closer to object-relations theory (p.35).

Melanie Klein (1882–1960) may be said to have furthered *Id psychology*. Born in Vienna, she came to Britain from Berlin in 1926 at the invitation of Ernest Jones, who had founded the British Psychoanalytical Society in 1919 (Grosskurth 1985). Like Anna Freud, she was a pioneer of child analysis and its use of play as a means of communicating with the child's fantasies and conflicts. In this way she analysed children as young as two years of age (Klein 1932). She became aware of their powerful, unconscious fantasy life, which she viewed as springing directly from instinctual drives. She thought that children have innate knowledge of sexuality and are innately aggressive, so developing Freud's controversial idea of a death instinct. Through her work with young children, Melanie Klein came to realize the early importance of the mother, so complementing Freud's greater emphasis on the role of father; it is perhaps no coincidence that Freud was a man and Klein a woman. In her view, Oedipal conflicts, or their precursors, begin much earlier than in the classical view of the Oedipus complex (p.43).

Klein especially emphasized primitive mental mechanisms such as introjection, projection, and splitting. In the earliest months, before the infant has clearly recognized the difference between fantasy and reality, between what is inside and outside itself, the death instinct, according to Klein, leads to feelings of destructive rage even without experiences of frustration, and images of a bad mother are split off and projected outside. The good feelings and images are introjected and kept inside, but threatened by the return of the projected 'persecutory' mother (the so-called *paranoid-schizoid position*). As the child learns that it is the same mother who both gratifies and frustrates, it has to cope with ambivalence, i.e., loving and hating the same person. This more mature *depressive position* allows for the coexistence of love and hate, and thus promotes concern for the other, and a wish to make amends and repair any damage the child imagines it has caused. Inadequately worked through, the depressive position can lead to unreasonable fears in later life that any hatred will damage or destroy a loved person. This is a way of viewing the clinical experience that death of a parent or sibling in childhood can result in the harbouring of deep feelings of guilt in later life (Pedder 1982). Kleinian analysts, in concentrating on primitive mental functions and fantasies, pay less attention to the real experiences of the developing child than do other psychoanalysts, and consider that an experience of bad mothering can be attributed to projected images of a bad mother created by the child (Segal 1964).

There has been a continuing to and fro debate within psychoanalytic circles as to whether externally imposed or internally imagined experiences are more important in development. Sigmund Freud had at first thought that the prime causes of neurosis were trauma and seduction, but when he realized that these may have been imagined, he considered inner psychic reality to be the more important. (Recent awareness of the extent of child abuse – see pp.14 and 33 – has led to a revision of this view; we consider internal and external realities as of equal importance, and as interacting.) Later on, in his structural theory, Freud re-emphasized the part played by external figures as they became internalized in the Superego. 'The superego enshrines the fact of personal object-relations' (Guntrip 1971:28). The Kleinians have given overriding importance to the role of internal fantasy, to the relative neglect of external reality. It was partly as a reaction to this that Bowlby (1952, 1969, 1973, 1980) set out to investigate the effects of one very obvious trauma, that of maternal separation (p.42), and Winnicott (1965) began to explore the importance of maternal provision and the 'facilitating environment'. Object-relations theory views the development of personality as inextricably linked with the internalized early relationships and the feelings associated with them, both good and bad.

Donald Winnicott (1896–1971), who came 'through paediatrics to psychoanalysis' as the title of his collected papers reminds us (Winnicott 1975), never lost his intense interest in the early mother-infant relationships. He developed his concept of the 'good enough mother' (1965) and the necessity for a degree of 'maternal preoccupation' for an infant to thrive. As Winnicott (1975:99) has said: 'There is no such thing as a baby', always 'a nursing couple.' Without mothering, a child perishes. Mother is needed not only to satisfy and look after his physical needs, but also to sense his emotional needs, to share his feelings with him and to modify them through her greater awareness of reality. She can feel anxious without feeling overwhelmed and helpless. Ideally, mother will at first encourage her infant's illusions of omnipotence, but later provide for 'gradual disillusionment'. Later in development, mother's presence is still needed to provide a sense of safety and space in which the child can play and be creatively himself; a role paralleled by that of the analyst in psychotherapy. Winnicott recognized that both fact and fantasy influence our development. It is the interplay between external and internal reality which psychoanalysis and its derivatives are uniquely able to investigate.

Winnicott was especially interested in the interplay between mother and infant in the first years of life. He introduced 'the terms "transitional objects" and "transitional phenomena" for designation of the intermediate area of experience, between the thumb and the teddy bear, between the oral eroticism and the true object-relationship' (Winnicott 1971:2). He repeatedly asks for the paradox of the transitional object to be respected. We must never ask, 'did you conceive of this or was it presented to you from without?' (ibid.:12). The transitional object is a joint creation of infant and mother; successful therapy is a joint creation of patient and therapist. 'Psychotherapy takes place in the overlap of two areas of playing, that of the patient and that of the therapist' (ibid.:38). Together they create a space and a shared language in which the patient comes to understand himself anew, much as an infant first discovers the world and learns to speak through mother. 'We experience life in the area of transitional phenomena, in the exciting interweave of subjectivity and objective observation, and in an area that is intermediate between the inner reality of the individual and the shared reality of the world that is external to individuals' (ibid.:64).

One result of these developments in psychoanalysis has been a greater appreciation of the uniqueness of each patient-therapist relationship and of how analysis takes place in a 'bi-personal field' to which both sides of the partnership contribute (Little 1951; Langs 1979b; Klauber 1981). Therapists are not dummy targets for patients' preformed transference reactions; their emotional and intellectual responsiveness to their patients' needs must vary, and their own personalities inevitably obtrude, for good or ill. The increasing recognition of the importance of countertransference as a therapeutic tool (see p.61ff) is part of this trend. Deepening appreciation of what the psychoanalyst himself provides parallels understanding of maternal provision in the very earliest, pre-verbal, stages of infant development. In turn these changes reflect the increase in the proportion of patients coming for psychoanalytic help, not with simpler neurotic problems stemming from later Oedipal stages, but with personality and character problems rooted in these earliest stages of development. They may be very unstable 'borderline personalities', easily tipped over the boundary into fragmentation and psychosis (Jackson and Tarnopolsky 1990); or 'narcissistic personalities' precariously and rigidly guarding a very vulnerable self-esteem (Kernberg 1975). Such people have suffered failures in the earliest stages of the parent-infant relationship. Balint has used a geological metaphor to describe such a failure of fit between mother and infant as leading to a Basic Fault – the consequence of a 'considerable discrepancy in the early formative phases of the individual between his bio-psychological needs and the material and psychological care, attention, and affection available during the relevant times' (Balint 1968:22). In consequence, analyses now usually last much longer than the year or so which was typical when Freud started.

In contrast to this trend towards longer and deeper analyses, efforts have been made from the days of Freud's disciple Ferenczi (1926) to speed up the process of analysis and to make it more widely available. Ferenczi's experiments with active techniques and relaxation, with the analyst adopting definite roles and attitudes, have not been accepted as part of psychoanalysis; manipulation and 'acting a part' by the therapist are contrary to the psychoanalytic values of self-responsibility and authenticity. But such attempts have been resumed in some of the new, less analytic techniques (pp.163ff), in behaviour therapy (p.89), and by therapists influenced by communications theory (Haley 1968).

Freud anticipated that 'the large scale application of our therapy will compel us to alloy the pure gold of analysis freely with the copper of direct suggestion'; he went on 'whatever form this psychotherapy for the people may take, whatever the elements out of which it is compounded, its most effective and most important ingredients will assuredly remain those borrowed from strict and untendentious psychoanalysis.' (Freud 1919:168). This is true of analytic psychotherapy, which, as we have already emphasized, shares common ground with psychoanalysis. Psychoanalytic concepts and techniques can be applied to psychotherapy conducted in other than the classical psychoanalytical way. This does not mean reverting to preanalytic common-sense, to suggestion or the mere dispensing of encouragement and advice. For example, it is possible to use knowledge of unconscious motives and transference without necessarily entering into detailed elucidation of the whole of a patient's past, or to bring psychodynamic understanding to bear on the management of cases where psychotherapy is not appropriate. Methods have been developed (for example, Malan 1963, 1979) to limit the extent of exploration by focusing on key problems or conflicts, as outlined below (p.117).

The UK Standing Conference on Psychotherapy (p.203) is currently aiming at a register of psychotherapists to bring some coherence into a fragmented field. The Psychoanalysis and Analytical Psychology Section comprises the British Psycho-Analytical Society and three smaller Jungian Training organizations, all based in London. The Analytical Psychotherapy Section consists of over 20 organizations throughout Britain. Both sections expect trainees to have long-term intensive personal therapy.

The setting

The generalization that the setting for dynamic psychotherapy is the relationship with the therapist (p.67) is especially true in psychoanalysis and analytic psychotherapy. Conditions are provided which foster a deepening concentration by both patient and therapist on their developing relationship.

For a patient to move safely to the deeper levels of therapy, the therapist has to pay careful attention to the reliability of the conditions he provides. While this is true at all levels of psychotherapy, here it is especially important. Great effort is made to ensure that the room is reasonably free from interruptions and intrusive noise. It is preferably furnished with a couch and comfortable chairs of comparable height, emphasizing the equality of the conversational exchange which, though asymmetrical with respect to what is talked about (Hobson 1974), is *mutual* as regards genuinness of feeling. While the same room should be used for each session, even more important is the reliability of time, duration, and frequency of sessions. The time and place become part of the containing environment offered by the therapist, which together with his sensitivity to their importance, help foster trust in the patient, who comes to see them as his own, and begins to use them as he needs.

Although therapists have to find their own way of working comfortably, a doctor, when beginning to work in a more psychotherapeutic way, may have to give up his more traditional models of sitting behind a desk and writing notes, or at least consider why he needs to retain them and the effect of doing so on the patient and his communications.

It will be remembered that Freud's psychological discoveries arose from his work as a neurologist (p.10). He first used hypnosis to dispel symptoms by suggestion, but later used this method to assist exploration of the origin and meaning of such symptoms and to facilitate catharsis of the associated emotional disturbance. He soon gave this up because of the difficulty of hypnotizing some patients, and his fear that the findings could be attributed to suggestion. Instead, for a while, he urged his patients to recall disturbing memories, often with his hand on their forehead, but this in turn he relinquished as he developed the technique of *free association* (Jones 1953:265).

Patients were encouraged to report whatever came into their mind, however trivial, irrational, or disturbing it might seem; this became known as the 'basic rule' of psychoanalysis. The emergence of this method of exploring the patient's experiences marked the beginning of psychoanalytic technique.

The couch, used by Freud for neurological examination and then for the induction of hypnosis, was retained to help patients with free-association. Many psychoanalysts give patients the freedom to choose whether or not they use the couch. Lying down comfortably, free from intrusion of external sights and sounds, including those of the analyst who sits behind him, the patient is enabled to attend increasingly to internal experiences; thoughts, feelings, and fantasies become available to be reported directly, or evaded. Sometimes, particularly in the early stages of analysis, a patient may be reluctant to use the couch. He may fear loss of control, or see it as seductive or humiliating, in which case, until the fear is understood and worked through, patient and analyst may use chairs, preferably set at an angle so that they can choose whether or not to look at each other. In less intensive or in briefer forms of analytic psychotherapy it is common to use chairs throughout.

Classically, *psychoanalysis* involves sessions of fifty minutes' duration four or five times a week, often for several years. The frequency and regularity of sessions contribute to the intensity of therapy, and therefore increase both the patient's ability to enter more fully into his inner experiences, and his sense of security in facing those which involve a lot of anxiety and pain. This provides time for the unfolding and exploration of the whole person and his psychopathology. The unhurried pace of psychoanalysis fosters regression, transference of feelings towards the analyst, and the recollection of forgotten memories. These become manifest within the patient-analyst relationship and thus available for mutual experience and exploration. The frequency of sessions, interrupted by the inevitable weekends and holiday breaks, allows for re-experiencing of the vicissitudes of attachment and separation, and recognition of their contribution to the genesis of patients' problems (Bowlby 1977).

Modifications of classical technique were spurred on by the need to help larger numbers of people in hospital and out-patient departments and clinics, particularly following World War One (p.69). *Analytic psychotherapy* is a term used to describe the commonest modification of psychoanalysis, in which the frequency of sessions is reduced to three, two, or one session per week. *Brief* or *focal psychotherapy* is a further development, limited in duration as well as frequency of sessions, though not necessarily in their intensity.

Patient's role

To engage in psychoanalysis or analytic psychotherapy, the patient needs to have some recognition that 1) the source of his problems is at least partially within himself, and 2) their solution can be facilitated by the fuller understanding of himself and his relationships, by questioning what had been taken for granted and, where appropriate, changing his attitudes and behaviour.

With the motivation to understand and change, if only in embryo, the patient joins in a therapeutic or working alliance (p.54) with the therapist, in which he undertakes to follow the basic rule (p.111), or at least gradually to try and overcome the resistance to communicate more openly and spontaneously. The patient gives the joint search for understanding priority even over the relief of symptoms and the avoidance of emotional discomfort. He attempts to talk about his feelings and fantasies as they emerge, and not to dismiss them or act them out, whether inside or outside therapy; for example, if angry with the therapist the patient is encouraged to say so rather than express it by coming late for a session or driving recklessly.

Through increasing awareness of the different levels of his experience of himself and others, and aided by the therapist's interpretations and comments, the patient comes to appreciate the continuing influence of the past in the present, of unconscious wishes and fears, and of maladaptive defences against them. He develops his capacity to differentiate between the objective and subjective aspects of the therapeutic relationship – between how it is and how it seems to be. Beyond this, he needs to integrate what he discovers, to test out new ways of viewing himself and others, and fresh methods of dealing with threats and opportunities, both within the therapeutic relationship and outside it.

Analytic psychotherapy, especially when of short duration, requires all these capacities of the patient, but also an ability to work hard in therapy, to think about it between sessions, and to tolerate the anxiety and frustration that can arise from waiting for up to a week between sessions. A study by Rayner and Hahn (1964) suggested that characteristics of the patient which favour a good outcome in brief analytic therapy include the capacity for self-responsibility, self-appraisal, and persistence.

Therapist's role

The first responsibility of the therapist is to create and maintain the therapeutic setting. Whilst this is true in all forms of psychotherapy, it is particularly so in those which allow for regression. If the patient is to be enabled to relinquish his more adult and defensive ways of experiencing himself and the therapist, the latter must be very sensitive to the effect of the environment he provides, and consider the impact of weekends, breaks for holidays or sickness, unexpected change of room or time, or the consequences of the patient's seeing the therapist or another of his patients outside the consulting room.

The therapist's attitude Freud (1912) described as one of 'evenly suspended attention', tuning in equally to the manifest and latent meanings of what the patient is saying, or has said in the past. He follows the flow of free-associations, noting resistances and evasions as well as the ideas and feelings conveyed by what the patient says, and the way he talks, moves and holds himself on the couch, in the chair or at the door. He is open to his own associations, fantasies, and feelings as well as to the patient's, monitoring them to ascertain whether they are likely to be springing from his own preoccupations or those of the patient. His preparedness to respond to the roles the latter draws him into has been called 'free-floating responsiveness' (Sandler 1976), a parallel to free-floating attention.

In contrast with the patient, who is free to say whatever comes into his mind, the therapist's interventions are aimed at furthering recognition and understanding of what has previously been avoided; these interventions may include confrontation, clarification, and interpretation (Greenson 1967) already defined on p.78. He should intervene mainly if the patient is blocked and not just to assert his own presence or to satisfy his wish to help or be clever. Choice, timing, and form of intervention can be crucial. An interpretation often puts into words something the patient has been aware of himself, however dimly or fleetingly. Sometimes it is best to delay an interpretation to enable the patient to arrive at it himself. As Winnicott (1971:117) said: 'Psychotherapy is not making clever and apt interpretations; by and large it is a long-term giving the patient back what the patient brings.' Just as the therapist should offer his interpretations with discrimination, so must he tolerate and use the countertransference feelings evoked rather than discharge them automatically (Heimann 1950). While it is the patient's privilege to discharge feelings, the therapist's responsibility is to contain and make use of his countertransference feelings.

Thus, the passivity of the therapist is more apparent than real. It provides the opportunity for the patient to experience the therapist in transference terms, as though he were a figure in his internal world seen in a 'mirror' (Freud 1912); and it gives the analyst the freedom to maintain free-floating attention, to listen with his 'third ear'. It enables him to retain a capacity for contemplation and detachment while at the same time remaining intuitively receptive. By letting himself be drawn into the patient's experience and then reflecting on it, he helps the patient to understand and modify his 'assumptive world'.

In brief or focal analytic psychotherapy (p.117), the therapist may be rather more active and directive than in classical psychoanalysis. He needs to keep in mind the limited duration of treatment and the psychodynamic formulation of the patient's principal problem which has been selected as the focus for psychotherapeutic work.

Therapeutic processes

Both psychoanalysis and analytic psychotherapy aim at the attainment by the individual of a fuller and more conflict-free experience of himself and his relationships by deepening and extending his contact with alienated parts of himself, and so furthering his individual development (see Understanding and Integration, pp.77–87). Both forms of therapy involve a mutual exploration of the patient's problems within the developing relationship with the therapist. Ideally, in psychoanalysis, there is time to explore all problems at all levels of personality development; in analytic psychotherapy, aims are more modest, and are usually restricted to the resolution of certain key problems and conflicts, freedom from which would then permit normal development to proceed.

Transference phenomena are encouraged and explored as the patient's conflicts become built into his relationship with the therapist. This *transference neurosis* is a re-creation in the present of the neurotic distortions springing from the patient's past disturbed family relationships. Repetition in the transference enables its vividness to be mutually experienced and examined by patient and therapist. This is the arena of what Alexander (1957) called the 'corrective emotional experience'. Intense transference feelings are experienced in which the past is alive, but the fact that the therapist does not respond as parents originally did in reality or in fantasy, for example, with rejection, punishment, or intrusion, provides a corrective emotional experience. Another way of looking at this aspect of therapy is to liken it to 're-parenting' (Sutherland 1976). The recognition and correction of transference distortions, as their nature and origin are discerned, deepen understanding and the patient's mastery of himself.

A man in his thirties was referred because of family difficulties, which had resulted in his wife's feeling neglected and his young son being scared of him. His careful politeness seemed to conceal a powerful and rebellious competitiveness. It emerged that he had been an assertive and aggressive child until, at the age of eight, he was sent to a convent boarding school across the road from where his parents and younger sister still lived. Fearing that he had been punished for his aggression, he became scared of physical violence, fearful of monsters in the dark, and started to wet his bed. His intense ambivalence towards his authoritarian and repressive father – wanting his acceptance but fearing his criticism and rejection – continued from childhood into his adult relationship with employers and, in due course, was expressed in reverse with his own son.

During psychotherapy these conflicts came into focus in the transference. In the session before a holiday break he started covertly to attack the therapist by quoting his sister's view that psychiatrists do nothing to prevent cruelty in the world, such as the large-scale massacres in a far-off country being at that time reported in the newspapers. Then, in scarcely concealed revenge at the therapist for leaving him, he announced defiantly that today he himself was going on a trip with a girl-friend. He stopped talking and waited. After a few minutes he began to laugh with relief; later he said he had felt intoxicated, with heart pounding, so fearful had he been that, like his father, the therapist would attack him for his defiance.

His previously distorted perception of people in the outer world, including the therapist, came home dramatically to him in this session. It played a part in gradually changing his relationship with his employers, and enabling him to give to his wife and son the interest he had previously withheld in revenge. His relationships were no longer so dominated by unconscious rage and guilt, as he began to modify his internal Super-ego and his projected images of a harsh and punishing father.

Strachey (1934) held the view that ultimately the only helpful or *mutative interpretations* are those aimed at transference distortions in order to modify a patient's overstrict Super-ego. Strachey's view of the analyst as an auxiliary Super-ego would now be regarded as unnecessarily restrictive; perhaps more often, especially in regressive states, he functions as an auxiliary Ego. But most psychotherapists would agree with Strachey's assertion that the greatest therapeutic effect takes place when the transference comes alive in the 'here and now' of therapy, as in the case described above. Psychoanalysis and analytic psychotherapy do not dwell on the past for its own sake; they are concerned to reveal its continuing effects, so that patients can free themselves from those that distort or restrict life in the present and future. All forms of analytic therapy aim at the resolution of conflicts by coming to face them and understand their roots in unreasonable fears or in previous development. The gradual overcoming of resistance to fuller acknowledgement and deeper understanding is what Freud meant by the analytic aim of making the unconscious conscious. 'Where id was, there ego shall be.' (Freud 1933).

These forms of therapy allow, and even encourage, *regression*: the re-living and discovery in therapy of earlier experiences, and of more childlike and irrational modes of thinking and feeling. Recognizing the child in the adult allows a greater awareness of impulses and fantasies, dreams and day-dreams. The purpose of regression is to regain contact with parts of oneself which have manifested themselves only indirectly, as a symptom, inhibition, or sense of being incomplete or false; and to re-experience some critical period of development in the more favourable setting of the therapeutic relationship. As this happens, forgotten early memories are frequently regained, and even without them, a tentative *reconstruction* is made possible of early events and relationships in the individual's life. 'Therapy in analysis results . . . from a . . . re-evaluation and reconstruction of the meanings of one's past, present and future in the crucible of transference.' (Gill 1977:589).

The patient can begin to master conflicts and traumas as he comes to place them in historical perspective, and to understand his own part in unnecessarily perpetuating them. This usually requires *working through* – that is, the repeated experiencing and resolving of them in different ways and at different times during therapy – until understanding and mastery are complete enough. The future can then be seen as a time of challenge and change, instead of only an extension of an imprisoning past. We return to the past in order to gather strength for a 'new beginning' (Balint 1965). There is a new chance for the patient to re-evaluate himself, his relationships, and his family of origin – understanding often allows forgiveness to mitigate blame – and to approach relationships outside in a more flexible and understanding way.

Short-term analytic psychotherapy, often termed *brief* or *focal therapy* may be less extensive than psychoanalysis, but it can still be intensive. Indeed Malan (1963) has shown that brief analytic psychotherapy is most effective when there is intense involvement by both patient and therapist, early development of transference, and when the patient is able to feel grief and anger about termination. In psychoanaly ;s there is time for intense involvement to develop slowly; in brief therapy it is needed from the start. The intensity is enhanced by the mutual motivation of patient and therapist, which can be increased by their awareness of the relatively short duration of therapy. In such time-limited therapy, a contract is entered into for a period of, say, three to twelve months. This restriction is made possible by focusing attention on certain key conflicts or problems, such as an unresolved grief reaction, an intellectual or sexual inhibition, a phobia or social anxiety (Malan 1963, 1979; Sifneos 1972; Davanloo 1978). Such short-term therapy is right for many patients, and is well-suited to conditions in the National Health Service (Stewart 1972). In these circumstances, if further, longer-term analytic treatment is indicated, brief individual therapy may be appropriately and usefully followed by a period of group psychotherapy.

GROUP PSYCHOTHERAPY

Man has always lived in family and social groups, and his problems are usually reflected in his group behaviour. The development of object-relations theory in psychoanalysis has helped us to understand the distorting effects that internalized early family relationships can have on current adult relationships. Groups are able to provide powerful support and encouragement, as well as a vivid setting in which problems based on such distorting effects can be explored and treated. That is, groups can be used at both the outer supportive levels and the deeper exploratory levels of psychotherapy.

Indeed, the therapeutic use of groups in modern clinical practice can be traced to the early years of this century, when the American chest physician Pratt (1907), working in Boston, described forming 'classes' of fifteen to twenty patients with tuberculosis who had been rejected for sanatorium treatment. Weekly social meetings provided instruction and mutual support, which led to striking improvements in morale and physical health. Subsequently, in the 1920s and 1930s, a number of psychiatrists applied such didactic and supportive measures to groups of mental hospital patients (Rosenbaum 1978; Ettin 1988). The term 'group therapy', however, was first used around 1920 by Moreno, whose main contribution was the development of psychodrama (p.169) in which groups were used as both cast and audience for the exploration of individual problems by re-enactment under the direction of the leader (Moreno 1948).

By the 1920s Freud was applying psychoanalytic insights to anthropology and to social groups. In *Totem and Taboo* (1913) he had explored the universality of the incest barrier, and in *Group Psychology and the Analysis of the Ego* (1921) he speculated on crowd behaviour, and the relationships of groups (such as Church and Army) to their leaders. The concept of the Super-ego (Freud 1923) recognized the internalization of social standards (p.47). Freud did not undertake anthropological fieldwork nor therapeutic work with groups himself; he left these to anthropologists such as Roheim (1950) and the psycho-analysts whose work is described in this section.

Adler parted from Freud in 1911, not only because he dis-agreed with Freud's view of instinct, but also because he attributed greater importance to social factors. He played a part in founding social and preventive psychiatry and had a direct influence on the development of day hospitals and therapeutic clubs (Bierer and Evans 1969). However, Adler did not himself explore the therapeutic use of groups beyond such innovations as conversation classes in kindergartens and among mothers of children attending child guidance clinics.

Exchange of information, education, encouragement, and mutual support are fundamental functions of therapeutic groups in their widest sense. Informal, non-professional self-help groups such as Alcoholics Anonymous are being developed and proving of value to many people who share problems such as alcoholism, agoraphobia, widowhood, or a handicapped child (Shaffer and Galinsky 1989:Ch.13). It will be apparent that these groups are primarily supportive rather than exploratory in aim.

The more analytic and exploratory use of groups in both hospital and out-patient settings was pioneered by a few Euro-pean psychoanalysts who emigrated to the USA, such as Paul Schilder who treated severely neurotic and mildly psychotic out-patients in small groups at Bellevue Hospital, New York.

However, each of his patients was also seen individually throughout the course of treatment, which was largely focused on individual psychopathology. Nevertheless, Schilder considered that some of the patients 'could not have been treated individually with classical analysis. They reacted only in the group. This is especially true of social neuroses' (Schilder 1939:97). In a group he found that patients 'realize with astonishment that the thoughts which have seemed to isolate them are common to all of them' (ibid.:91).

The power of groups was most influentially demonstrated in Britain during the Second World War, when several psychoanalysts and psychiatrists proved the value of group methods for officer selection in the War Office Selection Boards. A chance to run an Army psychiatric unit on group lines was then given to several of these pioneers, notably Bion and Rickman, followed by Foulkes and Main. The Northfield Military Hospital in Birmingham gave its name to what came to be called the two 'Northfield Experiments', which provided the impetus for the development since the war both of social therapy (p.149), i.e., the therapeutic community movement (Main 1946), and of the use of small groups for the treatment of neurotic and personality disorders (Foulkes 1964). Main (1977) has given us a vivid account of these pioneering days.

Another important influence in group work was that of the psychologist Kurt Lewin, a refugee from Nazi Germany working at the Massachusetts Institute of Technology, who coined the expression 'group dynamics'. He inspired the evolution in the USA of Sensitivity Training groups and Human Relations Laboratories, and developed his own field theory of social interaction, which involves the idea of psychological space and emphasizes the 'here and now' more than remote causes in the past. The effect of different styles of leadership on the functioning and social climate of groups was illuminated by his classic experiment comparing the effects of autocratic, democratic, and laissez-faire leadership (Lewin, Lippitt, and White 1939). Children in autocratically led clubs were dependent on the leader and self-centred in relation to their peers. When led democratically, the same children not only showed more initiative, friendliness, and responsibility, but they worked better and continued to work in the leader's absence. In laissez-faire groups, as well as those led autocratically, aggression was more common. Lewin's main influence has been through T-groups (training groups) organized to help people working in industry and other organizations to become aware of the effects of interpersonal behaviour, including styles of leadership (Frank 1964; Rice 1965). However, many processes emphasized in that field occur in therapy groups of both analytic and Encounter (p.166) type, such as 'self-disclosure', 'feedback', and 'unfreezing', i.e., the process of disconfirming the belief system previously held by an individual (Kaplan 1967).

Formal groups have been used for therapeutic and training purposes in many ways beyond analytic group therapy and T-groups, for example, Encounter, Gestalt, and Psychodrama groups which will be described in a later section, and groups used in Transactional Analysis and Behaviour Therapy. (Shaffer and Galinsky (1989) have written a valuable exposition of these many different models of group therapy and training.) We shall confine ourselves in what follows now to analytic group psychotherapy, which in the course of its development has been approached in three main ways: as analysis *in* the group, analysis *of* the group, and analysis *through* the group.

Analysis in the group makes the least use of group-dynamics. The therapist conducts psychotherapy of individuals in a group setting, as Schilder did, a method developed particularly in the USA, most notably by Wolf and Schwartz (1962). Their patients had often had a good deal of individual therapy or preparation, and so already had important individual relationships with the therapist. Sessions were held four times a week, two of them ('alternate' sessions) without the therapist. In this approach, there is an emphasis on individual transference relationships, and the therapist is active in directing therapeutic work on transference and resistance. The emergence of more spontaneous group processes is probably inhibited by focusing attention so much on the individual members and on the therapist.

Analysis of the group is associated with the particular interest in group dynamics developed in Britain by Bion and Ezriel at the Tavistock Clinic in London; group processes are seen to reflect the common motives, anxieties, and defences of the individuals in the group. Bion (1961) has contributed the idea of *basic assumptions*, or primitive states of mind which are generated automatically when people combine in a group. The fantasies and emotional drives associated with these basic assumptions unconsciously dominate the group's behaviour in a way that is apt to interfere with its explicit work task and so prevent creative change and development. In the case of a therapy group, the 'basic assumption groups' interfere with exploration by the 'work group' of the feelings and problems of individuals in it. Bion names the basic assumptions as *dependence* (expecting solutions to be bestowed by the therapist leader), *fight-flight* (fleeing from or engaging in battle with adversaries, particularly outside the group), and *pairing* (encouraging or hoping for a coupling of individuals which could lead to the birth of a person or idea that would provide salvation). These three attitudes, Bion suggests, are institutionalized respectively in the Church, Army, and Aristocracy. The relationship between basic assumption groups and work groups could be seen as analogous to that between primary and secondary process thinking (p.49). It is also possible to imagine the three basic assumptions of dependence, fight-flight, and pairing, as linked by fantasy systems associated with the oral-dependent, separation individuation, and Oedipal stages of individual development (Brown 1979). Bion worked with therapeutic groups for only a few years; his ideas have perhaps had more influence on our understanding of the dynamics of institutions, including therapeutic communities (p.151), committees with their hidden agendas, and training groups such as the T-groups organized by the Tavistock Institute of Human Relations in its Leicester Conferences (Rice 1965). Bion's ideas have helped us to understand the primitive factors disrupting group work rather than the positive processes promoting it. Whereas 'basic assumption' phenomena do occur, they may do so particularly in situations where 'democratic' dialogue is impossible, inappropriate, or not sought – as in some committees, institutions, and societies, and in 'autocratically' conducted therapy groups (Brown 1985).

Ezriel (1950, 1952) coined the expression *common group tension* to describe the group conflict resulting from a shared, wished-for but *avoided relationship* with the therapist, which arouses fear of the consequences if it were to be acknowledged (the *calamitous relationship*) and is resolved by the adoption of a compromise relationship with him (the *required relationship*). For example, hostility to the therapist for frustrating each patient's wish to be the only patient/child (avoided relationship), may lead to fear of retaliation by abandonment (calamitous relationship), and be resolved by concealing resentment under an attitude of helpful compliance (required relationship). Ezriel regarded the group therapist's task as first to discern the common group tension, and then to point out to each member of the group his own personal contribution and former solution to the conflict, based on his individual psychopathology. In this sense Ezriel combined analysis *of* the group and analysis *in* the group. These ideas can be useful in most groups, but their relevance is greatest in groups conducted along the lines of Bion and Ezriel, in which the therapist emphasizes his importance by being frustratingly impassive, or by being active in encouraging transference to himself.

Analysis through the group is particularly associated with the other main approach in British group psychotherapy, developed by S.H. Foulkes (1898–1976), the founder in London of the Group-Analytic Society in 1952. Like Bion and Ezriel, Foulkes was a psychoanalyst, but early in his career in Germany he worked alongside sociologists, and also for a time with the neurologist Kurt Goldstein, who was using the ideas of the Gestalt psychologists with their interest in the interrelation of sum and part, and of figure and ground. Foulkes was deeply impressed by the way in which a context affects not only what is seen, but also what happens within it.

Having made the experiment of seeing his individual analytic patients together in his waiting room in Exeter, Foulkes (1964) discovered at Northfield Military Hospital, during World War Two, that a freer, more democratic system could promote confidence and responsibility in previously demoralized and passively resentful patients. He regarded the group as the therapeutic medium, and the therapist's task as that of nurturing its therapeutic potential by allowing the individuals in it to function increasingly as active and responsible agents themselves. In group-analytic psychotherapy 'the individual is being treated *in the context* of the group with the active participation of the group.' (Foulkes and Anthony 1973:16). It is 'psychotherapy *by* the group, *of* the group, including its conductor.' (Foulkes 1975:3).

Foulkes came to see the individual as at a nodal point in a network of relationships, and illness as a disturbance in the network that comes to light through the vulnerable individual. This awareness of *transpersonal* phenomena anticipated the recent developments in our understanding of family processes and therapy. Furthermore, Foulkes discerned the many levels at which groups function, often simultaneously: (1) the level of current adult relationships; (2) the level of individual transference relationships; (3) the level of projected and shared feelings and fantasies, often from early pre-verbal stages of development; and (4) the level of archetypal universal images, reminiscent of Jung's Archetypes of the Unconscious. It will be seen that these levels range from more conscious objective 'everyday' relationships to increasingly subjective and unconscious fantasy relationships; from more to less clearly differentiated and individual relationships (Foulkes and Anthony 1957; Foulkes 1964). *Figure 9* illustrates the way these levels can be linked with the idea of Parent, Adult, and Child parts of the personality (p.55). Level 1 would be A ↔ A, Level 2 C → P, Level 3 C ↔ C, and Level 4 would join an infinite number of individuals.

The group-analytic approach of Foulkes is probably the most influential one in Britain today (Walton 1971; Pines 1983), and forms the basis of most of what follows in describing small group psychotherapy. In 1967 Foulkes started the journal *Group Analysis*, and in 1971 played a key part in founding the

Figure 9

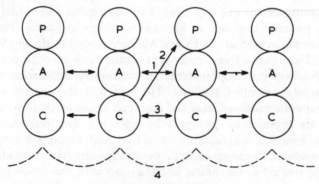

Foulkes's levels

1. current adult relationships (working alliance)
2. individual transference
3. shared feelings and fantasies
4. archetypal images

124

Institute of Group Analysis, the major training organization in analytic group psychotherapy with courses developing throughout Britain, and part of the Analytical Psychotherapy Section of UKSCP (p.203). Trainees are expected to have long-term intensive analytic group psychotherapy.

The setting

Six to eight patients, usually strangers to each other at the start, meet regularly for between one and one and a half hours, once or twice a week, for one to several years (most commonly two to three). The therapist (or pair of co-therapists) sits with them in a circle, in reasonably comfortable and equal chairs, perhaps with a small table in the centre as a focal point. Relative quietness and freedom from intrusion are as important as in individual psychotherapy, since the free flow of group discussion is the equivalent in a group of free-association in individual therapy.

Patients are expected to view group membership as a major commitment, to treat as confidential anything spoken of in the group, and not to meet outside without reporting it to the group. They are asked to notify the group of unexpected absences, to take holidays during the periods of several weeks a year set aside for this, and preferably to give at least a month's notice if they wish to leave. Most out-patient groups are *slow-open* groups, in that membership slowly changes as individuals leave at a time appropriate for them, and are replaced by others. Some are *closed* groups, with all patients starting and finishing together at the end of a given time, say one or two years, which has been previously arranged. Closed groups are more common for training purposes, to fit in with academic terms or courses, but have been used in centres where pressure of demand for group therapy makes it expedient, with good results (Dick 1975). Closed groups have the advantage that all members share the experience of termination together; while on the other hand, in a slow-open group, the experience of moving from a position of newcomer to one of senior, older sibling, is also valuable.

Most groups are deliberately composed of equal numbers of men and women, with sufficient similarity of background or ways of expressing themselves for communication to be facilitated and for no one to feel too much an outsider; e.g. the *only* single or coloured person may feel even more isolated than before joining the group. A range of personality type and experience is aimed for, as well as a variety of problem, in order to provide an atmosphere where people can interact fruitfully, learn from each other, and together represent the human condition in miniature. The idea of a group can often be threatening to patients who have social problems, or fear that their problems could not possibly be understood or tolerated by other people unless it were their job to do so. It is therefore important to prepare patients for a group by explaining what to expect, and to discuss their anxieties and possible inclination to leave the group soon after joining (Whitaker 1985:183ff). Sometimes an initial period of individual therapy will help a patient to make better use of a group (Malan *et al.* 1976).

The social nature of the setting provides opportunities to examine patients' difficulties in a situation reflecting the family and social networks in which their problems developed. In the National Health Service in Britain, group psychotherapy is the most generally available form of psychotherapy. This is not just an expedient; group psychotherapy is the treatment of choice for many people whose prime difficulty is relating to others.

Patient's role

The need for each patient to take responsibility for his problems and for seeking their solution through fuller understanding of himself and his relationships, exists in all exploratory insight-orientated analytic therapy, including that conducted in groups. Agreement to participate in group therapy already involves a tacit recognition that solutions cannot be expected from passive dependence on the therapist functioning as a parent/magician, but patients with uncertain motivation can find it strengthened by the example, support, and challenge of others. The therapeutic alliance needs to be forged, not only with the therapist, but also with fellow-patients, some of whom may be initially feared or even disliked, though the sharing of the endeavour on a more obviously equal footing can speed up the process, fostered by the discovery of how much each patient has in common with the others.

The greater his participation in the group, the more a patient will get from it. This involves being increasingly open about himself and his problems, but also increasingly responsive to and involved with others. Mere talking about himself, regardless of the needs or responses of others – 'hogging the limelight' – is usually counterproductive, leading to isolation and confirmation of stereotyped views of himself and others.

Some patients, silent for a while or for long periods, can still gain a lot from being in a group if they can allow themselves to think and feel in response to what is happening. In contrast with individual therapy, socially withdrawn and emotionally cut-off (schizoid) people can test themselves out gradually through involvement which is at first vicarious. What ultimately helps is joining in creating, responding to, and reflecting upon the experiences unfolding in the group, eventually putting into words what was previously unknown or inexpressible to themselves and others. Increasingly, each patient is enabled to take a therapeutic role in the group.

Therapist's role

The therapist is often called the *group conductor*. Like the conductor of an orchestra, he starts and finishes the proceedings, and helps to create an atmosphere in which honest communication can occur, with everyone giving of their best. By remaining relatively unobtrusive, he encourages the group to think, feel, and interact among themselves. This also allows him the opportunity to reflect on what is happening, using his own feelings and associations, including memories of previous sessions. He can attend not only to what individuals are saying, but how topics and associations link, and what the process reveals of common group preoccupations and conflicts. He may recognize that one individual is talking for others as well as for himself, for example, a more outspoken member might be able to criticize the conductor while others, more hostile but fearful, silently collude; or he may discern that talk about events in the outside world really concerns something being avoided in the group, for example, general discussion may develop about refugees, while an impending holiday break is not mentioned.

In the early stages, when individuals have not yet got to know and trust each other, the group usually adopts a regressive or dependent relationship to the conductor, looking to him for leadership and gratification of infantile wishes (Scheidlinger 1968). The group-analytic therapist, unlike those who follow the Tavistock model of Bion and Ezriel, will accept this as at first inevitable, because patients have to learn how to trust the new situation and to discover their own roles in it. The therapist may therefore facilitate, explain, and interpret more actively in the early stage, but relinquish this role of leadership when the group culture has become established.

However, the conductor's position as part of the group, yet different from the others, leaves him freer than the patients to maintain an analytic position of 'free-floating' attention. He can observe and may comment on how each person brings his problems into the group, creating a fresh blend in the 'here and now' of contributions from their current life outside, and from their past, including early family relationships. He is also able to tune into the atmosphere of the group, and might discern in the separate contributions of individuals, a common preoccupation or conflict. Some conductors find the concept of *group focal conflict* (Whitaker and Lieberman 1964) useful in orientating themselves. The conflict involves a *disturbing motive* in the group (such as the wish of each patient to have the therapist to himself), giving rise to a *reactive motive* (fear of disapproval by the therapist and fellow group members), and resulting in a *group solution*. Whitaker and Lieberman's group solution is not conceived as a fixed defence; it can change in the course of a session. A solution may be *restrictive*, directed only at alleviating the fear, or *enabling*, in which case some expression of the disturbing motive will be allowed, so that understanding and analysis is promoted. One common restrictive solution to the group conflict just described is that of 'spotlighting', where one patient at a time is given the whole group's attention. A more enabling solution is achieved when the hidden wish of all to be the only patient is acknowledged, so allowing a freer sharing of experiences. The concepts of group motives and solutions are really variants of those of wish, fear, and defence in classical psychoanalysis, and of Ezriel's avoided, calamitous, and required relationships.

The conductor's task is to help in creating a therapeutic atmosphere, and in the discovery, by the group, of such enabling solutions to the inevitable tensions it experiences. His interventions, including interpretations, may be especially needed when blockage occurs in the process of communication and exploration. It might be that issues are being avoided, or an individual is allowing himself to be ignored. Patients may still lack the confidence and skill to challenge someone (often the conductor), or to say something that they imagine would provoke a hostile or shaming response. At such times the conductor could intervene with a clarifying question, a confronting observation, or an interpretation. He might offer an encouraging comment or even divert attention if someone is too uncomfortably 'on the hook'. He does not confine himself to group interpretations, but talks to the group through the individual, and to the individual through the group. The conductor's interventions, like his attitude, have a modelling function from which patients increasingly find their own way of functioning as therapists, including interpreting wishes, feelings, and links with early family relationships.

As well as conveying a psychoanalytic attitude, the group conductor functions as a facilitator and model, in a rather more active role than the conventional picture of the psychoanalyst as a mirror, though even the latter is now an outdated view. His position, sitting in the group circle, would make it difficult and unnatural for him to hide himself and his feelings, even if he wanted to. However, therapists vary in their attitude to this issue of *therapist transparency* (Yalom 1985), some choosing to reveal more, some less. Most group therapists judiciously vary their approach, even within the same session. Both ends of the continuum have their advantages. A constantly impassive stance encourages the emergence of transference responses to the conductor, but provides a poor model of active concern and emotional or imaginative freedom. On the other hand, though patients do not want to be burdened with the conductor's personal life and problems, they usually appreciate and benefit from his example of openness and confidence in expressing himself. When the conductor takes the option to express and report his countertransference feelings and fantasies in response to what is happening in the group, patients may be helped to use their own feelings and fantasies more freely, and he can sometimes promote deeper levels of experience in the group.

Therapeutic processes

Analytic psychotherapy in groups, like that conducted on an individual basis, aims to help the individual to resolve conflicts, and gain greater understanding of himself and others, in the interest of fuller growth and development; the aim is insight, plus adjustment to relationships with others. The group setting in which these processes occur provides a context which has important consequences.

Because several people are taking part, interaction can be more varied and complex, at both conscious and unconscious levels, than in individual therapy. More experiences are drawn on from everyone's life situation, past and present, and a wider range of responses and attitudes is available. Because we are dealing with a multipersonal field *multiple transferences* can develop; that is, each person may transfer feelings not only to the therapist, but also to fellow patients and to the group as a whole; which can represent a mother, womb, or breast. Other patients may be experienced as siblings in rivalrous competition for the therapist/parent's attention, as in the example on p.59. At times, patients may experience others as though they represented unwelcome aspects of themselves, through projection and projective indentification (p.26).

Patients learn a lot about themselves by feedback from fellow group members. They can discover how their behaviour and attitudes are often self-defeating, and how they lend themselves to be misunderstood and to misunderstand others, for example, coercing them to fit in with a transference distortion, or expressing hostility to someone because they represent a feared aspect of themselves.

In one group, the mounting hostility between two members exploded in a session which allowed a homosexual man to see that he could not stand a recently married fellow member because he reminded him, in his gruff, withdrawn behaviour, of his rejecting and critical father.

At the same time the other man recognized that he himself was identifying with his own withdrawn father, who could not respond to the patient's longing for him, and that he feared his own affectionate feelings as feminine and therefore homosexual.

This is an example of what Foulkes called a *mirror reaction*. Through it the two patients saw more of themselves and their reactions, and thereby made contact with an important part of themselves. Following this they were able to communicate with and value each other better; and other patients had the opportunity to learn something too by sharing in the experience and applying it to their own developing understanding of themselves and others.

Neurotic conflicts can be seen as originating in relationships between the individual and his original family group. In the example given above, the two men were unable in childhood fully to express hostility or affection to their parents. Not only did they fear their fathers' responses, but also, the first man's mother had been temperamentally cold and critical, and the second man's had been unapproachable because of her chronic tuberculosis, which meant he was not allowed to give or receive demonstrations of love. The group provided a situation in which their previously private and incommunicable wishes and feelings could be expressed. As symptoms and inhibitions were translated into shared communication, they became understandable, and the outdated fears could be tested against the new reality of the therapy group and gradually relinquished.

Communication within and between people reverberates. Individual therapy allows for more detailed working within the single transference relationship with the therapist and more detailed reconstruction of each individual's developmental history, especially in its earlier infantile phase. But the setting of group therapy permits an analysis of the 'here and now' of the developing network of relationships, which for some can be both more varied and more vivid. Not only is there more input and response, at both transference and non-transference levels, which enables very intense emotional experiences to occur; but contrasts between the experience and behaviour of different individuals, and between those of an individual now, compared with an earlier occasion, can stand out very clearly. Therapeutic change is open to observation.

In a group, people can *resonate* to what occurs at different levels of consciousness and regression, according to their needs and preoccupations. From the common pool of themes and feelings they pick out what is most meaningful to them at the time. They respond to different levels of meaning from conscious to deeply unconscious, from mature to primitively infantile, according to what is stirred up in them.

In a group with two new members, an old member had just married and another's wife had just had a child. These events prompted envy and hostility in some of the others, as well as more readily expressed pleasure. Then, the therapist had to announce an unpopular change of arrangements, and for several sessions bad mothering became a shared theme which evoked memories and group dreams that were both intensely moving and illuminating. The shared painful longing and ambivalence, which led the more emotionally detached members to withdraw and the more depressive ones to burden themselves with guilt and excessive reparative behaviour, became clearer to all. The intensity evoked the impact of early traumatic experiences, which were now more tolerable because they were shared.

One depressed professional woman, excessively devoted to her work in helping others, had been emotionally deprived as a child because her very beautiful mother was incapacitated by chronic asthma. She dreamt during this period in the group that she met another group member, a more obviously attractive woman (representing mother), wearing a dress which was the same as her own but brighter in colour. They went to a cafeteria where the other woman poured out two cups of coffee, which spurted over the dreamer's dress. Still wet, she went into the next room which was full of desks piled with papers. She set to work on them until a man (representing the therapist) came in and told her she did not need to work so hard. In talking about the dream, the group recognized its clear symbolism of envy of her attractive mother, her mixed feelings about being fed by her, and her need to work hard to compensate for them. The patient realized that the man in the dream stood for the therapist, from whom she had learned that she did not need to go on making reparation for feelings she had had for her mother, now evoked in the group in relation to the other woman.

This is an example of the group dreams which are especially useful in group therapy, since they can be understood and worked on by everyone sharing the same 'here and now' experience. The detailed analysis of dreams, otherwise, plays a less important part in group therapy than in individual therapy.

Group therapy is rooted in the experiences fed into and emerging from the group. These build up into a unique developing culture with its own history and memory, as members relate ever more deeply and intimately. Foulkes called this the *group matrix*. In it each individual can immerse himself in experiences which are personal, interpersonal, and transpersonal. That is they spring from each individual's unique past and present outside the group, from fresh engagements between members 'here and now' in the group, and from deep shared motives and responses which transcend their separate individualities. In 'Group analysis: taking the non-problem seriously', Garland (1982) has described the value of patients entering a new system, the group, quite different from that in which their problems arose. The new task, relating more fully and honestly with strangers, takes priority over the restricted 'world view' of the presenting problem, which when it emerges can be seen more clearly as foreground against a healthier background. As patients immerse themselves in the group matrix, each individual can question their own preconceptions, boundaries and identity; they can regain aspects of themselves that they have disowned and projected, and re-emerge with fresh insights and ways of relating.

Yalom (1985) has described several therapeutic factors specific to groups. *Universality* refers to the discovery of shared basic preoccupations, fears, and conflicts, so that what had previously isolated individuals is now found to unite them. *Altruism*, caring for and helping others in need, follows as individuals emerge from isolation and painful preoccupation with themselves alone; the group situation provides opportunities for people to develop their strengths at the same time as revealing their weaknesses, to function increasingly as therapists as well as patients. *Corrective recapitulation of the family group* implies that what went wrong in the early family group can be repeated and recognized in the group, where now, in a more open and experimental atmosphere, less maladaptive ways of coping can be worked out. Sometimes a group provides something lacking in the original family, such as acceptance and encouragement, or the right to differ and express hostility. *Imitative behaviour* refers to the opportunity other group members, including the conductor, provide of different models of behaving and relating that can be followed in choosing alternatives to old restrictive and neurotic ways. *Interpersonal learning* indicates the experience the social setting provides for increasing interpersonal skills by discovering new ways of being oneself with others, in an environment which is much nearer to everyday life than is individual psychotherapy. This is what Foulkes meant when he described group psychotherapy as involving 'ego training in action'. Problems can be observed and worked with *in vivo*. *Cohesiveness* is the sense of solidarity that binds a group together, and makes it attractive to its members. The sense of belonging enables members to work through difficulties together, and is thus part of the therapeutic or working alliance. *Existential factors* include recognition of responsibility in the face of our basic aloneness and mortality.

Skynner (1986) has emphasized the way in which group membership provides opportunities to make up for developmental deficits and overcome blocks based on neurotic conflict, as the group itself moves towards greater understanding and maturation. He believes the conductor's role needs to be appropriate to the stage the group is recapitulating: supportive and nurturant in the initial dependent stage; firmer, more frustrating, and confronting when group cohesion and confidence is better established; and finally more open, personal, and playful when it has moved towards fuller intimacy and individuation. Like Foulkes, he holds that the therapist who grows and learns through the group provides the most effective model.

Various stages of group development have been described

in experimental group dynamic situations, well reviewed by Whiteley and Gordon (1979): Schutz (1958) related these to basic human needs of inclusion, control, and affection; Tuckman (1965) proposed four stages of forming, storming, norming, and performing that represent establishing a sense of belonging, emergence of conflict and resistance, arrival at intimacy, and new standards and roles, eventually sufficient for pursuit of group tasks. In an open-ended group, any such stages occur in a circular or spiral fashion, triggered by changing membership, crises, and destructive periods, but always hopefully in the direction of greater maturity.

Destructive forces in groups (Zinkin 1983) are based on primitive processes such as splitting, projection, and envy, often rooted in failures of the earliest environment to contain and modify severe anxiety, pain, and rage. They need to be faced up to and resolved for a move to take place in individual and group from the paranoid-schizoid to the depressive position (Klein, see p.106), or from what Winnicott (1963) called the stage of ruthlessness to the capacity for concern.

As mentioned, group therapy provides the greater part of long-term psychotherapy in the National Health Service in Britain today. Following assessment, when it becomes clear that a patient needs longer-term help to understand and modify his neurotic and interpersonal difficulties, a period of group therapy may be indicated if he has sufficient motivation for insight, sufficient Ego strength (see Selection and Outcome), and is prepared to commit himself to regular attendance for, say, at least a year. Where there is a range of psychiatric and psychotherapeutic facilities (still too rare in the NHS), group therapy can be part of an overall plan. It might be the first treatment offered; it may follow management of a crisis by supportive psychotherapy, medication, or hospital admission; or it might follow a shorter period of individual analytic therapy. Some patients who have responded to psychoanalytic therapy with only partial success can often begin to move, or apply what they have already learned, in the new atmosphere of a group. It has been stated, aphoristically, that 'after a successful psycho-analytic treatment a patient is definitely less neurotic (or psychotic) but perhaps not necessarily really mature; on the other hand, after a successful treatment by group methods the patient is not necessarily less neurotic but

135

inevitably more mature.' (Balint and Balint 1961:5). This difference probably results from the greater availability of non-transference curative factors in group therapy, the greater similarity of the setting to the natural groups in which people live, in the family and in society, and the activation of mutual responsibility and concern (Brown 1987).

FAMILY AND MARITAL THERAPY

The drama of family relationships has been the stuff of legend and literature since ancient times; but not until recently have psychiatrists recognized current family relationships as common sources of serious emotional disturbance, in addition to constitutional factors or intrapsychic conflicts and traumas rooted in early life.

The systematic study and treatment of family and marital problems have only emerged in the last few decades. Mittelman (1948), working in the USA, reported on his simultaneous but separate psychoanalytic treatment of husband and wife, which allowed him to understand their conscious and unconscious interaction and to treat successfully eleven out of twelve couples. At about the same time, the effect that some families have of predisposing children to schizophrenia was being studied. Fromm-Reichmann (1948) contributed the idea of the 'schizophrenogenic mother', and Lidz (1949) that of parental 'marital schism and skew', with consequent blurring of generation lines and promotion of irrational ideas. This type of study was continued by workers in the USA and Britain, some of whom believed that the immediate family of schizophrenics may be at least as ill as the patient. They were thought to communicate in deviant ways such as 'double binding' the patient (Bateson et al. 1956) by presenting to him contradictory overt and covert injunctions to which there is no correct response and from which there is no escape; for example, the mother who repeatedly asks her son to kiss her, but walks away when he moves towards her, and then accuses him of not being a good son. Such families may have disturbed styles of thinking including 'pseudo-mutuality' and illogicality which conceal underlying hostility (Wynne et al. 1958). Some believe that the family negate and virtually deny the patient's experience by 'mystification', so that a schizophrenic reaction is a natural self-protective response (Laing and Esterson 1964). In consequence, schizophrenia is seen by some as a family problem, and family therapy therefore as appropriate in certain cases. Doubts have been expressed about the validity of the observations on which this theory is based (Hirsch and Leff 1975), though the discrepant findings are almost certainly due in part to stricter criteria for diagnosing schizophrenia in Britain compared with the USA. In Britain the diagnosis is restricted to a clear-cut illness; in the USA it is used more broadly, covering more diffuse emotional reactions and personality problems.

While in Britain family conflicts are not generally seen as having a primary role in the aetiology of schizophrenia, it is well-established (Brown et al. 1972; Leff and Vaughn 1985) that patients who have had a schizophrenic breakdown are more liable to relapse in an emotionally charged family atmosphere. In any event, these studies have aroused interest in the role of the family in psychiatric disorders in general. Family relationships are now widely accepted as relevant to the understanding of many emotional and developmental problems.

Although it had long been customary in Child Guidance Clinics for a mother to be interviewed as well as her child, she was usually seen by a social worker while the child was interviewed and treated separately by a psychiatrist. However, in the 1950s, Ackerman (1966) began using family interviews in work with children and adolescents in the USA, and now this is being increasingly practised in Britain, where some child psychiatry clinics have been re-named departments of child and family psychiatry. Family therapy can be seen as a natural development of child psychiatry. Some departments of child psychiatry now offer a diagnostic interview to the whole family of any child newly referred (Bentovim and Kinston 1978) rather than the traditional method of mother and child being first seen separately

The usefulness of systems theory in analysing the problems of individuals and the natural groups in which they live has already been discussed (p.51). Skynner (1976, 1987), a leading exponent of family and marital therapy in Britain, developed his work through his interest in group psychotherapy and his practice as a psychiatrist in a child guidance clinic. He considers that what characterizes these newer forms of psychotherapy is their focus on the pathology and treatment of the natural systems formed by individuals in intimate relationships, rather than on individual psychopathology.

Therapy ideally helps the natural system of the family to move towards the patterns of interaction that characterize healthy families. Skynner (1987) has summarized studies of these in the USA, particularly those of the Timberlawn Psychiatric Research Foundation (Lewis 1979) which compared families at the extremes of health and dysfunction. At a level of statistical significance 'healthy' families (1) were affiliative rather than oppositional; (2) showed respect for separateness and individuality; (3) made open, clear communciations; (4) had a firm, equal parental coalition; (5) used flexible, negotiable control; and (6) interacted spontaneously, with wit and humour.

The many techniques used in family therapy have been well described by Glick and Kessler (1974), Skynner (1976), Walrond-Skinner (1976), Hoffman (1981) and Bentovim et al. (1987). As Bruggen and Davies (1977) have pointed out in a review of the field, methods range in a spectrum from the more analytic to the more active techniques. At the analytic end of the spectrum methods aim at insight through interpretation; at the other end, change in the disturbed system is sought through active intervention by the therapist using behavioural methods such as direct challenge and instruction, and active techniques such as role-playing, video-tape feedback, and 'family sculpting'. (In family sculpting 'the members of a family create a physical representation of their relationships at one point in time by arranging their bodies in space', in a tableau vivant (Simon 1972).)

The Milan school of family therapists (Selvini-Palazzoli et al. 1978) use their background as psychoanalysts to expose and undermine the unconscious 'rules of the game' which maintain family pathology. In their approach, psychoanalytic understanding is used for 'behavioural ends'. Family therapy is thus a fruitful meeting ground for dynamic and behavioural psychotherapists in many parts of the world. In 1977 they joined together to found the Institute of Family Therapy (London), now one of several organizations in the Family, Marital, and Sexual Therapy Sections of UKSCP (p.203). In contrast with individual and group analytical psychotherapists, family

therapy training does not insist on long-term personal psychotherapy experience.

The setting

The common element in family and marital therapy is the
focus on the family or marriage as the disturbed unit. Usually
one member has presented him or herself or (especially in the
case of children) has been referred as the patient to be treated.
The family or marital therapist will want to make a diagnosis
at the level of the whole family system and to interview as
many of the family as possible; if there is a marital problem,
he will want to see both partners. He will take pains to invite
the cooperation of the other members of the family (or the
spouse), and if possible interview them together. This *conjoint
interview* is often conducted by a pair of therapists, male and
female, which is particularly useful in marital therapy, as it
avoids some of the dangers of appearing to take sides. How
cooperative spouses or leading members of the family are, how
willing they are to help and share in taking responsibility
for the problems and their resolution, is itself of diagnostic
importance; for example, their insistence on making one
person the repository of all disturbance or blame suggests that
they need to see and keep it that way. An extreme example
is where a member of the family is falsely admitted to a mental
hospital by relatives who want rid of him or her. This has
been called the 'gaslight phenomenon' (Barton and Whitehead
1969) after the play *Gaslight* written in 1931 by Patrick Hamilton, which portrayed a husband trying to convince his wife
that she was mad. Family scapegoating is not new. In 1763, a
Select Committee of the House of Commons reported that
some people had been committed to asylums as a way of
solving family and social problems (Leigh 1961).

Sometimes family therapists will conduct their interviews in
the family home, particularly when they work on the *crisis
intervention* model. Psychiatric referral or requests for admission are then viewed as the result of a crisis in the network
of relationships in which the adult or adolescent patient lives,
usually at home, but perhaps also at school or work (Brandon
1970; Bruggen and Davies 1977). Such a crisis has usually
already existed for a period of a few days to six weeks before

either natural resolution or illness supervene. Timely therapeutic intervention can sometimes enable the crisis to be
resolved in a way that promotes learning and change. Some
psychiatrists, such as Scott (1973), recommend that all requests
for urgent admission should be first investigated at home,
in order to prevent unnecessary institutionalization. When
patients are seen in the context of their families, their problems
can often be encountered *in vivo*. This approach is probably
more appropriate where there is a settled population and families are living together than in bed-sitter land in city centres.

With less acute problems, interviews can take place in a
clinic or out-patient department, where it may be easier to
provide a suitable setting: sufficient equal chairs set in a circle
in a quiet room, with space in the centre for people to move
around in if they so wish. A one-way viewing screen or video-
camera is often used to allow supervision of the process, which
in some techniques is interrupted to allow consultation with
observing members of the team. Diagnostic interviews merge
into therapy sessions; two or three consultations at intervals
of two or three weeks may suffice, or weekly or fortnightly
sessions may continue for a year or two. Some family therapists, following the diagnostic interview with the whole family,
may concentrate therapeutic work on the most responsive
family member (often not the referred patient) or the parents
only (Bowen 1966); while, at the opposite extreme, others
(Speck and Attneave 1973) involve as many as possible of the
family and associated networks (work, school, neighbourhood
etc.) in meetings of up to fifty people! Yet others, especially
in hospital settings for adolescents, may have multiple family
groups discussing family relationships and intergenerational
problems. Most limit themselves to the nuclear family, perhaps
with key grandparents or with others sharing the home.

Marital therapy can also be conducted in various ways (Dicks
1967): in conjoint sessions, in which both spouses meet
together with one or a pair of therapists; in groups in which
three or four marital pairs meet with one or two therapists;
or by individual therapy conducted simultaneously with each
spouse by different therapists, who meet periodically to coordi-
nate their work, a method developed particularly by the Institute of Marital Studies at the Tavistock Clinic (Pincus 1960).
Indications and contra-indications for conjoint and individually-

based approaches have been described by Skynner (1976). It is widely accepted that the conjoint approach is particularly valuable where the couple do not function as fully separate individuals; for example, each may represent a disavowed aspect of the other and make extensive use of projective identification (Main 1966) as in the clinical example described below (p.146). Skynner holds that the conjoint approach is less suitable for people who have not yet mastered the 'depressive position' (p.106) that is, they have not learned to tolerate, without too much guilt, the coexistence of powerful feelings of love and hate.

Patients' role

Ideally members of a family or a marital pair accept that the problem they seek help with is a shared one, the solving of which is, at least to some degree, a joint responsibility. Often, however, some members exclude themselves, at least initially, but need to be kept in mind by the therapist. To establish a therapeutic alliance, which has to include other family members as well as therapists, there needs to be some residual mutual goodwill, and some hope that things might improve.

Cooperation of relatives can often be gained by asking them to provide information about the presenting patient or to help in deciding the best way of coping with the difficulties caused by his or her 'illness'. Not uncommonly some key member refuses, most often a husband or father; but having at first granted this involvement reluctantly, they may often be willing to join in examining the problem and their own part in it, if they are guided in an understanding, clear, and firm way.

Given the opportunity and any necessary guidance, members can begin to talk and interact, revealing much of what their difficulties are. If they respond to the safety of this unusual situation and to the example of the therapist(s) in trying to face the truth impartially, family members may discover they can communicate more openly, and confront each other with their views and feelings. Often it is the more 'ill' spouse, or, in a family, one of the children, who understands more or can provide the information or challenge which moves interaction on to a more creative plane, beyond the stereotyped complaint of symptoms or mutual blame.

If the initial interviews engage the family or couple, they may continue to communicate more openly between sessions, particularly as they come to recognize their mutual responsibility for change. This is one of the clear advantages of conjoint therapy: participants go on living together between sessions, and so have an opportunity to put into practice new ways of interacting begun in the sessions and to make the mutual adjustments which are necessary if the system is going to change for the better. When they slip back into the old maladaptive ways, they may point this out to each other; in other words they can continue as their own therapists. For this reason, family and marital therapy sessions are often held at less frequent intervals than those in individual therapy, or group therapy with strangers.

Therapists' role

This depends in part on the level at which they choose to work and on their methods; whether they are working within a more psychoanalytic insight-seeking framework, or in a more action-based and behavioural one. Family and marital therapy is developing on the borders of several psychotherapeutic fields, but whatever their approach, the therapists tend to adopt a more active and directive role than most other dynamic psychotherapists. They structure the interviews and use their power to challenge the existing family hierarchy and rules. As well as the more usual responsive and supporting role, they need to be authoritative and challenging because the disturbance of the family system is kept going by the interlocking of many relationships. Indeed the art of all psychotherapy is to find the right blend of support and challenge, or feminine and masculine elements. Too much of the former and the therapist might be overprotective, like a clucking mother-hen; too much challenge and invasion, and the patient may be driven away.

Family therapists discourage, and rarely draw attention to, transference feelings of family members towards *themselves*, unless they are interfering with the work in hand. Instead, to encourage interaction and exploration, they emphasize how members of the family or marriage are relating to *each other* consciously and unconsciously; and how members need to see others in certain ways, for example by repeating and avoiding patterns of relationship from their family of origin. Quite often therapists describe their own countertransference feelings evoked by the couple or family, either as a whole or by particular members. Also, more than most other therapists, they may talk about their own personal experiences. They function as models of openness and honesty, which can be particularly helpful when talking about sexual functions in a relaxed and direct way, so counteracting the influence of inhibited or restrictive parents.

Beels and Ferber (1969), in reviewing the work of many family therapists, gave a still useful description of three main types: *conductors*, *reactors*, and *systems-purists*. *Conductors* attempt as 'super-parents' to effect change in the family system towards more healthy functioning; educating by 'maternal' persuasion or 'paternal' criticism, whichever is more appropriate. Structural family therapy (Minuchin 1974) uses this approach. Therapy consists of redesigning the family system so that it will approximate to the normative model of clear but open boundaries between the subsystems of parents and children, and the sibling subsystem will be organized so that children have tasks and privileges appropriate to their age and sex in the cultural suprasystem to which they belong. Perhaps understandably, this approach originated in work with often chaotic families in underprivileged inner-city areas of the USA.

Reactor analysts, usually more psychoanalytically orientated, seek the family's *own* potential for change and growth and, by lowering their own defences, allow themselves to be drawn into its atmosphere and projections. This enables the therapists to experience the family's disturbance within themselves, as they come to feel confused, unskilled, or angry. Skynner (1976, 1987), who is influenced by Foulkes's group analytic approach (pp.123ff.), points out that such therapists are prepared to be drawn into the vulnerable role of child or patient rather than that of super-parent. Skynner himself, and Whitaker (1975), are prominent psychodynamic family therapists who make special use of their own subjective reactions.

The teenage son of a divorced couple was taken to his general practitioner by his father (with whom he lived) because of his gambling, which his father seemed to perpetuate by his over-solicitousness and by rescuing him from the scrapes he got into, so that the son never learned to be responsible for himself. Interviewed together with both parents, he was almost mute, while the estranged parents, sitting on either side of him, used the boy to complain about each other's failings. Mother claimed that father spoiled him. Father asserted he did this because she was as poor a mother as she had been a wife; he (father) was a much better mother. As they battled, each separately saying a lot that was true, one of the therapists felt himself increasingly oppressed and confused, and finally said so. He asked the son whether he felt the same. With relief the boy agreed, and turning to his father said: 'It looks as though *we* should be divorced.' The truth of this dawned on everyone, and father was enabled to give up some of his motherliness and to let his son separate and learn from his own mistakes.

Reactor therapists often operate in pairs, one letting himself be drawn into the family pathology in this way, the other standing by in a more detached way as if at the end of a lifeline. In psychoanalytic therapy both these roles are carried out by the therapist, alternately identifying with the patient and withdrawing into objectivity. In family therapy dividing the roles allows one therapist to enter into a maelstrom that may be potentially strong enough to drive a vulnerable family member into confusion, perhaps even psychosis.

The third type of family therapist is the *systems-purist*, who attempts to discern the ground-rules the family uses for its interaction, and in which it attempts to engage the therapist. He counters them, does not play their game, and attempts to induce them to change their immature or pathological way of behaving. This approach characterizes 'strategic' family therapy (Haley and Hoffman 1967; Watzlawick *et al.* 1968) and the 'systemic' family therapy of the Milan School (Selvini-Palazzoli *et al.* 1978).

Strategic family therapy originated in the USA. It uses active interventions designed to fit the specific problem presented and the details of how and when it occurs. Practitioners consider that symptoms are maintained by the family's habitual solution and seek ways to interrupt the vicious circle. These include issuing 'paradoxical injunctions', which challenge the family's declared wish to change, and use the oppositional qualities of most entrenched families by urging them to stay as they are or do the opposite of what would help them to change.

Systemic family therapy developed in Milan. Originally two therapists, a man and a woman, worked with a family while another two sat behind a one-way screen. More recently one therapist conducts the interview, one to three watch from behind the screen. The team discusses the referral or previous session beforehand, and carefully note non-verbal communication during the hour-long session, which is videotaped. The team again consults, and the therapist rejoins the family to put their recommendations to them. These involve proposing counter-paradoxes to oppose the paradoxes in which severely abnormal families are trapped through a process of circular causality. Having established 'the family game', e.g. that the whole problem is in a sick member, they accept it and even encourage it, but 'reframe it' in terms of the family needing a sick person. They then prescribe tasks or rituals to the family or part of it, which are designed to disrupt the systems of non-verbal signs that control collusive family denial, including 'double binds' (see p.136).

Which of these three types (conductor, reactor, or systems purist) a therapist fits into, no doubt depends on his own personality and background, as well as on his theoretical training.

Therapeutic processes

The theory and practice of family and marital therapy encompass counselling, behavioural, and action methods, as well as those based on analytic psychotherapy and group therapy. Therapeutic processes can therefore occur at all the levels described above (pp.87ff).

The outer level might suffice for less deeply entrenched problems and is common in a first interview or throughout a period of marital counselling. The opening up of communication, as members of the family or marriage allow themselves and each other to speak their minds and express their feelings to an unaccustomed degree, can lead to clarification of problems and recognition of mutual needs and responsibility, so that shared decisions can be reached and carried out by joint action. The so-called 'contract therapy' described by Crowe (1973) is a behavioural modification of this approach, involving agreement by spouses to reward one another for behaviour which each seeks from the other; for example a husband might help with the housework if his wife allows more sexual contact, which she might have previously withheld because she was so resentful about the unequal sharing of unwelcome domestic chores. Sexual problems such as impotence and frigidity can often be helped by the behavioural techniques pioneered by Masters and Johnson (1970), so long as they are not too deeply rooted in neurotic conflict or marital discord (Scharff 1982; Skrine 1989).

At a deeper level, when disturbance is more entrenched and resistances to change are greater, it may be necessary to work with less conscious processes, using concepts from psychoanalysis and group analysis. Avoided truths need to be faced and accommodated within the family so that collusive and coercive patterns of relating, such as mutual projection, are revealed, and responsibility for them acknowledged. For example, the exposure of unspoken family myths (Ferreira 1963; Byng-Hall 1973), such as 'safety is inside the family, danger outside', or 'a happy family is one where there are no disagreements', allows family members to discover their own ambivalence to each other, or permits an adolescent to begin to explore his own developing independence and sexuality. Family members may come to recognize their projection on to others of images of internalized parents or aspects of themselves, so allowing greater individuation and autonomy.

A middle-aged couple sought help after the wife's breakdown into a depressed state. The sale by her husband of his highly successful business, in order to start a second career as an artist, stirred up her anxieties stemming from a financially and emotionally insecure childhood. Their marriage had been based on her embodying the weak, helpless, and dependent parts of both of them, while he represented the tough and reliable parts; in consequence neither had achieved full separation and individuation. His change of career reflected an increasing dissatisfaction with being cut off from the previously feared intuitive and 'feminine' parts of himself, which he had associated with his mother. His wife was unprepared for this and reacted with anxiety and unexpressed resentment. In treatment they came to see the way they had both lost touch, through projective identification (p.26), with important parts of themselves which they were able to re-own; he by becoming more comfortably intuitive and receptive, she by allowing herself to be more assertive and independent.

Clarification of boundaries and re-distribution of power within a family system may have far-reaching effects. For example, recognition by parents that they have colluded with a child's wish to divide and rule the family, may require them to acknowledge and work on their own marital problem. This could free them to cooperate in helping all to find more appropriate roles, which are likely to decrease the child's anxieties and his consequent need to behave omnipotently. Another example would be when the principal bond of affection in the family is between one parent and one child, so that problems over power, resentment by the excluded parent and siblings, and anxieties about incestuous attachments, may have very distorting effects. The correction of these will require a clarification of the boundary between the parents' and children's sub-systems. Families often come to function better when a father, previously reduced to passivity and withdrawal, is enabled by the therapist to develop his authority and involvement (Skynner 1976).

Such changes may necessitate overcoming powerful resistance to change in entrenched family pathology, but if successful this can lead to dramatic improvement in conditions as serious as schizophrenia and anorexia nervosa (Selvini-Palazzoli et al. 1978).

Changes in a family system may lead to distress in members other than the presenting patient, as they come to face their own responsibility for the problems and their own personal difficulties. The reality that they have sought to avoid, say the poverty of their marriage, or the loss of their children's dependence on them, may be hard to face, and require a good deal of adjustment. Furthermore, some families cannot be helped by family therapy. They are locked in fixed or destructive patterns of interrelating, have insufficient concern for each other, or are too threatened by change. Then it may be necessary to help an individual patient, often an adolescent or young adult, to separate from the family by involving him in therapy for himself, either individually or in a group. Indeed a family is not necessarily the best place to be. One of the possible outcomes of a family or marital approach that has to be faced, may be a decision to split up. Therapy in such cases can often help to ensure that this is done in a constructive way.

Separate therapy might be needed to help members to differentiate and develop more fully as individuals. This can be the case with couples where one or both partners need help to overcome their own problems originating in early family relationships, which may have determined the choice of partner and which the marriage perpetuates. It can also be appropriate for children. Children and adolescents often present with medical or educational problems, or with delinquency, rather than with overt emotional or psychiatric disturbance. Such children may respond to family therapy directed at correcting unhealthy family interaction. In order to overcome the effects of ongoing (as well as past) trauma and conflict, and to release their developmental potential, some children require a different sort of relationship from that which they have with their parents and siblings.

Child Psychotherapy has grown in the last 70 years out of the pioneering work of psychoanalysts such as Hug-Hellmuth (1921), Klein (1932), Anna Freud (1966), and Winnicott (1975), who developed play techniques to analyse pre-school children not yet able to express themselves fully in words. With older children and adolescents it is possible to move towards more verbal communication in individual psychotherapy (Daws and Boston 1981) and in group psychotherapy (Riester and Kraft 1986); and there are now several therapeutic communities providing the benefits of Social Therapy (p.149) for disturbed children and adolescents, who often present with learning difficulties (Rose 1990). Most child psychotherapy in the UK takes place in community Child Guidance Clinics and in hospital Departments for Family and Child Psychiatry, where a family approach is usual. In some, Family Therapy is emphasized, in others parents are supported and guided while the main therapeutic effort is directed towards the child. A team approach is used, with the work of educational psychologists, teachers, educational therapists, and social workers integrated with that of psychiatrists and child psychotherapists.

Child Psychotherapy is now a growing discipline, with its own professional organization. The Association of Child Psychotherapists is represented at UKSCP (p.203) and has its own training programmes and its own journal, the *Journal of Child Psychotherapy*. The interested reader is referred to such texts as Daws and Boston (1981) on the work of child psycho-therapists in various settings; Laufer and Laufer (1988) on ado-lescent breakdown; and Sandler *et al.* (1990) on the work of Anna Freud and the Hampstead Child Therapy Centre.

SOCIAL THERAPY

The preceding three sections on individual, group, and family therapy have traced a widening perspective, from the indi-vidual and his inner world to his interpersonal and family relationships. This gives us different frames in which to view man, like using a microscope with lenses of varying powers of magnification. Parallel developments in psychoanalytic theory from 'one-body psychology' to two-, three-, and multi-body psychology were foreshadowed by Rickman (1951). How a person functions is dependent not only on his internalized family of origin, but also on the current family and social groups to which he belongs. His behaviour at any one time is affected by the social situation he finds himself in, including that in which he is treated when ill. When large groups such as institutions are studied, the insights of a psychoanalytic view can be usefully joined with the 'outsights' of a sociological one (Kreeger 1975; Pines 1975). Sociology was born out of the upheaval of the French Revolution and was christened by August Comte, who envisaged it would contribute to a new social order; it studies the relation between man and society – the ways in which man both creates society and is moulded by it (Hopper and Weyman 1975).

The less power individuals have, the more they are at the mercy of social forces and ideas imposed on them. For exam-ple, Karl Marx derived his concept of *alienation* from what he considered to be the helpless position of workers treated as 'hands', with no value or meaning in the social system other than in the work they produce. According to Marx, the more the worker produces materially, the poorer he will be in his inner life; similarly in the area of religious belief, the more he attributes to God the less he has in himself (Marx 1844). A sociological idea, readily linked with modern psychodynamic thinking, was Emile Durkheim's (1897) concept of *anomie*. This refers to the pathogenic vacuum of standards which results from the breakdown of stable social norms, familiar in the 'inner city disease' of today; it reminds us of the individual's need for structured relationships, identifications, and roles for a sense of fitting into a meaningful scheme, in order to feel securely himself. Durkheim considered anomie an important cause of suicide. The recent sociological work of G.W. Brown, also points to the social factors contributing to the high incidence of depressive states in working class women; in particular the lack of social contact through having a lot of children, no work outside the home, little support from husbands, and early death of mother (Brown and Harris 1978).

Social psychology and psychological sociology have flourished in the great social melting-pot of the USA. The pioneer psychologist William James (1890) recognized that the sense of self is bound up with the processes of social interaction, a view expounded and deepened by Erikson's (1965) more recent work on identity and psychosocial development (p.39). An early sociologist, Cooley (1902), had proposed the idea of 'the looking glass self', according to which a person's self-image is built up from how he imagines others view and judge him, and his own subsequent feelings, such as pride or mortification. This is not unlike Winnicott's (1971:111) more recent idea that the infant's self-image is built up through seeing himself reflected in his mother's face. Later sociologists (Parsons 1964) have interested themselves in the two-way process between man and his social world. Social institutions reflect man's psychic structure and vice versa; for example, the judiciary could be seen as representing man's collective external Super-ego, while some social and cultural standards are internalized in everyone's individual Super-ego. Both Super-ego and judiciary are 'decider subsystems' (p.53) which maintain a powerful controlling function in the larger systems of personality and of society respectively.

There can be a destructive as well as a creative interaction between man and the society he lives in, amply demonstrated by studies of closed institutions such as prisons and mental hospitals (Goffman 1961; Foudraine 1974), where humiliation and dispossession of familiar roles can destroy individuality and hope. Barton (1959) applied the term 'Institutional Neurosis' to these consequences of institutionalization, which can magnify or replace whatever disability brought a patient into hospital. The active rehabilitation and 'open doors' policies of the 1950s, reviving the 'moral treatment' of enlightened mental hospitals in the early nineteenth century, followed recognition of these adverse effects of prolonged hospital admission.

Main (1946), one of the pioneers of the Northfield Experiments (p.120), on the strength of his experience there gave the name *Therapeutic Community* to institutions where the setting itself is deliberately organized to restore morale and promote the psychological treatment of mental and emotional disturbance, and he went on to create an influential example in the Cassel Hospital in Surrey. This has been one of the few units in Britain where in-patients undergo individual analytic psychotherapy for neurotic and personality disorders, without recourse to drugs, in a setting where at the same time they engage in social learning.

In the 1950s Maxwell Jones (1952, 1968) founded the unit at Belmont, later to be called the Henderson Hospital. He emphasized the opportunity for *living-learning* processes when people live and work together in a setting where social analysis, rather than psychoanalysis, is practised. At the Cassel Hospital, the community is an adjunct to individual therapy; at the Henderson the community is the main focus. The Henderson Hospital has accepted people who tend to show their problems more in disturbed social behaviour and relationships, for whom individual treatment is less appropriate than for those whose problems are neurotic and internalized. A social context was provided where these 'sociopathic' disturbances could be expressed, confronted, and explored. The Henderson Hospital regime was (and still is) characterized by 'permissiveness, reality-confrontation, democracy and communalism' (Rapoport 1960). Its permissiveness encouraged the expression and enactment of disturbed feelings and relationships, so that they could be examined by fellow patients and staff. The differences between patients and staff were minimized by staff discarding uniforms and titles (as has been done in many units since), and by each freely contributing their feelings and opinions of events. Decision-making was shared by the community as a whole, including issues of admission and discharge. Rules were kept to the minimum necessary for the safety and well-being of everyone. This type of residential community is the prototype Therapeutic Community. Other examples have sprung up in many parts of the world, particularly in Britain, the USA, and Europe.

Clark (1977), in a valuable review of the history and present status of the Therapeutic Community, distinguishes between the Therapeutic Community, Therapeutic Milieu, and Social Therapy. The term Therapeutic Community or 'therapeutic community proper' (Clark 1964) should be reserved for the specific type of Therapeutic Milieu developed by Jones and his followers: 'a small face-to-face residential community using social analysis as its main tool' (Clark 1977). A Therapeutic Milieu is a social setting designed to produce a beneficial effect on those being helped in it; for example, a hospital ward, sheltered workshop or hostel, each with a social structure different from the others. Social Therapy (known as Milieu Therapy in USA) employs the idea that the social environment or milieu can be used as a mode of treatment. Of these three categories described by Clark, the Therapeutic Community is the most specific application of these principles; Social Therapy is the most general.

Clark points out that the enthusiastic idealism about the Therapeutic Community, widespread in the 1950s and 1960s, culminated in the founding of the Association of Therapeutic Communities in 1971. Such idealism has been tempered since then by recognition of the limitations of this means of treatment and by a move in society away from permissiveness. At the same time a clearer understanding of the principles of Social Therapy has led to their application in wider fields, such as the Richmond Fellowship hostels for psychiatric patients, communities for adolescents with behavioural and learning difficulties, and to their adaptation to other special needs. Some self-governing hostels for ex-drug addicts, for example, while retaining 'democracy, communalism and reality-confrontation' (Rapoport 1960) replace permissiveness by an authoritarian structure, with harsher punishments and degradations than would be tolerated in most organizations run by doctors and nurses. They are communities and they are therapeutic, but because of their authoritarian structure they are not 'therapeutic communities proper'. In hospital psychiatric units, the principles will also have to be adapted, but here to the broad range of psychiatric conditions, many of them acute. In such units, staff need to be free to make authoritative decisions, in order to cope with emergencies and maintain the safe structure that is especially important for acutely ill patients who are not yet able to take much responsibility. Awareness of the principles of social therapy helps staff to remain flexible in their roles, and share responsibility as patients become ready to assume it.

The essence of social therapy is *openness of communication* and *shared examination of problems*. Patients are encouraged to use their initiative in running their own lives. Hierarchy is played down and responsibility shared as much as possible between patients and staff. Group meetings play an important part in facilitating these processes, both small groups of a dozen or so, and large meetings of the total unit, patients *and* staff, in the community meeting.

The relationship between social therapy and psychotherapy in the *community meeting* is still being debated. Edelson (1970) distinguishes between them, claiming that the function of the community meeting is not group psychotherapy but facilitation of the day to day functioning of the unit. Others such as Springmann (1970) argue that there can be distinct potential for individual insight and change in community meetings, though they are not a substitute for more intimate small therapy groups. Springmann fosters a less structured and consequently more spontaneous meeting. However, large unstructured groups can produce a lot of anxiety even in 'normal' people; primitive anxieties of persecution and annihilation, and defences against them, such as withdrawal or omnipotent exhibitionistic behaviour, are not uncommon. In general psychiatric units, which cater for people with all degrees of disturbances and vulnerability, Pines (1975) favours a clear structure to the community meeting, particularly at its outset. This reduces anxiety and confusion induced by threats of anonymity, fear of loss of control, and of catching other people's madness. An elected chairman and an initial agenda of feed-back reports from groups of patients and staff can provide a useful structure from which more spontaneous information, preoccupations, and conflicts emerge later in the meeting. This procedure is followed at the Henderson Hospital, and has been adopted by many community meetings in psychiatric units.

Social systems can provide defences against primitive persecutory and depressive anxieties based on the paranoid-schizoid and depressive positions (p.106), or they can increase them (Jaques 1955). In creating a social system devoted to therapy, it is necessary to determine what level of anxiety and defence is appropriate for the patients and staff working together in it. The organization and methods used in a hospital or unit may be determined, understandably, by the need to provide staff with defences against anxiety, as much as by what is best for patients. For example, nursing hierarchies and rituals can protect nurses, many of them young and inexperienced, from the anxieties provoked by feeling too involved with the suffering they encounter (Menzies 1961); or, to counteract staff anxieties, psychiatric patients may be given drugs to quieten them rather than an opportunity to express and talk about their problems (Stanton and Schwartz 1954). Nevertheless, while social or institutional defences may be right and proper, they should not be so great as to hamper the therapeutic task of the institution. Getting the balance right can be a struggle (Hinshelwood 1987).

The idea of social therapy has been applied in a number of different settings, e.g. psychiatric hospitals, hostels for drug addicts, schools for emotionally disturbed and learning-impaired adolescents, even prisons. The methods used are even more numerous, and therefore description of them will be limited to a few general principles.

Most training in Social Therapy is gained 'on the job' in Therapeutic Communities and units using the Therapeutic Community approach. But the Association of Therapeutic Communities runs many courses, including a nine-month course in association with the Royal College of Nursing. Organizational dynamics can be experienced in group dynamic workshops such as the 'Leicester Conferences' organized by the Tavistock Institute of Human Relations; and the use of large groups, such as those used in Therapeutic Community meetings, in courses run by the Group Analytic Society (London) in association with the Institute of Group Analysis.

The setting

The boundaries of the social system in which social therapy is practised need to be distinct, whether it is a 'therapeutic community proper' or a 'therapeutic milieu' in a unit or hostel. This allows it to develop its own clear culture and rules. Clarity of the boundaries of the system also permits examination and understanding of happenings within it to be differentiated from events originating outside, such as intrusions from administrators, police, local inhabitants, or relatives.

The degree to which a unit can control its boundaries inevitably affects what happens inside it. This explains many of the differences between a 'therapeutic community proper' and a psychiatric unit operating as a 'therapeutic milieu' in a district general hospital, increasingly the basis of most psychiatric care in this country as old mental hospitals are closed down. A therapeutic community can control its admissions. It selects patients who, on the whole, want to play an active and responsible part in their own treatment, and are thought likely to fit into and benefit from the culture of the unit. In many therapeutic communities, more established patients play a part in deciding who will be admitted. Such control and selection is impossible in a district general hospital unit, because it serves a local catchment area and has to admit patients of all types and ages, and all degrees of intellectual capacity and emotional disturbance. In such a unit, the structure has to allow for patients who need traditional nursing and doctoring, at least for a while. The most acutely disturbed patient might need the provision of a good deal of structured care, as does a newborn child; but as the patient improves, he should be encouraged, like the growing child, to move towards the greatest autonomy possible.

The organization of any psychiatric unit should provide opportunities for sharing and learning from the reality of living together. Community meetings are held at least weekly, in some settings daily, attended by as many of the patients and staff as possible. It is important to have a room of sufficient size and shape for everyone to be accommodated, sitting comfortably in something approaching concentric circles, so that people can communicate with each other face to face. Decisions to exclude some patients (because, say, they are still too disturbed) or to agree that some staff do not attend (for example those not available all the time) need to be examined and faced openly, along with all other significant events.

In addition, small groups may exist for discussion of day-to-day problems in subdivisions of the unit (say wards) or for discussion of specific problems shared by a number of patients (arrival in the unit, impending discharge, women's rights, and so on). In a general psychiatric unit, more formal psychotherapy, which requires longer-term commitment, is best conducted in small out-patient groups which people usually join after discharge. For in-patients, opportunities are created in addition to discussion groups, for non-verbal expression and communication through Occupational Therapy and Art or Music Therapy. These can be extremely valuable in contacting patients who are withdrawn, inhibited, or unused to talking about themselves and their feelings. Some people can use these methods to get in touch with previously unexpressed aspects of themselves. We have already quoted Winnicott's (1971:38) saying that 'Psychotherapy has to do with two people playing together'; he went on, 'The corollary of this is that where playing is not possible then the work done by the therapist is directed towards bringing the patient from a state of not being able to play into a state of being able to play'. Art and Music Therapy may help people to find they *can* play.

Staff ideally meet together following (and sometimes before) community and small group meetings, to share and clarify their understanding of what has happened and to make any necessary decisions or contingency plans. In addition, staff often have their own meetings to discuss practical issues and planning. The more of a therapeutic community the unit is, the more likely it is that staff will air and face up to interpersonal tensions and conflicts in these meetings; otherwise it would be hypocritical to expect patients to do so, quite apart from the knowledge that unresolved conflicts between staff affect patients adversely (Stanton and Schwartz 1954).

A common feature in 'therapeutic communities proper' is the crisis meeting of either the whole community or one of the subgroups of patients and staff. This aims to examine a critical event, such as someone behaving in a disturbed or destructive way, in an honest and supportive manner. The extent to which this can happen might almost be a yardstick of how much a unit functions as a 'therapeutic community proper', i.e., by sharing responsibility and treatment between all members of the community, without slipping too much into the traditionally distinct roles of helpless sick patients and competent healthy staff.

Patients' roles

Patients learn that they have an active role to play in helping themselves and each other, by participating in communal life as they become able to do so. They have an opportunity to discover the personal and interpersonal nature of problems and conflicts which underlie symptoms. By facing up to the problems of living together and sharing in finding solutions, they can move away from isolation and a sense of abnormality. They have many chances to express feelings and talk honestly about themselves and others, and to learn new ways and attitudes. By playing an active role they have opportunities to rediscover, or discover for the first time, strengths and skills in handling problems. Being elected to the Chair of the Community meeting, and filling the role adequately, are often experienced as a graduation, particularly by previously unassertive patients and those with damaged self-esteem. Their success may encourage others.

Staff roles

In keeping with the ethos of social therapy, staff transcend the specific roles prescribed by their training in the disciplines of medicine, nursing, social work, occupational therapy, and so on. They work more as individuals in a multidisciplinary team. Though still practising their separate professional skills as necessary, they share socio-therapeutic attitudes and try to face up to any interdisciplinary tensions and rivalries which interfere with their work. As it is between disciplines, so it needs to be between different hierarchical levels within each staff subgroup; problems between seniors and juniors need to be resolved by honest confrontation and discussion. This is what is known as 'flattening of the authority pyramid' (Clark 1964:45). It does not mean that power and responsibility are dissipated; indeed one of the paradoxes of the therapeutic community movement is that the aims of democratization and sharing of responsibility have often been best achieved under the 'benevolent dictatorship' of charismatic leaders. However, a therapeutic milieu encourages the sharing of decisions and power among staff of different disciplines; it also tends to reduce 'social distance' between them. The same trends can be seen in the organization of industry and higher education, where greater consultation and shared decision-making are increasingly being sought. Desirable ideals in any organization are that power and responsibility are open and clear, and that their diffusion is in the interest of helping its members, in our case staff and patients, towards autonomy and growth, without losing direction and sight of the overall function of the unit.

Working in a therapeutic community demands openness and honesty. This means being able to say to fellow staff members, as well as to patients, things which are difficult to say and to accept, such as: 'I don't like the way you do that . . . Why on earth did you say that? . . . I feel it's your problem not the patient's.' An atmosphere and culture in which such confrontations can be made and received, without feelings being too hurt, is one which has to be built up and constantly maintained. Without it, destructive forces can prevail, e.g. through splitting and projection between subgroups of staff and patients (Main 1957).

Therapeutic processes

Social therapy involves open communication and confrontation of problems as they arise. Instead of using staff roles and hierarchies for unnecessary defence and evasion, it demands self-questioning and change. These characteristics produce an atmosphere which is lively and creative, but often stressful.

Not everyone, staff or patients, is comfortable in this atmosphere, though many adjust and learn to value it. The question of whether some may find it anti-therapeutic is still open to research. One of the disadvantages of social therapy is that it is difficult for patients to opt out if it does not suit them in the form provided in a particular unit, except by leaving or not cooperating. For this reason it is important for a general psychiatric unit aiming to function as a therapeutic milieu to have a range of programmes adaptable to a variety of different people and problems. Working well, a therapeutic milieu promotes the tackling of the inevitable problems of living with other disturbed people, in a way that facilitates their solution, and promotes learning about personal relationships.

A community meeting in the psychiatric unit of a general hospital had revealed an undercurrent of explosive irritability among patients, whose feed-back reports had glossed over several distressing events during the previous week, and hinted at shared anxieties and resentment about forthcoming staff changes. Some patients in particular, through the Chairman of the community meeting, who was one of their number, complained that they were not seeing enough of their doctors. This implied that the nurses were not good enough, and incapable of discerning deterioration in the condition of their patients. It emerged, in the staff group following the meeting, that some nursing staff were themselves demoralized by intense feelings of unexpressed resentment at their senior nurse who had not communicated with them openly and directly about his temporary absence, nor made arrangements for his replacement. When these feelings were shared with colleagues, and the problem acknowledged as one which needed to be tackled, the nurses felt freer to take action, and their morale began to improve. Opening up these issues also led, in the following community meeting, to a useful exploration of patient attitudes to staff, including their reluctance to recognize that staff too could have problems. The need for doctors to be idealized as strong and omniscient was seen to reflect the wish for a good reliable father on the part of many patients (including the Chairman), like the nurses' wish for a more reliable and concerned senior nurse.

The task of social therapy is to create a therapeutic milieu, and its paradigm is the therapeutic community, the core of which is the community meeting. Through it Pines has traced

the link between the social system and individual psychotherapy:

'The community meeting represents the creation of a new
social system that accepts as its fundamental problem
control, containment and treatment of mental illness. The
attempt is made to foster the development of a society
whose "shared understanding and common intellectual
and emotional discourse" (Earl Hopper) are based on the
insights of psychotherapy which state that mental illness
results in, and may arise from, faulty communication,
that mental illness has meaning that can be understood
and that all persons, sick or well, have more in common
than they can easily recognize. The psychotherapeutic
viewpoint emphasizes that emotional disturbances have
roots in failed developmental tasks which centre on the
resolution of issues of dependency, autonomy, authority
and sexuality. The resolution of these issues is renego-
tiable in the transactions of psychotherapy, and it is
expected that they will appear in the social transactions
of the group, and thereby offer opportunities for psychotherapeutic work. The psychotherapeutic effort is to raise
these issues to the level of conscious understanding
where they can be acted upon in more mature and adaptive ways than have been open to the individuals hereto-
fore . . .' (Pines 1975:303).

The therapeutic processes of social therapy are thus the treatment of conflicts and blocks in communication within the unit,
so creating a 'therapeutic milieu' in which practical problems
can be solved, interpersonal skills developed, and the psychotherapeutic functions of the unit can flourish. Whether the
latter be largely supportive or exploratory, both functions are
needed in a comprehensive caring service, and should be available within the National Health Service. Needs vary from
patient to patient, and often at different stages in the same
patient's care.

District general hospital units, now the basis of plans for
psychiatric care in Britain (Department of Health and Social
Security 1975) are expected to cope with all-comers from a
'catchment area', in a ratio of fifty in-patient beds and sixty-
five day places (more than half of which would be used by

the in-patients) for a population of 100,000. While appropriate and sufficient for a majority of patients, already the pressures on units of this type are such that patients may be discharged as soon as possible. Removal from stressful home circumstances, support, and effective medication can lead to rapid improvement. Patients may therefore be discharged before their capacity and wish to use more than supportive psychotherapy can be assessed, even if there are local facilities for deeper levels of psychotherapy. These are still very unevenly distributed through the country. The need in such a psychiatric unit to keep the average length of stay down to 6–8 weeks, might discourage a more gradual recovery, which does not depend so much on denial and allows contact with deeper feelings and resolution of underlying conflicts.

Alternative ways of working through emotional crises exist. Those who work on the crisis intervention model aim to keep people out of hospital by sorting out emotional crises in the home (p.139). In the group homes of the Arbours Housing Association and the Philadelphia Association, followers of Laing claim that patients can be supported and helped to work through their psychological disturbance in a way felt to be more creative, facing the suppressed imaginative parts of themselves rather than sealing them off with a rapid 'cure'. One does not need to accept Laing's view of mental illness *in toto* (p.137) to recognize that people vary in the time and conditions they need to work through their problems in a way that is right for them.

At the exploratory end of the psychotherapeutic spectrum, the existence of 'therapeutic communities proper' in such hospitals as the Cassel and Henderson depends on their being free from the pressures which constrain district general hospital units, so that they can make their facilities more widely available to patients likely to benefit from intensive psychotherapy and social therapy during a stay of 6–12 months. Ideally, perhaps, every region should have units of this type available for both in-patients and out-patients. At the opposite, supportive end of the spectrum, despite advances in psychiatric treatment, long-term care in conditions of true 'asylum' are likely to be needed for some chronically and severely handicapped patients, if necessary for the rest of their lives. As the large traditional mental hospitals are closed down, long-term units or group homes will be needed, and it is important that they have space, grounds, and adequate facilities for occupation and recreation.

There are disadvantages in trying to do everything together; neither support nor exploration can be easily provided, in full measure, in a compromise situation. Consequently there are dangers in a policy of concentrating psychiatric care in a uniform service based solely on district general hospitals, unless there is concurrent development of a wide range of psychotherapy services for out-patients and alternative therapeutic milieux.

The needs of many types of patient will have to be catered for in a comprehensive psychiatric service: some with acute emotional disturbance, others with chronic disability, some who need mainly support and medication, and others who can use an opportunity to work through problems and learn new solutions through psychotherapy, whether behavioural or dynamic. It is likely that the range of facilities required to augment district general hospital units will extend the work of some of the pioneer units described in this section. Sadly, 'Community Care' is still more a catch-phrase than a solid reality in many areas.

Despite the running down and closure of many large mental hospitals, and the laying down of official principles of community care (Griffiths 1988), community services are developing very slowly. The details of finance and organization have to be worked out in the face of many competing claims. In consequence the proportion of chronic psychiatric patients is rising among the destitute and homeless (Marshall 1989), who will require special out-reach schemes that are scarcely begun (Lowry 1990).

In many areas, however, psychotherapists are playing a growing part in the support and supervision of community psychiatric nurses, so helping in the psychodynamic management in the community of often very difficult patients. They are also cooperating with social workers, and others are already developing a more flexible service by adopting some of the principles of social therapy in facilities such as hostels and clubs. The idea of social therapy, that the social context affects what happens in it, can guide us in fitting the provisions to the needs of the patients for various types and levels of psychotherapy.

ENCOUNTER AND BEYOND

In this section we consider a variety of therapeutic movements which have emphasized, in a particular way, one aspect of therapy that has been present to some degree in classical psychoanalytical therapy, or was specially emphasized at some time in its development. These movements have attempted to correct what the proponents of each saw as a one-sided bias and limitation in psychoanalysis. It could be argued that they have mostly gone to an opposite one-sided and biased extreme.

Psychoanalysis began as a radical movement, challenging the established view of orthodox medicine and psychiatry. This may be one reason why it was more readily accepted in North America, with its democratic spirit of equality and opportunity for all, than in the Old World. However, in time, it encountered the problem of all revolutionary movements as they are taken over by, and become part of, the established order. The 'human potential movement', or 'humanistic psychology' as it is sometimes called, may be seen as the next revolution, reacting to what was felt to be conservatism in psychoanalysis. It was in many ways typically American (Kovel 1976), and with roots in inspirational religious revivalism (Marteau 1976) takes a basically optimistic view of human nature and its perfectibility. This contrasts with the rather pessimistic view of Freud (1930), towards the end of his life, as expressed in *Civilization and its Discontents*, that man is inevitably in conflict between the demands of instinct and those of culture. These movements attract many people who see themselves not as ill, but as 'blocked' or 'alienated' from their true selves and others.

Perhaps another, indirect, influence on these newer therapies has been the Existential movement in philosophy (Heidegger 1967), which has concentrated on *understanding* existence in contrast to the earlier Cartesian preoccupation with *thinking*; on *being* rather than *knowing*. In a sense it asserts *sum ergo cogito* as opposed to *cogito ergo sum*. The existential emphasis on the phenomena of the individual's experience and his need to face his mortality and aloneness, has led some philosophers,

163

like Sartre, to a position of stoicism in the face of anxiety and despair. It can also lead to a search for a meaningful 'I and Thou' relationship with God (Buber 1971) or with other human beings. Existentialist thinking has influenced several psychiatrists and psychotherapists (May *et al*. 1958; Laing 1960) who put conscious *awareness* of the self and others before consideration of unconscious processes or biological aspects of human behaviour. The title of Rogers's (1961) early book, *On Becoming a Person*, proclaims this attitude. In psychoanalysis, this humanistic trend has always existed, but has recently manifested itself in a growing interest in the experience of the Self, its development and vicissitudes (Jacobson 1964; Kohut 1977), and in narcissistic problems of self-esteem (Kernberg 1975). Over and above the more abstract notion of the Ego, the Self refers to the consistent images the individual has of himself, and their relation to his images of others (Fransella and Thomas 1988).

The 'human potential movement' is most typically represented by the Esalen Institute at Big Sur, California, where Rogerian psychotherapy, Encounter groups, Gestalt therapy, Bioenergetics, meditation, Yoga, and Zen flourish side by side. Similar 'growth centres' have been established in the Eastern USA, and introduced into Europe with the help of American 'missionaries'.

The most important departures from established psychotherapeutic practice have been in the nature of the therapist-patient relationship, the move from talk to action, and the emphasis on expression rather than on understanding. The basic elements of dynamic psychotherapy, as we have emphasized (pp.70ff) are a relationship of trust, communication in words, understanding, and integration. A relationship of trust remains the cornerstone of all psychotherapy, including these newer manifestations which, however, involve the therapist in a more active and self-revealing role. Rather than listening receptively, he engages the client in a series of technical exercises. Instead of patiently interpreting and working through resistances to self-awareness and change, the therapist aims at expression of the client's feelings by the facilitation of intense experiences. Treatment is shorter-term and often concentrated in weekend workshops or twenty-four hour 'marathons'. Feelings are considered to be more important than thoughts, getting them out (catharsis) more important than reflecting upon their origins. These therapists emphasize (a) 'body language' and the unity of body and mind, (b) treatment in the 'here and now' and, (c) the therapeutic impact of the real I-thou engagement between therapist and client. However, these concepts are basic to psychoanalysis and its more conventional derivatives. (a) Psychoanalysis has always concerned itself with the interplay of psychological and physical processes. (b) The concept of transference implies that the past is alive in the present, and psychoanalysis has long recognized that it is the 'here and now' quality of the experience of transference phenomena which gives them therapeutic impact (Strachey 1934). It is a common misunderstanding that psychoanalysts are only interested in discussing their patients' childhood at a distance, rather than as it is manifest in the 'here and now'. (c) Analysts also are well aware of the importance of their own personality and the 'real' as opposed to the transference elements in the therapist-patient relationship (Klauber 1981); it forms the basis of the therapeutic alliance (p.54).

Certainly a more active and directive therapist may do things that another might not do while in a psychoanalytic stance, but conversely there are things he may not be able to do. He can challenge defences more forcibly, and engineer changes when a patient or family is stuck in repetitive behaviour; but the quicker pace may not allow him to reflect on transference and countertransference phenomena, or attend to the slowly emerging communications of the patient. Further, there are dangers that the active, directive role, will attract therapists who seek to gratify their own needs for power. It is to counter such dangers that a personal analytic experience and supervision are considered such a vital part of most recognized forms of training in psychotherapy (Pedder 1989b).

While analytic therapy may lend itself to defensive thinking rather than feeling, especially in schizoid or obsessional patients cut off from their feelings, feeling alone can also be defensive. The intense experience of more active treatments can lead to great relief or euphoria, but without working through, the effect may be transient. Disregarding a person's need for defences can lead to psychiatric casualties – estimated at about 9 per cent – when such techniques as Encounter are used with people who are psychologically disturbed or vulnerable (Lieberman *et al.* 1973).

There have been many new developments (Dryden and Rowan 1988). Most of them, as can be seen from the following brief descriptions, reflect an aspect of Freud's thinking that was developed by one of his early followers. Whether such developments will die out, replace established methods, or be integrated into the mainstream of psychotherapeutic practice remains to be seen. Their methods however have stirred up a lot of interest and have enabled some people, especially those not formally designated as patients, to feel more fully alive and authentic; and they may help others, stuck in conventional therapy, to get moving again through the expressive methods of the creative therapies, using art, music, movement, and drama (Jennings 1983). James (1976), has described how useful some action techniques were in the early stages of group therapy with people unused to talking about feelings and relationships; later, as these people developed verbal skills, they chose to give up the action methods and concentrate on the more spontaneous and free-flowing discussion of analytic group psychotherapy.

Many of these approaches are included in forms of Humanistic and Integrative Psychotherapy represented in a section of the UK Standing Conference on Psychotherapy (p.203), with some fourteen constituent organizations. Their training programmes combine psychodynamic approaches with aspects of Gestalt, Transactional Analysis, body work, spiritual awareness, and so on. They expect some personal therapeutic experience of their trainees.

Encounter

Carl Rogers, the American evangelist turned academic psychologist, who developed non-directive counselling (p.95), later became a leading figure in the Encounter movement. As he pointed out (Rogers 1970), this grew out of the confluence of two streams. One started from the establishment of summer T-groups in Bethel, Maine in 1947, under the posthumous influence of Kurt Lewin (p.120). This led to the foundation of the National Training Laboratories, whose training groups in human relations skills have concentrated on helping managers and executives in industry to become aware of their interaction with others and the group dynamics inevitable in any organization. In the UK this work has been specially developed by the Tavistock Institute of Human Relations (Rice 1965). The other stream was started at about the same time when Rogers and his colleagues at the Counselling Centre of the University of Chicago set up brief but intensive training courses for would-be counsellors in the Veterans Administration Hospitals, which were then wrestling with the problems of servicemen returning from the Second World War. The trainees met for several hours a day to help their self-understanding and awareness of personal attitudes which, as counsellors, might be self-defeating. The training combined cognitive and experiential learning which often led, beyond improvement in interpersonal communication and relationships, to personal growth and development. Sensitivity or T-groups of this type are now being used in helping students and staff in psychiatric and many other institutions to learn about themselves and develop their skills. Coming to terms with oneself and learning through experience are part of the psychotherapeutic process, for therapists as well as for patients.

Encounter and sensitivity groups usually have from eight to eighteen members, and are relatively unstructured. They choose their own goals, which in Encounter groups proper would be an experience of personal authenticity and honesty in relation to others; in a staff sensitivity group it would be exploration of feelings and problems encountered in working together. Usually there is a leader, whose task is to help in the creation of a climate of safety which facilitates expression of members' feelings and thoughts in their immediate interactions. In this climate, trust can develop out of the freedom to express real feelings, hostile as well as appreciative, so that each member becomes more accepting of himself and others in the 'here and now', intellectually, emotionally, and bodily, without considering the past. With reduction of defensiveness, communication opens up, and new ideas and innovations can be welcomed rather than feared. Individuals learn to discard their masks and discover their hidden selves.

This is really another way of describing the communicative processes of all psychotherapy, (see *Figure 7* p.71). However, a certain sequence of events is characteristic of Encounter groups conducted in Rogers's non-directive way. After a period of 'milling around', in which people engage in defensive 'cocktail talk', a spontaneous structure emerges, usually after a member says something like 'shouldn't we introduce ourselves?' People then do so, but avoid real personal expression and exploration. When personal feelings finally do emerge, they are often feelings of hostility towards another member or the leader. The ice having been broken in this way, members begin to express and explore personal concerns; they may expose feelings of anxiety and pain which they have never shown to another person. The discovery that fellow group members respond in a spontaneously therapeutic way facilitates the extension and deepening of these revelations. As people feel more fully accepted as they really are, rather than for their social front, they can risk removing their masks more completely. The feedback that individuals get, sometimes with vigour and unwelcome honesty, enables them to take fuller stock of themselves and their behaviour. The counterbalancing sympathy and acceptance, sometimes with help extended outside the group situation, allows the increasing expression of closeness, affection, and gratitude. The real emotional and intellectual contact in the 'here and now' is what is meant by *basic encounter*.

To facilitate this basic encounter, certain techniques are sometimes used, such as guided daydreams or group fantasies, role-playing, and psychodrama (see below). Some Encounter leaders, such as Schutz (1967) emphasize physical and non-verbal experiences. For example, the need to make contact is explored by exercises in which everyone is blindfolded and has to find and explore each other only by touch. Competition is expressed by two people clasping hands and pushing each other. Trust and affection are learned and expressed by 'rocking and rolling', whereby one person at a time allows himself to fall into the arms of the others gathered around, who cradle and pass him around and rock him rhythmically. Rogers himself is distrustful of the over-ready use of such methods, preferring to use them only when they emerge spontaneously, and not as deliberate 'gimmicks'.

There is no doubt that people attain intense experiences in Encounter groups, and that some feel more acceptable and authentic as a result of the opportunity to be utterly frank about themselves, and learn a lot through the feedback from others. Some esoteric 'cultish' movements like EST and I Am apparently use a mixture of encounter techniques, group support, and pressure, along with suggestion and directive leadership, to enhance people's self-esteem and sense of mastery of their lives. But frankness and a superficial change of attitude do not in themselves ensure the elucidation and working through of deeply unconscious conflicts. Moreover, there are some casualties among the psychologically disturbed and vulnerable, as already mentioned. Adverse effects may be commoner in groups run by more directive, provocative, and charismatic leaders, who may use them for their own gratification.

Psychodrama

Psychodrama was the creation of Jacob Moreno (1892–1974). He was born in Romania and brought up in Vienna, where he not only studied philosophy and medicine, but became deeply involved in the arts and edited a literary journal. During the early 1920s he led impromptu play groups with children in the parks of Vienna, and went on to develop an improvized 'Theatre of Spontaneity' (Moreno 1948). Davies (1976) describes how Moreno discovered that an actress in this theatre, who usually played gentle, naive roles, behaved as a vicious person at home after marrying an actor friend of his. Moreno gave her more violent unsympathetic roles to play in the theatre with the result that her behaviour at home became transformed for the better!

After emigrating to the USA in 1925, Moreno applied his ideas to the treatment of emotional disturbance. He used groups (he is said to have coined the term 'group psychotherapy') in which members could explore and enact the role-conflicts which he saw as the essence of their neuroses; for example, a young woman may need to play the part of a gentle submissive female to please her father, and at the same time act as a confident assertive person to satisfy her mother's need for a successful achiever, a substitute for the son she never had. A common example nowadays is the role-conflict experienced by women who seek to be traditional wives and mothers while striving to achieve in competitive occupations. The therapist functions as a director, literally as in the theatre, and in some institutions a raised circular platform serves as a stage on which members of the group, usually 6–12 in number, meet for 1½–2 hours and take turns to enact their problems. The patient chosen as 'protagonist' will help the 'auxiliaries' to take up a role by describing the scene of his psychodrama in great detail. At times the director will instruct a member of the audience to step into the protagonist's role ('role reversal'), in order to foster identification and improvisation. Several people, from direct experience, can then join in the subsequent discussion about the protagonist's role-conflicts and how they might be overcome. The enactment and discussion, in a supportive and cohesive group atmosphere, aim to redefine the key conflict and allow the person to approach it from a number of different angles, until he achieves a sense of mastery.

The techniques of psychodrama may sometimes be useful in the course of more analytic individual or group therapy, to help patients work through a block in expression or communication. They can be particularly helpful in a hospital setting for those who are inhibited or find verbal expression difficult (Jennings 1987). They capitalize on the potential extraverted qualities in a patient, and probably appeal particularly to more extraverted therapists. In some psychiatric units, occupational therapists have developed special skills in these techniques, which become part of the range of creative therapies, like art and music therapy, used in helping patients to become more spontaneous and outgoing (Jennings 1983). Related role-playing exercises have been used in family therapy (p.138) and in training staff to appreciate what it feels like to be a patient or a member of a disturbed family. They have also been integrated into Gestalt therapy.

Gestalt

Gestalt therapy was developed by Frederick (Fritz) Perls (1893–1970). He was a man of great energy and restlessness, both a rebel and a synthesizer, who moved from Germany to South Africa, to New York, to the Esalen Institute in California, and finally to Vancouver, where he established a Gestalt Community. Trained in psychoanalysis in Germany, he felt it had become inflexible, particularly in its emphasis on mental and verbal processes. Like Foulkes, the pioneer of group psychotherapy, Perls had worked with the neurologist Kurt Goldstein. The latter had extended the concepts of Gestalt psychology to motivation, and saw human personality not as an aggregate of discrete habits but as striving for unity.

Perls considered neurosis to be caused by splitting in the Gestalten, that is the 'wholes', which unify mind and body, or an individual and his environment. Anxiety would be the manifestation of the organism's struggle for unification, not, as in classical psychoanalysis, a reaction to an inner danger. However, like Freud, and unlike Rogers, he considered that neurosis was caused by warding off forbidden trends or blocked-off needs of the total organism, mind plus body (Perls *et al*. 1951). In making particular use of bodily signs of tension and defence, Gestalt therapists followed the lead of Wilhelm Reich, an early adherent of Freud's who later left the psychoanalytic fold (p.172).

Gestalt therapy is practised individually or, more usually, in groups; but rather than making use of group processes, some individuals watch and participate vicariously on the sidelines while one of them is helped to be more whole through expanding his awareness of himself. Nor is transference encouraged; instead, dramatization is used to explore and express fuller awareness of the self in the 'here and now', utilizing certain rules and 'games'.

Levitsky and Perls (1972) identify several basic rules. *The principle of now*, whereby awareness is concentrated on current feelings – on the 'what' and the 'how', rather than the 'why' of remote causes – implies that if the past needs attention, it has to be brought into the present, not 'talked about'. (This is also true of analytic therapy, although in the latter the 'here and now' and 'there and then' are seen as in dynamic interaction; too much talk about either may be considered defensive.) *I and thou* is another principle followed in the struggle for immediacy; patients are urged to talk *at* rather than *to* others. *It language* is eschewed; that is, when people talk about parts of their body they have to translate 'it' into 'I' language; for example, 'my legs are tense' becomes 'I am tense'. Passive expressions like 'I am choked' are translated into the active 'I am choking myself'. *No gossiping* means that people should be addressed directly, not talked about as though they were

171

absent. Statements are demanded when questions distance the questioner and evade direct confrontation.

Gestalt 'games' are techniques devised to foster immediacy of awareness. In *Dialogue*, the patient is asked to create a conversation between two split parts of himself (for example, over-conscientious and resentfully compliant, or masculine and feminine parts) or between himself and some other significant person who can be imagined sitting on an empty chair in the room. The patient will play both roles in turn. *Making the rounds* involves the patient in replacing a general remark about the group by a process of addressing the remark individually to each in turn, or translating it into more emotional body language (for example, caressing, or giving vent to hostility). *Unfinished business* refers to bringing into the treatment situation, and facing directly there, unresolved feelings from the patient's earlier life, for example about parents or siblings. In *Exaggeration* a patient is asked to act out the feeling he complains of in accentuated form; in *Reversal* to enact its opposite.

Gestalt therapy thus aims at an intense immediacy of awareness. Words tend to be distrusted as defensive 'bullshitting' (a characteristic phrase), and feelings and bodily expression to be regarded as more reliable. While psychoanalysts, too, watch out for wordy defensiveness in their own practice, on the other hand they would regard total reliance on immediacy and feeling as equally defensive and misleading.

Bioenergetics

This has been called a 'biofunctional therapy', based on the assumption that neurosis involves interference with man's fundamentally biological nature, and that therapy should aim to remove the results of such interference. This had been Freud's original view of one type of neurosis he called *Actual Neurosis*, based on his first anxiety theory (p.21). Incomplete discharge of libido was thought to be converted into anxiety through unnatural sexual practices such as coitus interruptus. Wilhelm Reich (1897–1957), one of the original followers of Freud, became especially interested in the way that bodily tension and posture – 'character armour' – could reflect and maintain psychological character defences (Reich 1933). Often these have to be confronted and interpreted before any repressed feelings and fantasies can emerge. Such ideas became part of psycho-analysis and influenced Anna Freud's (1936) view of defence mechanisms (p.25). However, Reich eventually left the psycho-analytic fold as his own notions developed a more and more revolutionary flavour, equating the overthrow of Fascism with the overcoming of repressions which prevent the attainment of full 'orgastic potency' and sexual release. Perhaps because of his revolutionary zeal, Reich had the unique distinction of being expelled from both the Communist Party and the International Psychoanalytical Association (Rycroft 1971). Reich even came to believe that he could record and store (in the famous Orgone box) the 'sexual energy' flowing freely within and between people.

Essentially, Reich seemed to be reverting to one-body psy-chology and to Freud's first anxiety theory. He ignored the importance of intrapsychic life and object relations. He adopted an active confrontational style to challenge a person's character defences. Interpreting a fixed smile or military bearing would sometimes release a flood of dammed up emotion, e.g. rage or passive yearning for affection. He introduced physical tech-niques, such as massage and attention to breathing, to help the thawing of frozen postures and attitudes. This is a return to Freud's early cathartic methods for the release of 'strangulated affects' (Breuer and Freud 1895) or even Freud's own early use of massage to promote free association. Catharsis still plays an important part in more orthodox therapies, perhaps most commonly when helping someone to ventilate previously unexpressed grief.

Reich's work has been continued as 'bioenergetic therapy' by his former pupil Lowen (1967), who has corrected some of the excessive physical bias of Reich's methods, by using more varied physical exercises, and verbal forms of psychotherapy, including group work. Many current 'body work' therapies, such as yoga and Autogenic Training, aim to correct the flow and balance of bodily forces and their integration with mental ones.

Primal therapy

The Primal Scream is the name of a book by Arthur Janov (1970) describing a theory and treatment of neurosis. He believed that all neurosis is an attempt to ward off mental pain which has been inflicted on the infant from outside and creates tension leading to secondary defences. Like Freud, he sees the neurotic as someone struggling with unresolved problems from the past. But he does not allow, as Freud later did, for the interaction between actual events and intrapsychic fantasies based on the child's instinctual wishes. Like Reich, who inflated Freud's early idea of actual neurosis and the harm that can be caused by an unhealthy sexual life, Janov takes as the form of his treatment the discharge of intense emotion. In Primal Therapy, this is the 'scream' generated in infancy by intense pain, but not expressed sufficiently in an adequately supporting relationship, and consequently sealed off.

The pain experienced by the child as a sense of being intensely hurt or wronged has recently been traced by Janov and others, including Laing, to what they regard as the first trauma, that of birth. Freud (1926) himself had proposed that the 'trauma' of birth was the prototype of traumatic neuroses, as opposed to those caused by internal conflict. This idea was exaggerated by another of Freud's early followers, Otto Rank (1929), who thought that the sudden expulsion from the protecting environment of the womb constituted a trauma which was the precursor of *all* later experiences of anxiety, and believed that many patients were seeking to re-experience their birth. The obstetrician Leboyer (1977) drew attention to the insensitivity with which children are often received into the world in hospital, with bright lights, clashing noises, and rapid removal from their mothers. He reintroduced quieter and less traumatic methods, which include putting mother and child into immediate skin contact. While still controversial, these ideas have a natural appeal to many obstetricians and paediatricians, and are nearer to the normal practice of most midwives doing home deliveries. There have been reports that minimization of the traumatic separation of mother and infant, and their early re-introduction, foster subsequent 'bonding' between them. Perhaps this seemingly romantic movement is no more than a timely reassertion of human values in the face of excessive hospital technology. It is also part of women's demand to have more say and control of how they give birth, a practical fruit of the Women's Movement.

Giving so much importance to birth trauma seems too

reductionist; after all, everyone has to be born, but only some develop neuroses. Yet there are patients with a history of early trauma who experience a need to scream in therapy, and, in a regressed state, some do appear to experience birth-like bodily sensations. Although there have been reports of dramatic cures from severe neurosis and psychosomatic states following guided re-experience of birth (Lake 1978), we cannot take them as proof of a causal connection; suggestion in a state of intense arousal and emotional vulnerability can have powerful effects.

In Janov's hands, primal therapy involved a full-time intensive initial phase, lasting three weeks. This was followed by return to normal life, whilst continuing treatment for six months in a 'Primal Group', which provided a supportive background in which each individual sought repetition of his own primal experiences.

Other therapies

In addition to the forms of therapy already described, all deriving historically from some elements of psychoanalysis (*Figure 10*), several others have recently gained some prominence and are represented at the United Kingdom Standing Conference on Psychotherapy (p.203). We cannot fully do them justice, or include them in *Figure 10*, but will say something brief about them to extend our overview of current forms of therapy that have at least peripheral connections with the main forms of dynamic psychotherapy described in this book.

Hypnotherapy. It will be recalled (p.11) that Freud first used hypnosis in an attempt to remove neurotic symptoms, later to release repressed memories and ideas by putting his patients into a light trance. He soon relinquished deliberate suggestion and replaced hypnosis by the technique of free association. Others, however, continued to investigate hypnotic phenomena (Heap 1988) and to use it for therapeutic ends with neurotic, behavioural, and addictive problems; to help in the management of psychosomatic disorders, and the management of pain in obstetrics and dentistry (Kroger 1963; Erickson and Rossi 1979). Good hypnotic subjects not only attain a heightened susceptibility to suggestion, but under its influence appear to 'regress' to earlier periods of their lives, and recall traumatic events, often with considerable emotional catharsis

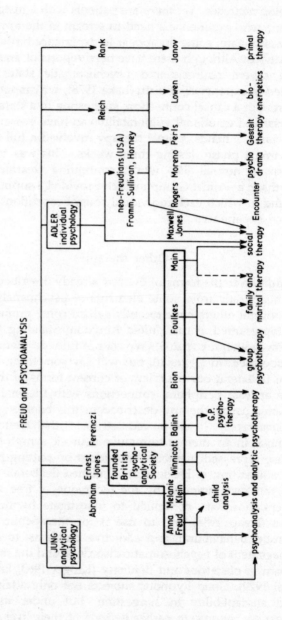

Figure 10

and vividness. They can then be reassured, 'forgiven', and offered explanations of a link between these experiences and their current difficulties. This can bring relief which, even if only short term, can break a cycle of symptoms and distress.

The relationship of patient to therapist needs to be submissive and trusting. The power of transference is used in hypnosis rather than revealed by exploration and interpretation as in analytical psychotherapy. The practice of hypnosis as part of psychotherapy has been confined to the periphery of orthodox medicine, dentistry, obstetrics, and psychiatry. In this country, however, the British Society of Medical and Dental Hypnosis has continued as a focus for professional development, and there are now a few training bodies which are attempting to organize and control work in this field, and are represented in a separate Hypnotherapy section within the UK Standing Conference on Psychotherapy (p.203).

Neuro-Linguistic Programming (NLP). An influential figure in hypnotherapy has been the powerful personality of Erickson whose language patterns, like those of other charismatic therapists (Perls, Satir) were studied by Bandler and Grinder (1981) to form the therapeutic system known as NLP (O'Connor and Seymour 1990). This explores the models of the world people create based on the pre-verbal raw material of their dominant perceptual mode – visual, auditory, or kinaesthetic-emotional. Hypnosis is used to varying extents by different NLP practitioners to help clients change their restricted models to more flexible and adaptive ones. Practitioners use close observation of sensory cues – eye movements, breathing, skin colour changes, head nods, and so on – to determine the deeper, unconscious responses of clients to questions and suggestions in establishing rapport, and in guiding themselves towards what is 'right' for the client.

Personal Construct Therapy (PCT) engages with patients to discover their maladapative ways of construing themselves and the world, using more cognitive and traditional verbal methods than does NLP. However, practitioners of these two types of therapy have recently joined together to form a separate section, Experiential Constructivist Therapies, within the UKSCP. Both approaches have what they describe as an equality of interest between therapist and client, and emphasize the 'here and now' and 'continuing processes of reconstruction' in helping patients to free themselves from the 'prisons' of their past. However, while NLP requires a knowledge of well-developed techniques and interventions, in Personal Construct Therapy, techniques for helping the process of reconstruction are used more empirically. PCT uses the Personal Construct Psychology of George Kelly (Fransella and Thomas 1988), who devised the *repertory grid*. This studies the cognitive constructs underlying our evaluation of significant figures in our lives, past and present. Repertory grids have also been used by research-orientated psychoanalysts and psychotherapists to study transference problems, identification, and sense of identity (Feldman 1975; Ryle 1990).

Cognitive Therapy could be seen as having links with Personal Construct Therapy, being avowedly cognitive and 'rational' in its approach. It was originated by Beck (1976) and aims to help patients recognize and modify those attitudes and patterns of thought about themselves and their relationships which trap them in depression and some other restricting states. It has proved useful, though less so in people with deeply seated depression, biological or characterological (Scott *et al.* 1989). Even then it can help people begin to move enough for them to make use of more dynamic forms of therapy. Ryle (1990) has recently brought together aspects of cognitive, personal construct, and psychodynamic approaches in a method of brief psychotherapy he calls Cognitive-Analytic Therapy (CAT).

As defined by Gelder, standard Cognitive Therapy describes a group of treatments intermediate between dynamic psychotherapy and Behaviour Therapy:

'They resemble Behaviour Therapy in being active, directive and structured. They differ from Behaviour Therapy in being founded on the idea that cognitions have a central role in behaviour disorders; abnormalities of behaviour (and mood) are thought of as the consequences of primary abnormalities in cognitions. Dynamic psychotherapy and Cognitive Therapy resemble one another in being concerned more with mental content than behaviour. They differ in the priority given in Cognitive Therapy to thinking over feeling and to cognitions that are, or can easily be made, conscious.'

(Gelder 1983)

There are three main procedures: cognitive restructuring, cognitive behaviour therapy, and anxiety management. Gelder concluded that cognitive procedures had a more powerful effect with depressive disorders than with anxiety and phobic neuroses; that the more effective procedures contain behavioural as well as cognitive techniques (anxiety management for anxiety and phobic neuroses, and cognitive behaviour therapy for depressive disorders); and that cognitive procedures may help to avoid relapse as much as aid recovery. Clinical psychologists have played a major part in developing Cognitive Therapy, as they have with Behavioural Psychotherapy.

By this time, however, we are on the fringes of *Behavioural Psychotherapy*, which deliberately plays down the existence of unconscious processes, including transference, which many proponents of Behavioural Psychotherapy actively deny.

None of the organizations promoting these forms of therapy (hypnotherapy to cognitive therapy) requires their practitioners to have a personal psychotherapeutic experience. Taking the first and last of these forms of therapy as extremes, one could say that hypnotherapists aim to induce regression and catharsis, bypassing the patient's defences, and maximize the effects of suggestion; and cognitive therapists aim to reconstruct attitudes without taking into account underlying unconscious motives, feelings, and fantasies within the patient. A psychodynamic psychotherapist would take such factors into account within themselves as well as their patients. Although sometimes symptomatically effective, it could be argued that at their extremes, hypnotherapy and cognitive therapy may keep apart aspects of a total personality that the psychodynamic approach attempts to integrate.

Looking at the various new therapies described in this section, it will be apparent that each one picks up and inflates one of the elements in the work of Freud and of mainstream analytic psychotherapy, while excluding others. Rogers emphasized frankness, as though unburdening and acceptance are the whole of psychotherapy. Perls stressed immediacy in the 'here and now' and therapist activity, as though reflectiveness and the emergence of transference were nuisances (as Freud had thought when he first started his work with Breuer). Reich came to believe that the discharge of pent-up feelings and sexual energy was all that was necessary, reverting to Freud's first anxiety theory and earliest cathartic model of therapy. Janov takes the idea of infantile emotional trauma to an extreme that excludes everything else. And as already discussed, hypnotherapy and cognitive therapy, at their extremes, may keep apart aspects of the self. In *Figure 10* we have attempted to show the derivation from Freud's ideas of most of the forms of therapy described in this book. The lines of influence should be read as our own view. They would not necessarily be acknowledged by those mentioned, nor do they always imply an apostolic succession of analyst and analysand. The 'family tree' illustrates our contention, expressed in the Foreword (p.vii) and Introduction (p.5) that all forms of dynamic psychotherapy derive from the work of Freud and psychoanalysis.

SELECTION AND OUTCOME

For whom should psychotherapy be considered?

In order to answer this question we need to specify what type of psychotherapy for what sort of problem. Furthermore, since psychotherapy is not an impersonal medical technique, we cannot avoid taking into account the individual characteristics of patient and therapist, who must be able to work together. Ultimately a decision about embarking on psychotherapy can only be arrived at when both patient and therapist show what they could bring to the therapeutic relationship.

In assessing suitability for different types of psychotherapy, the doctor or therapist will listen attentively and try to enter imaginatively into the patient's experience, if necessary encouraging him to amplify his account of what troubles him. Comments by the doctor/therapist which show awareness of the patient's anxieties about the interview are often particularly helpful in establishing rapport. In attempting to understand and look below the surface of the presenting complaints, he may offer interventions (or test interpretations) at varying levels. For example, he may say to a depressed and agitated middle-aged woman, devoted to caring for her aged parents: 'It seems that you are trying not to think about your feelings of resentment at the restrictions this imposes on your life'; or to a promising student who always fails his examinations: 'I wonder if you are afraid of succeeding because that would be like triumphing over your unsuccessful father?' The responses they make could help in assessing their preparedness to think about difficulties in a new way. Unthinking rejection or passive acceptance of an interpretation are usually bad auguries for dynamic psychotherapy; a thoughtful response, with expression of emotion or meaningful associations, or even 'I don't think so', are preferable. Sometimes it is possible to make transference interpretations linking a patient's attitude to the interviewer (for example, fearful of criticism or anxious to please) to his attitude to a parent. If the patient can make use of interpretations it suggests that he will continue to do so if he enters therapy.

The therapist's personality and the extent to which he is interested and involved are key factors. Research work has shown (p.95) that 'empathy, warmth and genuineness' are therapist characteristics which predispose to favourable outcome in non-directive therapy. These factors are probably relevant to some degrees in all types of psychotherapy. But even this cannot be seen in isolation. What matters is how patient and therapist get on together. This can often be assessed at a first interview by the degree of emotional contact, or rapport, that is made between them, by the feelings that the patient expresses (sometimes to his surprise) and by the therapist's own countertransference responses.

We have already indicated (pp.87ff) that psychotherapy can occur at several levels, from supportive to exploratory, and that it can take place within both informal and professional relationships. *Any* person in difficulties benefits from support and help to maintain or restore morale; this is psychotherapy in the general sense (Level 1). However, certain questions arise when considering exploratory psychotherapy in the special dynamic sense (Level 3), which aims to promote change. These are as important as the formal psychiatric diagnosis, or presenting problem, in deciding who would make use of dynamic psychotherapy (*Table 6*).

Table 6 Selection criteria for psychotherapy

	supportive (level 1)	*exploratory* (level 3)
understanding of problems in psychological terms		
patient's motivation for insight and change	not essential	necessary
ego strength		
capacity to form and sustain relationships		

Are the person's difficulties understandable in psychological terms?

Beyond making a psychiatric diagnosis, based on the symptoms and signs elicited at the interview, it should be possible to make a tentative *psychodynamic formulation* of the patient's problems, taking into account both current life situation and earlier development. For example, the depressive state of Mrs A., described in the Prologue, became understandable when her response to the prospect of her daughter's leaving home was viewed in the context of her own early history of separation. The patient's preparedness to think about problems in psychological terms is a parallel requirement. Response to test interpretations, as described above, can help in assessing this. Perhaps of greater significance is the way in which both interviewer and patient can enter into sharing the essence of a provisional psychodynamic formulation, before moving on to discuss treatment options at the end of the interview (Brown 1991).

Is there sufficient motivation for insight and change?

A patient expresses his wish for insight by the way he asks for help and engages in discussion about himself and his problems. If he is rigidly defensive and remains very guarded, or restricts himself to complaining about symptoms, or to blaming someone else for his troubles, he is unlikely to want to understand his own contribution to his problems and how he can change. If he pours out his difficulties, as though using the interviewer as a wastebin, or he seems to be looking for 'magical solutions' from an omnipotent parent/therapist, he is probably not yet ready to join in an effective *working alliance* (p.54), though he might do so in time. Mrs A.'s reappraisal of her separation experiences, past and present, in a joint exploration with the interviewer, indicated her readiness for insight and augured well for her ability to use dynamic psychotherapy. A degree of introspectiveness, average intelligence, and verbal fluency are desirable, otherwise patients will find it difficult to reflect and to think about their feelings, rather than act them out impulsively; and their capacity to communicate through talking may be restricted. However, patients' capacities for introspection and verbal communication can develop during therapy. Sometimes these are fostered by the use of action techniques, such as those mentioned in the previous section, but as yet these have not been widely integrated into the mainstream of psychotherapy.

A patient's *earliest* memories can be used in dynamic interviewing and formulation. A marked degree of childhood amnesia may indicate prominent repression and restriction of personality. The capacity to remember dreams is another useful indicator of the ability of patients to contact unconscious parts of themselves, without feeling unduly disturbed. Resistance to insight and change can be based on anxieties about the danger of deep exploration or unwillingness to upset a balance which brings advantage to the patient or their family.

Has the patient adequate Ego strength?

He must be able to evaluate his experience and integrate the competing demands of motivational drives (Id), conscience (Super-ego) and external reality, while coping with the tensions they create. He needs to take stock of perceptions arising from the external world and from within himself, and to distinguish between them. He has to be able to sustain feelings and fantasies without impulsively acting on them, without being overwhelmed by anxiety, and without losing, for long, the capacity to think and talk rationally. Further, he must keep in touch with his adult self and maintain the working alliance with the therapist, at the same time as he contacts the disturbed and often helpless child in himself. Then, before leaving a session, he must return to functioning as a reasonable coping adult until the next session, which during holiday breaks he may need to do for several weeks. Repeated hospital admissions or frequent suicidal attempts may suggest insufficient Ego-strength for dynamic psychotherapy. Repeated risk-taking, an established and destructive pattern of addictive behaviour, or serious somatization into major psychosomatic disorder can indicate overrunning of the person's capacity for integration (Malan 1979:Ch.18). In addition, a history of repeated dropping out of relationships and failure to complete ventures can be bad auguries for sticking at therapy.

In general, patients with acute psychotic disorders are not amenable to exploratory psychotherapy, because their Ego functions are too impaired. During a schizophrenic breakdown, patients suffer impaired Ego boundaries, and they are already flooded by unconscious primitive material. They may no longer be certain whether their thoughts and feelings are their own or someone else's (which gives rise to the phenomena of thought transference and insertion). Severely depressed patients may be too slowed up and unresponsive to engage in psychotherapy, while at the same time a hypercritical Superego might produce severe guilt feelings or even delusions. Ego functions may be so impaired that the voice of conscience is no longer recognized as internal, but projected outwards and experienced as a hallucinatory voice making derogatory remarks. The transference relationships made by psychotic patients are often frighteningly intense, and cannot be seen by the patient in 'as if' terms; for them, the doctor or nurse *is* their mother or father. Primitive transference responses to the therapist are likely to overwhelm the working alliance. On the other hand, however, psychotic patients benefit from supportive psychotherapy aimed at strengthening the Ego while they receive medication, often in hospital. At a later stage, when they have recovered from an acute episode, cautious exploration of underlying conflicts may sometimes be appropriate.

Is there a capacity to form and sustain relationships?

It might seem paradoxical that this should be a criterion for dynamic psychotherapy. After all, most of the difficulties with which people come for help are ultimately relationship problems. However, as we have said, psychotherapy operates within or through the relationship of patient and therapist, without which there can be no working alliance, let alone analysis of transference. Even one sustained or reliable relationship in the patient's past or current life suggests a firmer basis from which to start therapy. This is particularly important in short-term analytic psychotherapy. Whereas in long-term analytic psychotherapy there is time to develop trust and become more fully engaged, in brief therapy intense involvement is required from the start (p.117).

Given that these criteria are satisfied, many people with neurotic and character problems, if they genuinely want to change, can be helped by analytic psychotherapy, either individually or in a group. Their problems may have been brought to light by life events or developmental crises, such as leaving home for the first time, parenthood, or bereavement. Others may be more chronically dissatisfied with themselves and their relationships, or may feel inhibited or unduly anxious. They may be unable to realize their potential or to cope with aggression or sexuality. If successful, benefit usually extends beyond any presenting symptoms. For example, a man who initially complained only of impotence discovered that he was afraid of the consequences of his aggressive feelings towards women, a fear that originated through his relationship with his mother; as he resolved this conflict, he discovered that he could also be more appropriately assertive in other areas of his life. Some patients with psychosomatic disorders which are not too deeply ingrained in their physical or psychological constitution, can be helped by dynamic psychotherapy, if they are able to consider psychological causes and solutions. Likewise some perversions and addictions can be modified, if they are not symptoms of a seriously damaged personality or a defence against breakdown and disintegration.

Selection for psychotherapy may appear to some to involve an objectionable introduction of elitist values. Psychotherapists have been chided for tending to take on young, intelligent, and personable patients; but equally they are asked to take on difficult patients for whom psychiatrists have little to offer. While surgeons perform relatively brief operations on inert anaesthetized patients, psychotherapists spend a lot of time in a unique personal relationship with their patients. Personal feelings are therefore bound to influence who is accepted for treatment by therapists, just as referrals to them are influenced by the feelings of the family doctor or general psychiatrist. Indeed, referrals may be motivated either by a wish to do everything possible for someone, or conversely by a wish to get rid of a difficult or even untreatable patient. The therapist has to decide the level and type of psychotherapeutic help the patient is able to use, as well as who can best provide it. Part of the task is to engage the patient in this decision-making, and to respect his right to reject a therapist he does not feel he can work with. For this reason a network of therapists, as well as a range of therapies, is desirable in a full psychotherapy service.

What type of psychotherapy?

We have already outlined different levels of psychotherapy. The *outer levels* (p.91) involving unburdening, ventilation of feelings (catharsis), and discussion of problems, include counselling and supportive psychotherapy, and are indicated for those who do not want, or could not tolerate, deeper exploration and uncovering. Those who want help with particular problems, for example, relating to adolescence, unwanted pregnancy, or marital difficulties, can get valuable help from special counselling agencies. Patients with long-term disability and impairment, chronic psychosis, or personality severely affected by early deprivation, may need long-term support to help them cope with the inevitable stresses of life. People who are reacting to an acute crisis in their lives, such as bereavement, divorce, or loss of a job, and whose personality is basically strong and capable of adjusting to difficulties, might need only relatively short-term supportive psychotherapy or counselling to restore their defences and stability to the *status quo ante*. If after a while their emotional distress has not begun to resolve, it is possible that the crisis has thrown up underlying conflicts and problems which may be helped by more exploratory, dynamic psychotherapy. Therapists who work with a crisis model (p.139) may attempt to intervene at an early stage in a family crisis, hoping thereby to increase the chances of constructive change and learning.

At *intermediate levels*, the question arises of whether the patient should be referred for general psychiatric treatment, behaviour therapy, or for dynamic psychotherapy. If a person has symptoms of anxiety and depression it is often appropriate to put it to him that there are different ways of viewing the problem. His symptoms could be seen as part of an illness of unknown cause, which will be relieved by medication; or he might want to try and discover why he has developed into the kind of person who reacted in this sort of way at this time, in which case psychotherapy may be more appropriate. The two views are not mutually exclusive – symptomatic relief from drugs might be helpful first and then further exploration via psychotherapy if desired. When given this choice people are very often able to decide what is best for themselves. As Balint and Balint (1961:47) said, 'one of the chief aims of every diagnostic interview is, if at all possible, to enable the patient to decide for himself what his next step should be – a decision which, as a rule, he has been unable to take before the interview'. People differ according to age, education, and background. One patient may say 'Give me the pills, doctor, there's no point in talking about it'; another more reflective person may say 'What's the good of suppressing symptoms with medication if they only recur? I want to get to the bottom of it and understand why I'm like this.' Psychotherapy is more akin to an educational process that engages the client as an active participant, than to a conventional medical treatment, where the patient remains a passive recipient.

On another occasion, the choice might be between dynamic and behavioural psychotherapy. Suppose the presenting problem was the sudden realization by a formerly happily married man of homosexual impulses; again there are different ways of viewing the problem. It could be seen as a 'bad habit' which the patient merely wants to be rid of, in which case behaviour therapy might be appropriate. Alternatively he may want to know why this had happened at this particular time; was it perhaps due to his jealousy at feeling excluded by his wife following the birth of a child? In this case dynamic psychotherapy would be appropriate. One patient who presented with just this problem was a vicar who found himself suddenly attracted to choirboys. When presented with the choice as above, his response was, 'I certainly don't want to know any more about it; it threatens my whole life; I just want it abolished'. In this case behaviour therapy was successfully pursued.

Where there are marital difficulties, one couple might prefer to tackle a sexual problem, such as impotence or frigidity, by the sexual training techniques pioneered by Masters and Johnson (1970); while to another couple it may make more sense to view it as a reflection of something amiss in their relationship and of what each brings to it, and therefore to seek more dynamic marital therapy.

Behaviour therapy and dynamic psychotherapy can complement each other in the treatment of some patients. For example, a period of dynamic psychotherapy following behaviour therapy enabled the woman with a phobia of thunder (p.85) to understand her conflicts, to change her attitude to herself and her family, and to establish a healthier adjustment which stood the test of time. Dynamic psychotherapy had not been possible before she received behaviour therapy. Similarly, some socially inhibited and unassertive patients, who would at first be too overwhelmed by the idea of joining a group, are able to make use of analytic group psychotherapy following social skills training. Conversely, there are patients who improve in many ways through dynamic psychotherapy, without fully overcoming their symptoms, and subsequently obtain relief through techniques of behaviour modification, for example, desensitization for residual phobic symptoms.

At the *deeper* levels of exploratory psychotherapy, we need to consider the developmental origin of the underlying conflicts and problems. This can be seen in terms of the three developmental phases described in Part I (pp.41–4). (1) In the phase of total dependence on mother (0–1 yr) lie the roots of many psychotic conditions and severe character problems described as borderline. These patients have a poor sense of their own boundaries and are extremely easily hurt and overwhelmed by feelings and fantasies. (2) In the phase of growing separation and individuation (1–3) many problems originate concerning attachment and separation, wilfulness and compliance. These include separation anxiety, depression, defensive detachment, and obsessional problems. (3) In the phase of increasing differentiation and rivalry within the family (3–5), known as the Oedipal stage, can be seen the roots of many neurotic and sexual problems, inhibitions, and phobias. By this time a child can move about, talk, identify with others (for example, father as well as mother), distinguish the sexes, and more securely differentiate fantasy from reality. By the end of this phase the child has begun to internalize parental and social standards, and can be said to have organized his/her personality more securely into Ego, Super-ego, and Id.

The more mature a patient's personality, and the later the developmental phase in which his principal conflicts and problems originated, the more likely he is to respond to shorter-term analytic psychotherapy or group therapy. Conditions with roots in earlier phases are likely to need longer term treatment. Patients severely damaged by early environmental failure, such as inadequate mothering, if suitable for analytic therapy, might need over a long period to experience the analyst more concretely as mother and his words as feeds, in a recapitulation of the earliest developmental phase. At such a time the provision of a relationship may be more important than the intellectual content of interpretations. Such patients can be treated in groups, but often their need to regress and re-experience the earliest phase of total dependence, though in a new and more favourable environment, makes them extremely intolerant of other group members; or they may comply and make no deep therapeutic progress. Some therapists have used combined individual and group therapy for such very deprived patients with good results (Jackson and Grotjahn 1958).

Group psychotherapy is the treatment of choice for many patients with problems in relating to others since the group setting provides particular opportunities for interpersonal learning. Even members who are initially reluctant to talk much about themselves learn from others. In the course of a few months, isolated or schizoid people may allow previously cut off feelings to emerge. Those with character problems perpetuated by restricting their relationships may, in a group, discover for the first time how unsatisfactory have been their solutions to underlying problems; they can then begin to seek new solutions with the help of the group. However, patients who are extremely demanding, paranoid, or severely depressed have difficulty in tolerating or being tolerated by a group. Ultimately, whether they become part of the group depends on its composition, atmosphere, and stage of development.

In considering whether individual, group, or family therapy is appropriate, Skynner's (1976:168) notion of *minimum sufficient network* can help in deciding whom to include in treatment when one member of a family presents or is presented as a problem. Skynner applies the idea that a well-functioning individual needs to have Ego, Super-ego, and Id working in harmony. All three are needed in individual therapy to allow a reasonable degree of reality-testing, control of impulses, and emotional spontaneity respectively. Working with families, often from deprived and chaotic backgrounds, he found that these families needed to integrate and harmonize their functions, which previously they had split off into different members of the family (for example, sensible mother, critical father, and delinquent child), or lodged in the family's relationship with the community (for example, concerned school, punishing police, and demanding, violent family). What is needed is to reintegrate the parts so that they can begin to modify each other. As discussed in the section on family and marital therapy, when a disturbance is located in the family or marriage, the presenting patient may not be the sickest member nor the one most open to change. Bringing the family together for treatment can often mobilize understanding and constructive change in the *system*, producing sufficient relief of stress for a more satisfactory adjustment to be achieved without deep exploration of individual members.

Skynner and Brown (1981) have pointed out that although it is individuals who are usually referred, and individual therapy most often thought of, a family approach (to diagnosis if not therapy) has wide applicability in terms of types and level of pathology and capacity for insight. If it can be arranged, a family consultation provides information about the interaction of many key people in addition to the presenting patient, who may not be the sickest nor the most amenable to direct therapeutic influence. And even without motivation for insight a few sessions can have a big effect by changing the whole system of interaction (Howells and Brown 1986).

Group therapy of different types also has a wide spectrum of applicability, and in analytical group therapy even patients who initially have poor motivation for insight and little capacity for emotional expression can be helped; they can learn from others and change gradually over time. Individual therapy has the advantage of flexibility in that the needs of each person, including the frequency of sessions, can be catered for.

Between 1979 and 1982 Clarkin and Frances reviewed the selection criteria for Family Evaluation and Therapy, Group Therapy, Brief Psychotherapy, and No Treatment. They provide useful guidelines based on research literature and clinical consensus which we summarize under headings of (1) family or marital evaluation, (2) group psychotherapy, (3) brief psychotherapy, and (4) no treatment, in Appendix 2 (p.204).

Why is help sought now?

This is often a pertinent question when a patient asks for help, from either family doctor or psychiatrist. The answer may throw light on factors which disturb the individual's adjustment, and give an idea of his Ego strength and coping capacities. It could throw into relief the interaction between chronic and acute stresses, for example, between long-term frustration of needs or wishes and the final blow of disappointment or loss. It might reveal a sequence of successful attempts to cope with challenges, before tension and other non-specific signs of crisis arise prior to the final 'breakdown' into an organized psychological or physical disorder. The crisis may have been precipitated by some sudden or mounting stress in the family, or at work, or even in the patient's relationship with his family doctor; in which case help may be most appropriately directed at a family or marital problem, or at supporting the doctor in coping with a burdensome long-term patient.

It may take more than one meeting, but eventually having defined and located the problem, patient and doctor/therapist are usually in a better position to decide whether ongoing psychotherapy is needed, and if so, which level and form of therapy makes most sense to both of them. The *level* will range from support and counselling, augmented if necessary by symptomatic relief with medication, to various levels of analytic exploration. In addition, the *form* of therapy may depend on the degree of directiveness likely to be required in order to influence the problem, and also on whether the patient is more likely to respond to behavioural and action methods rather than those based on insight and understanding.

Figure 11 places the psychotherapeutic methods described in Part II in a range from interpretation to action, between the individual and group.

Figure 11

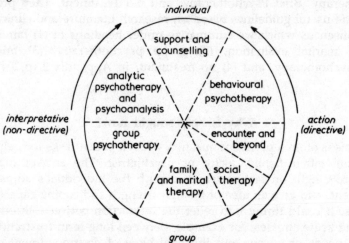

Whatever the problem and however full the range of possible psychotherapeutic methods, assessment and selection for psychotherapy does not involve examination by an active doctor of a passive and inert patient, as in some areas of medicine. We need the patient's active cooperation. Moreover, 'The other cardinal difference is that in organic medicine it is sufficient if the therapy makes sense to the doctor; what is required from the patient is merely that he should reliably carry out the doctor's prescriptions. Contrariwise in psychological medicine it is essential that the therapy should make sense both to the patient and to the doctor.' (Balint and Balint 1961:206).

What evidence do we have that psychotherapy does any good?

This is as hard to answer simply as the question 'For whom should psychotherapy be considered?', and for similar reasons: few studies have taken into account all the relevant variables, such as the level and type of psychotherapy, the sort of patient and problem, the personality and skill of the therapist, and how patient and therapist get on together. It is difficult to measure the relevant changes in human adjustment and to standardize treatments which by their nature involve unique experiences at many levels.

Controlled double-blind trials of drug treatments are simple in comparison, because every pill is the same, and control groups of patients can be given dummy pills without their realizing it, so giving a measure of the 'placebo effect'.

'The more an illness resembles an accident, the better are the results of hospital medicine, and it is here in this field that the proper application and value of the double-blind experiment lie. On the other hand, the more an illness is due to a lack of integration the less effective will be the so-called scientific treatments and the less applicable will be the double-blind experiment.'

(Balint and Balint 1961:126)

In psychotherapy each therapeutic relationship is unique and every session is different. Even in one session the key experience might be one *mutative* interpretation, the withholding of an interpretation, or, in a group, the impact of someone else's experience. Controlled trials of psychotherapy are difficult to construct because of the problems of matching relevant variables and allowing sufficient time for therapy and follow-up. Many people get better spontaneously, without formal treatment, through time, maturation, and 'therapeutic' experiences in relationships outside. If a patient improves, can one say with certainty that he did so because of treatment, or something else in his life? In considering both selection and research, it is helpful to bear in mind that dynamic psychotherapy is more comparable to an educational process than to a medical treatment.

Thus, a question put in such general terms as 'What evidence do we have that psychotherapy does any good?' would be as meaningless as asking it about surgery. Yet a great deal of heat has been generated in trying to answer it, particularly by those who seem committed to discover that psychotherapy is no more effective than the passage of time. Eysenck (1952; 1965), in his often-quoted reviews of evidence then available, asserted that two-thirds of neurotic patients improve whether they are treated or not, but his view has been sharply criticized. Indeed, it is amazing how much mileage these articles have had when one considers that they compared out-patients who improved in analysis with in-patients considered well enough to be discharged from state mental hospitals within a year; the groups were scarcely comparable in terms of type and severity of illness, social background, or criteria of change. The figures if offered by anyone else, would hardly escape Eysenck's own criticism. Reviewing evidence about spontaneous remission, Bergin (1971) believed that a figure of 30 per cent would be a truer assessment, though this figure in its turn has been challenged. Clearly an appreciable number of people do improve with time, for whatever reason, and any trial of psychotherapy must take this fact into account. Frank (1961) has reminded us of the need to distinguish between spontaneous improvement, the effect of any form of treatment where a patient expecting help meets a socially sanctioned healer, and the specific benefits claimed for a particular form of treatment.

Outcome studies are complicated by the fact that assessments by the patient, the therapist, an independent assessor, and relatives often correlate poorly. The relevant criteria include the level of symptoms (most often emphasized by behavioural psychotherapists); social and sexual adjustments; and personal growth and insight (more often emphasized by humanistic and analytic psychotherapists).

After examining in detail the huge literature on trials of different types of psychotherapeutic intervention, Meltzoff and Kornreich (1970) found 101 studies in which the outcome was compared with some form of control group, either a period of non-treatment or a group of patients treated in some other way. Criteria of outcome included observed behaviour, questionnaires, independent ratings, projective tests, and Q-sorts (testing differences between a patient's view of himself as he is and as he would like to be). In eighty-one studies the outcome was favourable, in twenty it was not.

'The weight of experimental evidence is sufficient to enable us to reject the null hypothesis. Far more often than not, psychotherapy of a wide variety of types and with a broad range of disorders has been demonstrated under controlled conditions to be accompanied by positive changes in adjustment that significantly exceed those that can be accounted for by the passage of time alone. The therapists represent a cross-section of those who do therapy in the various settings in which the research has been done. As a group, they were not selected for their outstanding ability.'

(Meltzoff and Kornreich 1970:175)

Bergin (1967) has drawn attention to the 'deterioration effect' in psychotherapy; while some patients get better in therapy, others may get worse. It could hardly be otherwise if we are dealing with a treatment of any power (just as with drugs or radiotherapy), but, as Bergin pointed out, if a substantial number of patients do deteriorate, the benefit in others may be obscured when overall effects are measured. Mistakes in selection or technique, or poor match between therapist and patient could all contribute to such adverse effects.

The importance in research of taking into account characteristics of both individual patients and the treatment they receive, emerged from the Psychotherapy Research Project of the Menninger Foundation (Kernberg 1972) and the work on brief analytic psychotherapy carried out at the Tavistock Clinic in London by Malan (1963, 1973). Malan has demonstrated the value of designing outcome criteria appropriate to each patient. After careful psychodynamic assessment, but before therapy begins, a decision was made by Malan's research team as to which changes would be accepted as evidence, in each case, that the focal conflict underlying the patient's symptoms had been resolved or modified. For example, in the case of a socially anxious woman whose underlying conflict is related to fear of entering a relationship with a man, the evidence sought might be that, by the end of treatment or follow-up, she should have a long-term heterosexual relationship. Reduction in social anxiety alone would not be accepted as evidence of dynamic change. So far, however, practical problems have defeated valiant attempts to complete a controlled trial conducted along these lines.

In a joint study between the Tavistock Clinic and the Maudsley Hospital in London (Candy et al. 1972) which invited referrals from more than fifty consultant psychiatrists in the London area, insufficient cases fitting the selection criteria were collected in the time available for the trial. The first problem was that those who had firm views in favour of the value of psychotherapy were not prepared to submit patients to the uncertainty of a controlled trial in which there was a 1 in 3 chance of their not receiving treatment. Second, many consultants preferred to refer patients to their own, local psychotherapy services. Third, the psychotherapists reserved the right only to accept into the trial those likely to benefit from psychotherapy – whether or not they were to receive it. They have been criticized on the grounds that they should have accepted cases regardless of their suitability. However, we feel such criticism misses a crucial difference between psychotherapy and drug therapy. A physician might be prepared to admit a patient to a short controlled trial of a new drug whether or not he thought it would be effective (so long as it was not thought likely to be harmful). A psychotherapist, like a violin teacher, may not consider it worthwhile to spend long hours with someone who had no aptitude for the enterprise; nor might the patient or pupil.

The problem of assessing outcome in psychotherapy remains an important challenge. It is unlikely to be tackled adequately unless methods are devised which match the complexity and subtlety of human beings and their problems, and the many variables in patient, therapist, and psychotherapeutic technique used. However, it is hard for those with strong humanistic faith in the value of personal relationships to wait for incontrovertible evidence of the sort demanded by hardheaded critics. After all, the development of educational and social services has followed man's conviction of what is right and just, and has not been delayed until controlled trials have been conducted on the efficacy of schooling or family allowances, however desirable such trials might be. Confirmation of the value of a psychotherapeutic approach may come from unexpected indirect sources, such as the sociological evidence (p.150) that the lack of supportive relationships contributes to the development of depressive states.

As mentioned in discussing selection, the choice of type of treatment (and, one could add, of therapist) should depend on the patient as well as the therapist. The choice is often limited because of restricted local provision. This is an additional factor not often considered by critics hostile to psychotherapy, nor in scientific assessment of the comparative effect of different forms of psychotherapy. Luborsky *et al.* (1975) reviewed the research literature on comparative effectiveness and concluded there was no reason to suppose that overall there was any significant difference between long- and short-term therapy, individual and group therapy, Rogerian counselling and traditional psychotherapy, or behavioural and dynamic psychotherapy. Bloch (1982) has suggested that this could be interpreted as evidence for the importance of non-specific factors in all forms of psychotherapy. In a more recent publication, summing up the Penn Psychotherapy Project, Luborsky *et al.* (1988) have identified core conflictual relationships as critical in predicting response to psychodynamic psychotherapy. Reduction of the intensity and pervasiveness of these problems, and the early establishment of a positive therapeutic alliance, significantly improve outcome.

In the last decade there has been a lot of controversy about the statistical treatment of very large numbers of separate studies of different forms of psychotherapy for many different conditions and in widely different settings. This so-called meta-analysis (Smith *et al.* 1980) calculates an index of effect size (ES) by subtracting the untreated (waiting-list) group mean from the treatment group mean and dividing by the control group standard deviation (Gwynne Jones 1985). On this basis over 500 studies of various psychological therapies, verbal and behavioural, were judged as showing, overall, a superiority of therapy over no therapy. The average patient receiving treatment was better off than more than 80 per cent of the untreated controls. This approach has been severely criticized on methodological grounds and Prioleau *et al.* (1983) concluded that the results of the original study could be re-interpreted as showing no clear benefit from psychotherapy. This conclusion has in its turn been criticized (Aveline 1984; Bloch and Lambert 1985). Whether placebo or waiting-list controls are necessary or possible is still fiercely debated but, as a recent investigator states (Gwynne Jones 1985), 'More realistic is the prediction of "spontaneous" change over a period of study based on knowledge of the natural history of the condition treated. In my experience dramatic changes may be induced merely by patients' decisions to refer themselves for treatment.'

Indeed, even a consultation can have a pronounced effect. In a controlled trial of psychiatric treatment in eczema (Brown and Bettley 1971), comparing dermatological treatment alone with such treatment plus psychiatric treatment, it was found that several patients in the control group had done very well at six-months follow-up. They attributed it to talking to the psychodynamically orientated psychiatric interviewer, which they experienced as therapy. When the design of the study was modified, so that controls were given questionnaires but not seen by the psychiatrist, as a group they did particularly badly throughout follow-up over 18 months.

The issue of effectiveness of psychotherapy is of increasing importance today when financial stringency in the National Health Service makes it necessary to justify all services in terms of cost-effectiveness. This is entirely proper, and a challenge to both detractors of psychotherapy (Shepherd 1979) and proponents (Aveline 1984; Kolvin et al. 1988). Ideology can blind, or at least lead to tunnel vision. This is particularly dangerous when narrow criteria are used to justify axing the still-too-rare psychotherapy provisions in the NHS, when their wider cost-benefits are not taken into account. In-patient psychotherapy at the Cassel Hospital (see p.151) was threatened because of a short-term financial crisis in the District Health Authority, even though a careful study (Denford et al. 1983; Rosser et al. 1987) showed that psychotherapy there led to substantial long-term savings by relieving psychiatric and social services of people previously chronically dependent on them. In Germany this has been so well established that private in-patient and out-patient psychotherapy, including psychoanalysis, is covered by government medical insurance (Brocher 1988). In Finland psychotherapy is regarded as a form of rehabilitation by the National Social Insurance Institution, which subsidizes analytically orientated and supportive psychotherapy for two to three years to improve people's capacity to work and study. Careful assessment of the results indicates that more than 80 per cent benefited and about one-third were symptom-free; those suffering from neurotic disorders particularly benefited (Seppala and Jamsen 1990).

The complex issues involved in assessing the efficiency of

psychotherapy services have recently been analysed with great thoroughness by Fonagy and Higgitt (1989). They conclude that it is possible to find indicators that reflect the value of a psychotherapy service to the local community, and that we urgently need to agree on the appropriate parameters to evaluate this. Holmes and Lindley (1989) provide a powerful rebuttal of 'the case against psychotherapy' (Ch.2) in their own review of research findings. They make an eloquent plea for the more widespread availability of publicly funded psychotherapy services, comparing the current view that this is a luxury rather than a basic right with attitudes to education a century ago.

Our contention that psychotherapy has more in common with education than with medical treatment is lent indirect support by findings that emerge from examination of a study by Sloane *et al*. (1975) in Philadelphia. They studied patients suffering from a variety of moderately severe neuroses and personality disorders, who, after a lengthy initial assessment (which could itself be therapeutic), were randomly allotted to one of three groups for four months. One group was treated by behaviour therapists, one by analytically-orientated psychotherapists, and the third remained on a waiting list with the promise of eventual treatment (and were kept in telephone contact). Within four months the severity of target symptoms had declined significantly in all three groups, but in both treated groups more than in the waiting-list group; and in both treatment groups outcome was very much related to the quality of the relationship between patient and therapist. However, while only the behaviour therapy group had improved in four months on both work and social adjustment ratings, during the subsequent eight month follow-up, *after treatment had stopped*, the psychotherapy group continued to improve with regard to social adjustment. It seems that, despite the short duration of psychotherapy, they had internalized the learning process.

These findings support those of an earlier study in Baltimore, comparing the outcome in patients who had six months of either individual, group, or supportive therapy, and were followed up for five years:

The results add some confirmation to the supposition that psychotherapy produces two distinguishable but related types of effect – relief of distress and improvement in personal functioning. Symptom relief results primarily from the patient's expectation of help, so that it occurs rapidly, is independent of the particular type of therapy, and can be duplicated in some patients by administration of a placebo. Improvement in personal functioning occurs more gradually and seems to be related to the kind of therapeutic experience, suggesting that it may be the result of a learning process.

(Frank 1961:214)

It would seem that successful psychotherapy initiates a process of learning which develops its own momentum. This starts in the relationship between patient and therapist, the crux of all dynamic psychotherapy, whether at the outer levels of support and counselling, or the deeper levels of exploration and analysis.

What sort of outcome can we look forward to, for an individual patient, at the end of psychotherapy?

We began with a Mrs A. as an example of someone helped by an initial psychotherapeutic approach. Where do we hope to have got after more extensive psychotherapy? Freud defined mental health as the capacity to find satisfaction in work and love. Perhaps we should add a capacity for play or, in other words, define health as the ability to find satisfaction in work, play, and loving relationships. If this sounds rather ideal, it is less so than the definition adopted by the World Health Organization in its Charter that 'health is a state of complete physical, mental and social well-being'! Such magical solutions psychotherapy cannot provide, but at best it can help launch people in the direction of greater freedom and growth. We will give the last words to another patient.

Miss Z. was referred by her family doctor for psychotherapy in a depressive crisis, which followed a second abortion. In the past she had lurched from one relationship and crisis to the next. Part of her was again inclined to 'pull herself together' as in the past, and forget about her difficulties till the next crisis arose. She had spent her life trying to be 'pleasant' to people and fulfil their expectations. Another part of her knew that this time she really needed help to break the cycle of failed relationships.

During psychotherapy it became clear that the abortion, which precipitated her depression, had revived her earlier childhood feelings of loss when her parents' marriage broke up, since when she had learnt to hide all her feelings behind a controlled and courteous front.

Slowly she began getting in touch with the lost child part of herself and was able to develop a more appropriate and satisfying relationship with a man, whom she later married. After a comparatively brief period of psychotherapy, once or twice a week for eighteen months, she felt, in her own words, *'the door had been pushed open a bit, the stiffness of the hinges overcome'* and she both wanted and felt able to go on opening it herself.

Some time after leaving she wrote: 'I would like to let you know that on leaving I felt none of the sadness of parting I had expected but, to my astonishment, quite the reverse: an immense cheerfulness at having found someone to talk with, past, present, and future. And so, for the first time I can remember a feeling of solid confidence in myself to face life itself still confusing but not so frightening any longer. The feeling of being able to be and exist and give of myself without feeling the threat of an infinite void, of falling off a very high roof, but rather of having myself, and contact with the world all around, continues.'

APPENDICES

APPENDIX 1

BRIEF DESCRIPTION OF TRAINING AND ROLES OF SOME PROFESSIONALS IN THE FIELD OF THE PSYCHE

Psychiatrists are medically qualified doctors who have gained postgraduate experience and training in the treatment of emotional and mental disturbances. Like general physicians in the medical field, they have overall repsonsibility for the assessment and management of all types of psychiatric in-patients and out-patients, including those with organic and functional psychoses, neuroses, and personality problems. Their treatment may be more often physically based, especially for the psychoses, using drugs and ECT, but also offers the vital support of hospital admission or day-care essential in many conditions. Supportive psychotherapy (p.92) is provided by the general psychiatrist and other members of his team, such as social worker, nurse, or occupational therapist. Some training in psychotherapy is now recommended for every psychiatrist (Royal College of Psychiatrists 1986), but he may also draw on the services of any of the following.

Psychologists are usually not medically qualified, but have a degree in psychology – the study of mental processes and behaviour, normal and abnormal; after graduation they may specialize in academic, educational, industrial, or clinical psychology. Clinical psychologists in the past were chiefly employed to administer intelligence and personality tests, but are now becoming more autonomous and developing an important therapeutic role. They have played a leading part in furthering Behavioural Psychotherapy and Cognitive Therapy (pp.89 and 178), but many are active in dynamic psycho-therapy, and some go on to train in the special fields of psycho-analysis, group analysis, and family and marital therapy.

Psychoanalysts are more often medically qualified than not, and if so have usually trained as psychiatrists before seeking further training at a recognized institute of psychoanalysis, which includes having a personal psychoanalysis. Those who are not medically qualified come from backgrounds such as psychology and social work, but usually arrange for a doctor to take medical responsibility for the patients they treat. Psychoanalysis can be viewed as one type of psychotherapy, albeit the most radical and intense in its aims.

In the UK, *psychotherapist* as a designation implies no specific professional training as yet. This has disadvantages and advantages. The fact that anyone can call himself a psychotherapist means that untrained people can exploit those in emotional distress. Following concern about Scientology, the Foster Report (1971) recommended that in order to ensure professional and ethical standards, a register of *specialist* psychotherapists should be set up indicating those with a recognized training such as qualified psychoanalysts, group-analysts, and psychotherapists trained by certain established institutes.

To this end a Professions Joint Working Party was formed which led to the publication of the Sieghart (1978) Report, then a series of annual 'Rugby' Psychotherapy conferences, and finally the inauguration of the UK Standing Conference for Psychotherapy (UKSCP) in 1989 (Pedder 1989b). UKSCP is pursuing issues of standards of training, ethics, and registration, and whether or not specialist psychotherapists should largely be drawn from the core professions of medicine, psychology, social work, and nursing. These developments have been given impetus by the establishment of a single market within the European Community in 1992. Reciprocal arrangements will have to be arrived at whereby qualifications to practise psychotherapy are recognized between countries. In some, legislation exists to restrict practice and health insurance cover to registered psychotherapists and their clients.

In its *general* sense, the practice of psychotherapy should not be restricted to full-time psychotherapists. Everyone in the helping professions should have a psychotherapeutic attitude, be familiar with the simpler psychotherapeutic methods, and be aware of the scope and availability of more specialized forms of psychotherapy.

APPENDIX 2

SELECTION CRITERIA FOR DIFFERENT KINDS OF THERAPY

(1) *Family or Marital Evaluation* (Clarkin *et al.* 1979) is almost *always* essential when the presenting patient is a child or adolescent, the presenting problem is sexual difficulty or dissatisfaction, or the problem is clearly a family one, and when psychiatric hospitalization is being considered; and *commonly* indicated when more than one family member is in psychiatric treatment at the same time, or when improvement in one leads to deterioration in another.

(2) *Group Psychotherapy* (Frances *et al.* 1980) is divided into *heterogeneous* and *homogeneous* forms. The former deals with varied problems, the latter with a single problem. Analytic groups are most often heterogeneous and are indicated when (a) patients have important problems in current interpersonal relationships, (b) get locked into regressive transference, are excessively intellectual, cannot tolerate dyadic intimacy, or elicit harmful countertransference responses in an individual therapist, and (c) are open to others and willing to share. Homogeneous groups (more usual in self-help or counselling groups) are indicated when (a) patients share the same problem, (b) see their symptoms as a problem, (c) experience shame and isolation because of them, and (d) do not have a sustaining social network. These criteria are seen to be a combination of indications for group psychotherapy and contra-indications for individual therapy.

(3) *Brief Psychotherapy* (Clarkin and Frances 1982) is considered through a three-step 'decision tree' to guide the selection of (a) crisis intervention, (b) brief vs. long-term therapy, and (c) one particular form of brief psychotherapy, psychodynamic, problem-solving, marital/family, or behavioural. The main criteria for (a) crisis intervention are severe distress, precipitating stress, recent onset, and adequate social and family networks; for (b) brief as opposed to long-term therapy, a clearly defined focus, adequate but limited motivation and goals, ability to

separate from treatment, and/or likelihood of reacting to long-term treatment negatively (e.g. secondary gain, transference psychosis); for (c) the different types of brief therapy – psychodynamic, problem-solving, marital/family, or behavioural – criteria are complex and we shall describe here only those for brief *psychodynamic* therapy. Indications are wide, but 'patient enabling factors' are demanding and there are therefore many contra-indications unlike the other forms of brief therapy.

These criteria are more exacting than those we gave in *Table 6* (p.182), for dynamic psychotherapy in general, and are basically the same as those for brief psychotherapy laid down by Malan (1963, 1979) Sifneos (1972), and Davanloo (1978).

Indications for brief psychodynamic therapy are (a) a problem understandable as related to a *focal intrapsychic conflict* to do with separation, Oedipal issues, narcissistic injury, or post-traumatic stress disorder; (b) the goal of treatment is at least circumscribed *character change*. The stringent *'patient* enabling factors' are (a) at least one significant early relationship; (b) the patient *quickly and flexibly* relates to the assessor and can *freely express feelings*; (c) the two can agree on a *focal conflict*, which becomes clearer as they explore it, the patient responding to interpretations about it; (d) the patient is motivated to *understand and change*, and to make *sacrifices* for it; (e) can experience, tolerate, and discuss *painful feelings*; and (f) has relatively high *ego-strength* and *verbal intelligence*.

(4) *No Treatment* (Frances and Clarkin 1981), declining to offer formal psychotherapy, is indicated for (a) 'negative responders' (3–28 per cent in different studies are made worse by therapy) likely to be borderline and masochistic personalities with low motivation; (b) 'non-responders' (30–35 per cent in different studies) often chronically dependent, treatment addicted, poorly motivated, or with incapacitating symptoms, anti-social or with self-induced illnesses they 'need'; and (c) 'spontaneous improvers' (43 per cent as median of well-controlled studies, but only in terms of symptoms, not character change), e.g. those recovering from recent stress.

The danger and wastefulness of offering intensive psychotherapy to some patients can be underestimated by overenthusiastic beginners in the field – as most of us have been – and by referrers anxious to pass on responsibility. Sometimes the best a consultant psychotherapist can do is to spot the dangers and disadvantages, and support the referrer in helping the patient to face up to the limitations of what can realistically be offered.

REFERENCES

Acharyya, S., Moorhouse, S., Kareem, J., and Littlewood R. (1989) 'Nafsiyat: a psychotherapy centre for ethnic minorities', *Bulletin of Royal College of Psychiatrists* 13: 358–60.

Ackerman, N.W. (1966) *Treating the Troubled Family*, New York: Basic Books.

Adler, M.H. (1970) 'Panel on Psychoanalysis and Psychotherapy', *International Journal of Psychoanalysis* 51: 219–31.

Alexander, F. (1957) *Psychoanalysis and Psychotherapy*, London: George Allen & Unwin.

Ansbacher, H.L. and Ansbacher, R.R. (eds) (1957) *The Individual Psychology of Alfred Adler*, New York: Harper Torchbooks.

Argyle, M. (1972) *The Psychology of Interpersonal Behaviour*, Harmondsworth: Penguin Books.

Ashurst, P. and Hall, Z. (1989) *Understanding Women in Distress*, London: Tavistock/Routledge.

Aveline, M. (1984) 'What price psychiatry without psychotherapy?', *Lancet* 2: 856–9.

Balint, M. (1957) *The Doctor, His Patient and the Illness*, London: Tavistock Publications.

—— (1965) *Primary Love and Psychoanalytic Technique*, London: Tavistock Publications.

—— (1968) *The Basic Fault*, London: Tavistock Publications.

Balint, M. and Balint, E. (1961) *Psychotherapeutic Techniques in Medicine*, London: Tavistock Publications.

Balint, M., Ornstein, P.H., and Balint, E. (1972) *Focal Psychotherapy: An Example of Applied Psychoanalysis*, London: Tavistock Publications.

Balint, M., Hunt, J., Joyce, D., Marinker, M., and Woodcock, J. (1970) *Treatment or Diagnosis: A Study of Repeat Prescriptions in General Practice*, London: Tavistock Publications.

Bandler, R. and Grinder, J. (1981) *Neuro-Linguistic Programming and the Structure of Hypnosis*, Moab, Utah: Real People Press.

Barton, R. (1959) *Institutional Neurosis*, Bristol: John Wright.

Barton, R. and Whitehead, J.A. (1969) 'The gas-light phenomenon', *Lancet* 1: 1258–60.

207

Bateson, G., Jackson, D.D., Haley, J., and Weakland, J.H. (1956) 'Towards a theory of schizophrenia', *Behavioural Science* 1: 251–64.

Beck, A.T. (1976) *Cognitive Therapy and the Emotional Disorders*, New York: International Universities Press.

Beels, C.C. and Ferber, A. (1969) 'Family therapy: a view', *Family Process* 9: 280–318.

Bentovim, A. and Kinston, W. (1978) 'Brief focal family therapy when the child is the referred patient', *Journal of Child Psychology and Psychiatry* 19: 1–12.

Bentovim, A., Gorell Barnes, G., and Cooklin, A. (1987) *Family Therapy*, London: Academic Press.

Bentovim, A., Elton, A., Hildebrand, J., Franter, M.C. and Vizard, E. (eds) (1988) *Child Sexual Abuse within the Family*, London: Wright.

Berger, R.J. (1969) 'The sleep and dream cycle', in A. Kales (ed.) *Sleep Physiology and Pathology*, Philadelphia: Lippincott. Reprinted as Ch.13 in S.G.M. Lee and A.R. Mayes (eds) (1973) *Dreams and Dreaming*, Harmondsworth: Penguin Books.

Bergin, A.E. (1967) 'Some implications of psychotherapy research for therapeutic practice', *International Journal of Psychiatry* 3: 136–50.

—— (1971) 'The evaluation of therapeutic outcomes', in A.E. Bergin and S.L. Garfield (eds) *Handbook of Psychotherapy and Behaviour Change*, New York: John Wiley & Sons.

Berne, E. (1961) *Transactional Analysis in Psychotherapy*, New York: Evergreen.

—— (1966) *Games People Play*, London: André Deutsch.

Bertalanffy, L. von (1968) *General System Theory*, New York: Brasiller.

Bettelheim, B. (1975) *The Uses of Enchantment*, Harmondsworth: Penguin (1978).

Bierer, J. and Evans, R.I. (1969) *Innovations in Social Psychiatry*, London: Avenue Publishing Co.

Bion, W.R. (1961) *Experiences in Groups*, London: Tavistock Publications.

Bloch, S. (1977) 'Supportive psychotherapy', *British Journal of Hospital Medicine* 16: 63–7.

—— (ed.) (1979) *An Introduction to the Psychotherapies*, Oxford: Oxford University Press.

—— (1982) *What is Psychotherapy?*, Oxford: Oxford University Press.

Bloch, S. and Lambert, M.J. (1985) 'What price psychotherapy? A rejoinder', *British Journal of Psychiatry* 146: 95–8.

Bowen, M. (1966) 'The use of family therapy in clinical practice', *Comprehensive Psychiatry* 7: 345–74.

Bowlby, J. (1952) *Maternal Care and Mental Health*, Geneva: World Health Organization.

—— (1960) 'Separation anxiety', *International Journal of Psychoanalysis* 41: 89–113.

—— (1969) *Attachment and Loss. I. Attachment*, London: Hogarth Press.

—— (1973) *Attachment and Loss. II. Separation: Anxiety and Anger*, London: Hogarth Press.

—— (1975) 'Attachment theory, separation anxiety and mourning', in

REFERENCES

D.A. Hambourg and H.K. Brodie (eds) *The American Handbook of Psychiatry*, Vol. VI, New York: Basic Books.
—— (1977) 'The making and breaking of affectional bonds. II. Some principles of psychotherapy', *British Journal of Psychiatry* 130: 421–31.
—— (1980) *Attachment and Loss III. Loss: Sadness and Depression*, London: Hogarth Press and Penguin.
Brandon, S. (1970) 'Crisis theory and possibilities of therapeutic intervention', *British Journal of Psychiatry* 117: 627–33.
Breuer, J. and Freud, S. (1895) *Studies on Hysteria*. The Standard Edition of the Complete Psychological Works of Sigmund Freud, Vol. 2, London: Hogarth Press and the Institute of Psychoanalysis.
Brocher, T. (1988) 'Psychoanalytic psychotherapy services in West Germany', unpublished paper to conference of Association for Psychoanalytic Psychotherapy in the NHS, London, November.
Brook, A. (1967) 'An experiment in general practitioner/psychiatrist co-operation', *Journal of College of General Practitioners* 13: 172–31.
Brown, D.G. (1967) 'Emotional disturbance in eczema: a study of symptom-reporting behaviour', *Journal of Psychosomatic Research* 11: 27–40.
—— (1977) 'Drowsiness in the countertransference', *International Review of Psycho-Analysis* 4: 481–92.
—— (1979) 'Some reflections on Bion's basic assumptions from a group-analytic viewpoint', *Group Analysis* 12: 204–10.
—— (1985) 'Bion and Foulkes: basic assumptions and beyond', in M. Pines (ed.) *Bion and Group Psychotherapy*, London: Routledge & Kegan Paul, Ch.10.
—— (1987) 'Change in the group-analytic setting', *Psychoanalytic Psychotherapy* 3: 53–60.
—— (1991) 'Assessment and selection', in J. Roberts and M. Pines (eds) *The Practice of Group Analysis*, London: Routledge.
Brown, D.G. and Bettley, F.R. (1971) 'Psychiatric treatment in the management of eczema: a controlled trial', *British Medical Journal* 272: 729–34.
Brown, G.W. and Harris, T. (1978) *Social Origins of Depression*, London: Tavistock Publications.
Brown, G.W., Birley, J.L.T., and Wing, J.K. (1972) 'Influence of family life on the course of schizophrenic disorders: a replication', *British Journal of Psychiatry* 121: 241–58.
Brown, J.A.C. (1961) *Freud and the Post-Freudians*, Harmondsworth: Penguin Books.
Bruch, H. (1974) *Learning Psychotherapy*, Cambridge, Mass.: Harvard University Press.
Bruggen, P. and Davies, G. (1977) 'Family therapy in adolescent psychiatry', *British Journal of Psychiatry* 131: 433–47.
Buber, M. (1971) *I and Thou* (trans. W. Kaufmann), Edinburgh: Clark.
Butler, S. (1872) *Erewhon*, Florin Books edn, London: Jonathan Cape.
Byng-Hall, J. (1973) 'Family myths used as defence in conjoint family therapy', *British Journal of Medical Psychology* 46: 239–49.
Candy, J., Balfour, F.H.G., Cawley, R.H., Hildebrand, H.P., Malan,

D.H., Marks, I.M., and Wilson, J. (1972) 'A feasibility study for a controlled trial of formal psychotherapy', *Psychological Medicine* 2: 345–62.

Casement, P. (1985) *On Learning from the Patient*, London: Tavistock Publications.

Cawley, R.H. (1977) 'The teaching of psychotherapy', *Association of University Teachers of Psychiatry Newsletter* January: 19–36.

Clark, D.H. (1964) *Administrative Therapy*, London: Tavistock Publications.

—— (1977) 'The therapeutic community', *British Journal of Psychiatry* 131: 553–64.

Clarkin, J.F. and Frances, A. (1982) 'Selection criteria for the brief psychotherapies', *American Journal of Psychotherapy* 36: 166–80.

Clarkin, J.F., Frances, A.J., and Moodie, J.L. (1979) 'Selection criteria for family therapy', *Family Process* 18: 391–403.

Cooley, C.H. (1902) *Human Nature and the Social Order*, New York: Scribner.

Crisp, A.H. (1967) 'The possible significance of some behavioural correlates of weight and carbohydrate intake', *Journal of Psychosomatic Research* 11: 117–31.

Crowe, M.J. (1973) 'Conjoint marital therapy: advice or interpretation?', *Journal of Psychosomatic Research* 17: 309–15.

Darwin, C. (1871) *The Descent of Man*.

Darwin, C. (1872) *The Expression of the Emotions in Man and Animals*. Chicago: University of Chicago Press (1965).

Davanloo, H. (ed.) (1978) *Basic Principles and Techniques in Short-term Dynamic Psychotherapy*, New York: SP Medical & Scientific Books.

Davies, M.H. (1976) 'The origins and practice of psychodrama', *British Journal of Psychiatry* 129: 201–6.

Daws, D. and Boston, M. (eds) (1981) *The Child Psychotherapist: Problems of Young People*, London: Karnac Books.

Denford, J., Schachter, J., Temple, N., Kind, P., and Rosser, R. (1983) 'Selection and outcome in in-patient psychotherapy', *British Journal of Medical Psychology* 56: 225–43.

Department of Health and Social Security (1975) *Better Services for the Mentally Ill*, London: HMSO.

Dick, B.M. (1975) 'A ten year study of out-patient analytic group therapy', *British Journal of Psychiatry* 127: 365–75.

Dicks, H.V. (1967) *Marital Tensions: Clinical Studies Towards a Psychological Theory of Interaction*, London: Routledge & Kegan Paul.

Dixon, N.F. (1971) *Subliminal Perception: The Nature of a Controversy*, London: McGraw-Hill.

Dryden, W. and Rowan, J. (eds) (1988) *Innovative Therapy in Britain*, Milton Keynes: Open University Press.

Durkheim, E. (1897) *Suicide: A Study in Sociology* (trans. J.A. Spaulding and G. Simpson), London: Routledge & Kegan Paul (1952).

Edelson, M. (1970) *Sociotherapy and Psychotherapy*, Chicago: University of Chicago Press.

Ellenberger, H.F. (1970) *The Discovery of the Unconscious*, London: Allen Lane.

Engel, G.L. (1967) 'A psychological setting of somatic disease: the giving up, given-up complex', *Proceedings of the Royal Society of Medicine* 60: 553–5.

Epstein, L. and Feiner, A.H. (eds) (1979) *Countertransference*, New York: Jason Aronson.

Erickson, M.H. and Rossi, E.L. (1979) *Hypnotherapy*, New York: Irvington Publishers.

Erikson, E.H. (1965) *Childhood and Society*, Harmondsworth: Penguin Books.

Ernst, S. and Maguire, M. (eds) (1987) *Living with the Sphynx: Papers from the Women's Therapy Centre*, London: The Women's Press.

Ettin, M.F. (1988) ' "By the crowd they have been broken, by the crowd they shall be healed": the advent of group psychotherapy', *International Journal of Group Psychotherapy* 38: 139–67.

Eysenck, H.J. (1952) 'The effects of psychotherapy, an evaluation', *Journal of Consulting Psychology* 16: 319–24.

—— (1965) 'The effects of psychotherapy', *International Journal of Psychiatry* 1: 99–144.

Ezriel, H. (1950) 'A psycho-analytic approach to group treatment', *British Journal of Medical Psychology* 23: 59–74.

—— (1952) 'Notes on psycho-analytic group therapy: II. Interpretations and research', *Psychiatry* 15: 119–26.

Fairbairn, W.R.D. (1952) *Psychoanalytic Studies of the Personality*, London: Tavistock Publications.

Feldman, M.M. (1975) 'Body image and object relations: exploration of a method utilizing repertory grid techniques', *British Journal of Medical Psychology* 48: 317–32.

Ferenczi, S. (1926) 'The further development of an active therapy in psychoanalysis', in *Further Contributions to the Theory of Psychoanalysis*, London: Hogarth Press.

Ferreira, A. (1963) 'Family myth and homeostasis', *Archives of General Psychiatry* 9: 457–63.

Findlay, A. (1948) *A Hundred Years of Chemistry* (2nd edn), London: Duckworth.

Fonagy, P. and Higgitt, A. (1989) 'Evaluating the performance of departments of psychotherapy', *Psychoanalytic Psychotherapy* 4: 121–53.

Fordham, M. (1978) *Jungian Psychotherapy*, London: Wiley.

Foster, Sir John (1971) *Practice and Effects of Scientology*, London: HMSO.

Foudraine, J. (1974) *Not Made of Wood*, London: Quartet Books.

Foulkes, S.H. (1964) *Therapeutic Group Analysis*, London: Allen & Unwin. (Marlsfield Reprints 1984.)

—— (1975) *Group-Analytic Psychotherapy*, London: Gordon & Breach. (Marlsfield Reprints 1986.)

Foulkes, S.H. and Anthony, E.J. (1957) *Group Psychotherapy: The*

Psychoanalytic Approach, Harmondsworth: Penguin Books. (Marls-field Reprints 1984.)

Frances, A. and Clarkin, J.F. (1981) 'No treatment as the prescription of choice', *Archives of General Psychiatry* 38: 542–5.

Frances, A., Clarkin, J.F., and Marachi, J. (1980) 'Selection criteria for out-patient group psychotherapy', *Hospital and Community Psychiatry* 31: 245–50.

Frank, J.D. (1961) *Persuasion and Healing*, Baltimore: Johns Hopkins University Press.

—— (1964) 'Training and therapy', in L.P. Bradford, J.R. Gibb, and K.D. Benne (eds) *T-Group Theory and Laboratory Method: Innovation in Education*, New York: Wiley.

Fransella, F. and Thomas, L. (eds) (1988) *Experimenting with Personal Construct Psychology*, London: Routledge & Kegan Paul.

Fraser, C. (1976) 'An analysis of face-to-face communication', in A.E. Bennett (ed.) *Communication between Doctors and Patients*, London: Nuffield Provincial Hospitals Trust and Oxford University Press.

Freud, A. (1936) *The Ego and the Mechanisms of Defence*, London: Hogarth Press.

—— (1958) 'Adolescence', *Psychoanalytic Study of the Child* 13: 255–78.

—— (1966) *Normality and Pathology in Childhood*, London: Hogarth Press. Reissued by Karnac Books, 1989.

—— (1976) 'Psychopathology seen against the background of normal development' (The forty-ninth Maudsley Lecture), *British Journal of Psychiatry* 129: 401–6.

Freud, S. (1894) *The Neuro-Psychoses of Defence* (I). Standard Edition of the Complete Psychological Works of Sigmund Freud, Vol. 3, London: Hogarth Press and the Institute of Psychoanalysis.

—— (1900) *The Interpretation of Dreams*, Standard Edition, Vols 4 and 5.

—— (1901) *The Psychopathology of Everyday Life*, Standard Edition, Vol. 6.

—— (1905) *Three Essays on the Theory of Sexuality*, Standard Edition, Vol. 7.

—— (1911–15) *Papers on Technique*, Standard Edition, Vol. 12.

—— (1912) 'Recommendations to physicians practising psychoanalysis', in Standard Edition, Vol. 12.

—— (1913) *Totem and Taboo*, Standard Edition, Vol. 13.

—— (1914) 'Remembering, repeating and working through', in Standard Edition, Vol. 12.

—— (1917) 'Mourning and melancholia', in Standard Edition, Vol. 14.

—— (1919) 'Lines of advance in psycho-analytic therapy', in Standard Edition, Vol. 17.

—— (1921) *Group Psychology and the Analysis of the Ego*, Standard Edition, Vol. 18.

—— (1923) *The Ego and the Id*, Standard Edition, Vol. 19.

—— (1925) *An Autobiographical Study*, Standard Edition, Vol. 20.

—— (1926) *Inhibitions, Symptoms and Anxiety*, Standard Edition, Vol. 20.

REFERENCES

—— (1930) *Civilization and its Discontents*, Standard Edition, Vol. 21.

—— (1933) *New Introductory Lectures*, Standard Edition, Vol. 22.

Fromm-Reichmann, F. (1948) 'Notes on the development of treatment of schizophrenics by psychoanalytic psychotherapy', *Psychiatry* 11: 263–73.

Frosh, P. (1987) *The Politics of Psychoanalysis: An Introduction to Freudian and Post-Freudian Theory*, London: Macmillan Educational.

Garland, C. (1982) 'Group analysis: taking the non-problem seriously', *Group Analysis* 15: 4–14.

Garland, C. (1991) 'External disasters and the internal world: an approach to understanding survivors', in J. Holmes (ed.) *Handbook of Psychotherapy for Psychiatrists*, London: Churchill Livingstone.

Gay, P. (1988) *Freud: A life for our time*, London: Dent.

Gelder, M.G. (1983) 'Is cognitive therapy effective?', *Journal of the Royal Society of Medicine* 76: 938–42.

Gill, C. (1973) 'Types of interview in general practice: "The Flash" ', in E. Balint and J.S. Norell (eds) *Six Minutes for the Patient*, London: Tavistock Publications.

Gill, M.M. (1977) 'Psychic energy reconsidered: discussion', *Journal of the American Psychoanalytic Association* 25: 581–97.

Gittings, R. (1975) *Young Thomas Hardy*, London: Heinemann.

Glick, I.D. and Kessler, D.R. (1974) *Marital and Family Therapy*, New York: Grune & Stratton.

Goffman, E. (1961) *Asylums: Essays on the Social Situation of Mental Patients and Other Inmates*, Harmondsworth: Penguin Books.

Gonda, T.A. (1962) 'The relation between complaints of persistent pain and family size', *Journal of Neurology Neurosurgery and Psychiatry* 25: 277–81.

Greenberg, J.R. and Mitchell, S.A. (1983) *Object Relations in Psychoanalytic Theory*, Cambridge, Mass.: Harvard University Press.

Greenson, R.R. (1965) 'The working alliance and the transference neurosis', *Psychoanalytic Quarterly* 34: 155–81.

—— (1967) *The Technique and Practice of Psychoanalysis*, London: Hogarth Press.

Griffiths, R. (1988) *Community Care: Agenda for Action*, London: HMSO.

Grosskurth, P. (1985) *Melanie Klein: Her World and Her Work*, London: Hodder & Stoughton.

Guntrip, H. (1961) *Personality Structure and Human Interaction*, London: Hogarth Press.

—— (1971) *Psychoanalytic Theory, Therapy and the Self*, London: Hogarth Press.

Gwynne Jones, H. (1985) 'Psychotherapy research', *Journal of the Royal Society of Medicine* 78: 3–6.

Hafner, R.J. (1977) 'The husbands of agoraphobic women and their influence on treatment outcome', *British Journal of Psychiatry* 131: 289–94.

Haley, J. (1968) *Strategies of Psychotherapy*, New York & London: Grune & Stratton.

Haley, J. and Hoffman, L. (1967) *Techniques of Family Therapy*, New York: Basic Books.

Hamilton, J.W. (1976) 'Early trauma, dreaming and creativity: the works of Eugene O'Neill', *International Review of Psychoanalysis* 3: 341–64.

Hampson, J.L. and Hampson, J.G. (1961) 'The ontogenesis of sexual behaviour in man', in W.C. Young (ed.) *Sex and Internal Secretions*, London: Bailliere, Tindall.

Harlow, H. (1958) 'The nature of love', *American Journal of Psychology* 13: 673–85.

Harlow, H.F. and Harlow, M. (1962) 'Social deprivation in monkeys', *Scientific American* 207: 136–46.

Hartmann, H. (1939) *Ego Psychology and the Problem of Adaptation*, London: Imago.

Hawthorne, N. (1850) 'The Scarlet Letter', in *The Scarlet Letter and Selected Tales*, Harmondsworth: Penguin Books, 1970.

Heap, M. (ed.) (1988) *Hypnosis: Current Clinical, Experimental and Forensic Practices*, London: Croom Helm.

Heidegger, M. (1967) *Being and Time*, Oxford: Blackwell.

Heimann, P. (1950) 'On counter-transference', *International Journal of Psychoanalysis* 31: 81–4.

Hersen, M. and Bellack A.S. (eds) (1985) *Handbook of Clinical Behaviour Therapy with Adults*, New York: Plenum.

Hill, D. (1956) 'Psychiatry', in J. S. Richardson (ed.) *The Practice of Medicine*, London: Churchill.

—— (1977) Correspondence, *British Journal of Psychiatry* 131: 217–19.

Hinshelwood, R.D. (1987) *What Happens in Groups: Psychoanalysis, the Individual and the Community*, London: Free Association Books.

Hirsch, S.R. and Leff, J.P. (1975) *Abnormalities in Parents of Schizophrenics* (Maudsley Monograph no. 22), London: Oxford University Press.

Hobson, R.F. (1974) 'Loneliness', *Journal of Analytical Psychology* 19: 71–89.

Hoenig, J. (1985) 'The origin of gender identity', in B. Steiner (ed.) *Gender Dysphoria: Development, Research, Management*, New York: Plenum Press, pp.11–32.

Hoffman, L. (1981) *Foundations of Family Therapy*, New York: Basic Books.

Holmes, J. and Lindley, R. (1989) *The Values of Psychotherapy*, Oxford: Oxford University Press.

Home, J.H. (1966) 'The concept of mind', *International Journal of Psychoanalysis* 47: 42–9.

Hopkins, P. (ed.) (1972) *Patient-centred Medicine*, London: Balint Society and Regional Doctor Publications.

Hopper, E. and Weyman, A. (1975) 'A sociological view of groups', in L. Kreeger (ed.) *The Large Group*, London: Constable.

Howells, J.G. and Brown, W. (1986) *Family Diagnosis*, Madison, Wis.: International Universities Press.

Hug-Hellmuth, H. von (1921) 'On the technique of child analysis', *International Journal of Psycho-Analysis* 2: 287–305.

Jackson, J. and Grotjahn, M. (1958) 'The treatment of oral defences by combined individual and group psychotherapy', *International Journal of Group Psychotherapy* 8: 373–81.

Jackson, M. and Tarnopolsky, A. (1990) 'Borderline personality', in R.S. Bluglass and P.M.A. Bowden (eds) *Forensic Psychiatry*, London: Churchill Livingstone, Ch.27.

Jacobson, E. (1964) *The Self and the Object World*, New York: International University Press.

James, D.C. (1976) Unpublished paper, read to academic meeting at St Mary's Hospital, Department of Psychiatry.

James, W. (1890) *The Principles of Psychology*, London: Macmillan.

Janov, A. (1970) *The Primal Scream*, New York: Dell Publishing Co.

Jaques, E. (1955) 'Social systems as a defence against persecutory and depressive anxiety', in M. Klein (ed.) *New Directions in Psychoanalysis*, London: Tavistock Publications.

—— (1965) 'Death and the mid-life crisis', *International Journal of Psychoanalysis* 46: 502–14.

Jennings, S. (ed.) (1983) *Creative Therapy*, Banbury: Kemble Press.

—— (1987) *Dramatherapy*, London: Routledge.

Joffe, W.G. and Sandler, J. (1965) 'Notes on pain, depression and individuation', *The Psychoanalytic Study of the Child* 20: 394–424.

Jones, E. (1953) *Sigmund Freud. Life and Work*, Vol. I, London: Hogarth Press.

—— (1955) *Sigmund Freud. Life and Work*, Vol. II, London: Hogarth Press.

—— (1957) *Sigmund Freud. Life and Work*, Vol. III, London: Hogarth Press.

Jones, M. (1952) *Social Psychiatry: A Study of Therapeutic Communities*, London: Tavistock Publications.

—— (1968) *Social Psychiatry in Practice: The Idea of the Therapeutic Community*, Harmondsworth: Penguin Books.

Jung, C.G. (1933) *Modern Man in Search of a Soul*, London: Routledge & Kegan Paul.

—— (1946) *Psychological Types*, London: Routledge & Kegan Paul.

Jung, C.G. (ed.) (1964) *Man and His Symbols*, London: Aldus Books.

Kafka, F. (1920) *Diary: Kafka Shorter Works, Vol. 1* (transl. and ed. Malcolm Pasley), London: Secker & Warburg, 1973.

Kalucy, R.S., Brown, D.G., Hartman, M., and Crisp, A.H. (1976) 'Sleep research and psychosomatic hypotheses', *Postgraduate Medical Journal* 52: 53–6.

Kaplan, S. (1967) 'Therapy groups and training groups: similarities and differences', *International Journal of Group Psychotherapy* 17: 473–504.

Keats, J. (1817) 'Letters, 32, To G. and T. Keats. 21 Dec. 1817', *Letters of John Keats* (selected by F. Page), London: Oxford University Press, 1954.

Kempe, C.H., White Franklin, A., and Cooper, C. (1980) *The Abused Child in the Family and in the Community*, Oxford: Penguin.

Kernberg, O.F. (1972) 'Summary and conclusions. Psychotherapy and psychoanalysis: Final Report of the Menninger Foundation Psychotherapy Research Project', *Bulletin of the Menninger Clinic* 36: 181–99.

—— (1975) *Borderline Conditions and Pathological Narcissism*, New York: Jason Aronson.

Kestenberg, J.S. and Brenner, I. (1986) 'Children who survived the Holocaust', *International Journal of Psychoanalysis* 67: 309–16.

Klauber, J. (1981) *Difficulties in the Analytic Encounter*, New York: Jason Aronson.

Klein, M. (1932) *The Psycho-Analysis of Children*, London: Hogarth Press.

Knight, L. (1986) *Talking to a Stranger: A Customer's Guide to Therapy*, London: Fontana/Collins.

Koestler, A. (1964) *The Act of Creation*, London: Hutchinson.

Kohut, H. (1977) *The Restoration of the Self*, New York: International Universities Press.

Kolvin, I., Macmillan, A., Nicol, A.R., and Wrate, R.M. (1988) 'Psychotherapy is effective', *Journal of the Royal Society of Medicine* 81: 261–6.

Kovel, J. (1976) *A Complete Guide to Therapy*, New York: Pantheon.

Kreeger, L. (ed.) (1975) *The Large Group: Dynamics and Therapy*, London: Constable.

Kroger, W.S. (1963) *Clinical and Experimental Hypnosis in Medicine, Dentistry, and Psychology*, Philadelphia: Lippincott.

Lader, M. (1975) *The Psychophysiology of Mental Illness*, London: Routledge & Kegan Paul.

Laing, R.D. (1960) *The Divided Self*, London: Tavistock Publications.

Laing, R.D. and Esterson, A. (1964) *Sanity, Madness and the Family*, London: Tavistock Publications.

Lake, F. (1978) 'Treating psychosomatic disorders related to birth trauma', *Journal of Psychosomatic Research* 22: 228–38.

Langs, R.J. (1979a) 'The interactional dimension of countertransference', in L. Epstein and A.H. Feiner (eds) *Countertransference*, New York: Jason Aronson, Ch.4.

—— (1979b) *The Therapeutic Environment*, New York: Jason Aronson.

Laufer, M. (1975) *Adolescent Disturbance and Breakdown*, Harmondsworth: Penguin Books.

Laufer, M. and Laufer, M.E. (1988) *Developmental Breakdown and Psychoanalytic Treatment in Adolescence*, Newhaven & London: Yale University Press.

Leboyer, F. (1977) *Birth without Violence*, London: Fontana.

Leff, J.P. and Vaughn, C. (1985) *Expressed Emotion in Families: Its Significance for Mental Illness*, New York: Guilford Press.

Leigh, A.D. (1961) *The Historical Development of British Psychiatry*, Vol. 1. *The Eighteenth and Nineteenth Century*, Oxford: Pergamon.

Levitsky, A. and Perls, F. (1972) 'The rules and games of Gestalt therapy', in J. Huber and L. Millman (eds) *Goals and Behaviour in Psychotherapy and Counseling*, Ohio: Charles Merrill.

Lewin, K., Lippitt, R., and White, R.K. (1939) 'Patterns of aggressive behaviour in experimentally created social climates', *Journal of Social Psychology* 10: 271–99.

Lewis, I.M. (1979) *How's Your Family?*, New York: Brunner/Mazel.

Lidz, R. and Lidz, T. (1949) 'The family environment of schizophrenic patients', *American Journal of Psychiatry* 106: 322–45.

Lieberman, M.A., Yalom, I.D., and Miles, M.B. (1973) *Encounter Groups: First Facts*, New York: Basic Books.

Little, M. (1951) 'Countertransference and the patient's response to it', *International Journal of Psychoanalysis* 32: 32–40.

—— (1957) ' "R" – the analyst's response to his patient's needs', *International Journal of Psychotherapy* 38: 240–58.

Littlewood, R. and Lipsedge, M. (1989) *Aliens and Alienists: Ethnic Minorities and Psychiatry*, 2nd edn, London: Unwin/Heinemann.

Lorenz, K. (1966) *On Aggression*, London: Methuen.

Lowen, A. (1967) *The Betrayal of the Body*, London: Collier Macmillan.

Lowry, S. (1990) 'Health and homelessness', *British Medical Journal* 300: 32–4.

Luborsky, L., Singer, B., and Luborsky, L. (1975) 'Comparative studies of psychotherapies: is it true that everyone has won and all must have prizes?', *Archives of General Psychiatry* 32: 995–1008.

Luborsky, L., Crits-Christoph, P., Mintz, J., and Auerbach, A. (1988) *Who Will Benefit from Psychotherapy? – Predicting Therapeutic Outcomes*, New York: Basic Books.

Luft, J. (1966) *Group Processes: An Introduction to Group Dynamics*, Palo-Alto: National Press.

McDougall, J. (1974) 'The psychosoma and the psychoanalytic process', *International Review of Psycho-Analysis* 1: 437–59.

Maeterlinck, M. (1901) *The Life of the Bee* (trans. A. Sutro), London: George Allen & Unwin.

Mahler, M.S., Pine, F., and Bergman, A. (1975) *The Psychological Birth of the Human Infant*, London: Hutchinson.

Main, T.F. (1946) 'The hospital as a therapeutic institution', *Bulletin of the Menninger Clinic* 10: 66–70.

—— (1957) 'The ailment', *British Journal of Medical Psychology* 30: 129–45. Reprinted in T.F. Main *The Ailment and Other Psychoanalytic Essays*, London: Free Association Books, 1989.

—— (1966) 'Mutual projection in a marriage', *Comprehensive Psychiatry* 7: 432–49.

—— (1968) 'Psychoanalysis as a cross-bearing', *British Journal of Psychiatry* 114: 501–7.

—— (1977) 'The concept of the therapeutic community: variations and vicissitudes', *Group Analysis* 10(2) (supplement): 1–16.

—— (1989) *The Ailment and Other Psychoanalytic Essays*, London: Free Association Books.

Malan, D.H. (1963) *A Study of Brief Psychotherapy*, London: Tavistock Publications.

—— (1973) 'The problem of relevant variables in psychotherapy research', *International Journal of Psychiatry* 11: 336–46.

—— (1979) *Individual Psychotherapy and the Science of Psychodynamics*, London: Butterworth.

Malan, D.H., Balfour, F.H.G., Hood, V.G., and Shooter, A.M.N. (1976) 'Group psychotherapy: a long-term follow-up study', *Archives of General Psychiatry* 33: 1303–14.

Marks, I.M. (1981) *Cure and Care of Neuroses: Theory and Practice of Behavioural Psychotherapy*, New York: Wiley.

Marshall, M. (1989) 'Collected and neglected: are Oxford hostels for the homeless filling up with disabled psychiatric patients?', *British Medical Journal* 2099: 706–9.

Marteau, L. (1976) 'Encounter and the new therapies', *British Journal of Hospital Medicine* 15: 257–64.

Marx, K. (1844) 'Economic and philosophical manuscripts', in K. Thompson and J. Tunstall (eds) *Sociological Perspectives*, Harmondsworth: Penguin Educational Books, 1971.

Masters, W.H. and Johnson, V.E. (1970) *Human Sexual Inadequacy*, London: Churchill.

May, R., Angel, E., and Ellenberger, H. (1958) *Existence: A New Dimension in Psychiatry and Psychology*, New York: Basic Books.

Mayer-Gross, W., Slater, E., and Roth, M. (1977) *Clinical Psychiatry*, 3rd edn, London: Bailliere Tindall.

Meares, R.A. and Hobson, R.F. (1977) 'The persecutory therapist', *British Journal of Medical Psychology* 50: 349–59.

Meltzoff, J. and Kornreich, M. (1970) *Research in Psychotherapy*, New York: Atherton.

Menzies, I.E.P. (1961) *The Functioning of Social Systems as a Defence against Anxiety: A Report on a Study of the Nursing Service of a General Hospital*, Tavistock Pamphlet no. 3, London: Tavistock Publications.

Menzies Lyth, I. (1989) 'The aftermath of disaster: survival and loss', in *The Dynamics of the Social*, London: Free Association Books.

Merskey, H. and Spear, F.G. (1967) 'The concept of pain', *Journal of Psychosomatic Research* 11: 59–67.

Michaels, R.M. and Sevitt, M.A. (1978) 'The patient and the first psychiatric interview', *British Journal of Psychiatry* 132: 288–92.

Milner, M. (1971) *On Not Being Able to Paint*, 2nd edn, London: Heinemann.

Minuchin, S. (1974) *Families and Family Therapy*, London: Tavistock Publications.

Mittelman, B. (1948) 'The concurrent analysis of married couples', *Psychoanalytic Quarterly* 17: 182–97.

Money, J., Hampson, J.G., and Hampson, J.L. (1957) 'Imprinting and the establishment of gender role', *Archives of Neurology and Psychiatry* 77: 333–6.

Moreno, J.L. (1948) *Psychodrama*, Beacon, New York: Beacon House.

Mullan, H. and Rosenbaum, M. (1978) *Group Psychotherapy: Theory and Practice*, New York: Free Press of Glencoe.

Nemiah, J. and Sifneos, P. (1970) 'Affect and fantasy in patients with psychosomatic disorders', in O.W. Hill (ed.) *Modern Trends in Psychosomatic Medicine – 2*, London: Butterworth.

Newsome, A., Thorne, B.J., and Wyld, K.L. (1973) *Student Counselling in Practice*, London: University of London Press.

O'Connor, J. and Seymour, J. (1990) *Introducing Neuro-Linguistic Programming*, Bodmin, Cornwall: Crucible.

Ogden, T.H. (1982) *Projective Identification and Psychotherapeutic Technique*, New York: Jason Aronson.

Parkes, C.M. (1972) *Bereavement: Studies of Grief in Adult Life*, London: Tavistock Publications.

Parsons, T. (1964) *Social Structure and Personality*, London: Collier Macmillan.

Pedder, J.R. (1977) 'The role of space and location in psychotherapy, play and theatre', *International Review of Psychoanalysis* 4: 215–23

—— (1982) 'Failure to mourn, and melancholia', *British Journal of Psychiatry* 141: 329–37.

—— (1987) 'Some biographical contributions to psychoanalytic theories', *Free Associations* 10: 102–16.

—— (1989a) 'The proper image of mankind', *British Journal of Psychotherapy* 6: 70–80.

—— (1989b) 'Courses in psychotherapy: evolution and current trends', *British Journal of Psychotherapy* 6: 203–21.

Perls, F., Hefferline, R.F., and Goodman, P. (1951) *Gestalt Therapy: Excitement and Growth in the Human Personality*, Harmondsworth: Penguin Books (1973).

Piaget, J. (1953) *The Origins of Intelligence in the Child*, London: Routledge & Kegan Paul.

Pincus, L. (ed) (1960) *Marriage: Studies in Emotional Conflict and Growth*, London: Methuen.

Pines, D. (1986) 'Working with women survivors of the Holocaust', *International Journal of Psychoanalysis* 67: 295–307.

Pines, M. (1975) Overview, in L. Kreeger (ed.) *The Large Group*, London: Constable.

—— (ed.) (1983) *The Evolution of Group Analysis*, London: Routledge & Kegan Paul.

Pirandello, L. (1954) *Six Characters in Search of an Author* (transl. Fredrick May), London: Heinemann.

Pontalis, J.B. (1974) 'Freud in Paris'. *International Journal of Psychoanalysis* 55: 455–8

Pratt, J.H. (1907) 'The class method of treating consumption in the homes of the poor'. *Journal of the American Medical Association* 49: 755–9.

—— (ed.) (1983) *The Evolution of Group Analysis*, London: Routledge & Kegan Paul.

Prioleau, L., Murdoch, M., and Brody, B. (1983) 'An analysis of psychotherapy versus placebo studies', *Behavioural and Brain Sciences* 6: 275–85.

Racker, H. (1968) *Transference and Countertransference*, New York: International Universities Press.

Rangell, L. (1954) 'Similarities and differences between psychoanalysis and dynamic psychotherapy', *Journal of the American Psychoanalytic Association* 2: 734–44.

Rank, O. (1929) *The Trauma of Birth*, London: Routledge & Kegan Paul.

Rapoport, R.N. (1960) *Community as Doctor: New Perspectives on a Therapeutic Community*, London: Tavistock Publications.

Rayner, E.H. and Hahn, H. (1964) 'Assessment for psychotherapy', *British Journal of Medical Psychology* 37: 331–42.

Reich, W. (1933) *Character Analysis*, London: Vision Press (1950).

Rice, A.K. (1965) *Learning for Leadership*, London: Tavistock Publications.

Rickman, J. (1951) 'Number and the human sciences', in W.C.M. Scott (ed.) *Selected Contributions to Psycho-analysis*, London: Hogarth Press (1957).

Riester, A.E. and Kraft, I.A. (eds) (1986) *Child Group Psychotherapy*, Madison, Wis.: International Universities Press.

Rogers, C.R. (1961) *On Becoming a Person*, London: Constable.

—— (1970) *Encounter Groups*, Harmondsworth: Penguin Books.

Rogers, C.R. and Dymond, R.F. (1954) *Psychotherapy and Personality Change*, Chicago: University of Chicago Press.

Roheim, G. (1950) *Psychoanalysis and Anthropology*, New York: International University Press.

Rose, M. (1990) *Healing Hurt Minds: The Peper Harrow Experience*, London: Tavistock/Routledge.

Rosenbaum, M. (1978) 'Group psychotherapy: heritage, history and the current scene', in H. Mullan and M. Rosenbaum *Group Psychotherapy: Theory and Practice*, New York: Free Press of Glencoe.

Rosenblatt, A.D. and Thickstun, J.T. (1977) 'Energy, information and motivation: a revision of psychoanalytic theory', *Journal of the American Psychoanalytic Association* 25: 537–58.

Rosser, R., Birch, S., Bond, H., Denford, J., and Schachter, J. (1987) 'Five year follow-up of patients treated with in-patient psychotherapy at the Cassel Hospital for Nervous Diseases', *Journal of the Royal Society of Medicine* 80: 549–55.

Rowley, J. (1951) 'Rumpelstiltskin in the analytic situation', *International Journal of Psychoanalysis* 32: 190–5.

Royal College of Psychiatrists (1986) 'Guide lines for the training of general psychiatrists in psychotherapy', *Bulletin, Royal College of Psychiatrists* 10: 286–9.

Rycroft, C. (1966) 'Causes and meaning', in *Psychoanalysis Observed*, Harmondsworth: Penguin Books (1968).

—— (1971) *Reich*, London: Fontana.

—— (1972) *A Critical Dictionary of Psychoanalysis*, Harmondsworth: Penguin Books.

—— (1979) *The Innocence of Dreams*, Oxford: Oxford University Press.

Ryle, A. (1990) *Cognitive-Analytical Therapy*, Chichester: Wiley.

Samuels, A. (1985) *Jung and the Post-Jungians*, London: Routledge & Kegan Paul.

Sanders, K. (1986) *A Matter of Interest: Clincial Notes of a Psychoanalyst in General Practice*, Strath Tay: Cluny Press.

Sandler, J. (1974) 'Psychological conflict and the structural model', *International Journal of Psychoanalysis* 55: 53–62.

—— (1976) 'Countertransference and role-responsiveness', *International Review of Psycho-analysis* 3: 43–7.

Sandler, J. and Joffe, W.G. (1969) 'Towards a basic psychoanalytic model', *International Journal of Psychoanalysis* 50: 79–90.

Sandler, J., Dare, C., and Holder, A. (1972) 'Frames of reference in psychoanalytic psychology. II. The historical context and phases in the development of psychoanalysis', *British Journal of Medical Psychology* 45: 133–42.

—— (1973) *The Patient and the Analyst: The Basis of the Psychoanalytic Process*, London: George Allen & Unwin.

Sandler, J., Kennedy, H., and Tyson, R.L. (1990) *The Technique of Child Psychoanalysis: Discussions with Anna Freud*, London: Karnac Books.

Scharff, D.E. (1982) *The Sexual Relationship*, London: Routledge & Kegan Paul.

Scheidlinger, S. (1968) 'The concept of regression in group psychotherapy', *International Journal of Group Psychotherapy* 18: 3–20.

Schilder, P. (1939) 'Results and problems of group psychotherapy in severe neurosis', *Mental Hygiene* 23: 87–98.

Schutz, W.C. (1958) *FIRO: A Three-dimensional Theory of Interpersonal Behaviour*, New York: Holdt Rinehart & Winston.

—— (1967) *Joy: Expanding Human Awareness*, New York: Grove Press.

Scott, J., Williams, J.M.G., and Beck, A.T. (eds) (1989) *Cognitive Therapy in Clinical Practice*, London: Routledge.

Scott, R.D. (1973) 'The treatment barrier', *British Journal of Medical Psychology* 46: 45–67.

Searles, H.F. (1979) *Countertransference and Related Subjects*, Madison, Conn.: International Universities Press.

Segal, H. (1964) *Introduction to the Work of Melanie Klein*, London: Heinemann.

Selvini-Palazzoli, M., Boscolo, L., Ceccin, G., and Prata, G. (1978) *Paradox and Counterparadox*, New York: Jason Aronson.

Seppala, K. and Jamsen, H. (1990) 'Psychotherapy as one form of rehabilitation provided by the Finnish Social Insurance Institution', *Psychoanalytic Psychotherapy* 4: 219–32.

Shaffer, J.B.P. and Galinsky, M.D. (1989) *Models of Group Therapy and Sensitivity Training*, 2nd edn, New Jersey: Prentice-Hall.

Shepherd, M. (1979) 'Psychoanalysis, psychotherapy, and health services', *British Medical Journal* 2: 1557–9.

Shepherd, M., Cooper, B., Brown, A.C., and Kalton, G. (1966) *Psychiatric Illness in General Practice*, London: Oxford University Press.

Sieghart, P. (1978) Statutory Registration of Psychotherapists: Report of a Professions Joint Working Party, Cambridge: Plumridge.

Sifneos, P.E. (1972) *Short-term Psychotherapy and Emotional Crisis*, Cambridge, Mass.: Harvard University Press.

Simon, R. (1972) 'Sculpting the family', *Family Process* 11: 49–57.

Skrine, R.L. (ed.) (1989) *Introduction to Psychosexual Medicine*, London: Montana Press.

Skynner, A.C.R. (1976) *One Flesh: Separate Persons*, London: Constable.

—— (1986) 'What is effective in group (and family) therapy', *Group Analysis*, 19: 5–24.

—— (1987) *Explorations with Families*, London: Methuen.

Skynner, A.C.R. and Cleese, J. (1983) *Families and How to Survive Them*, London: Methuen.

Skynner, A.C.R. and Brown, D.G. (1981) 'Referral of patients for psychotherapy', *British Medical Journal* 282: 1952–5.

Sloane, R.B., Staples, F.R., Cristol, A.H., Yorkston, N.J., and Whipple, K. (1975) *Psychotherapy versus Behaviour Therapy*, Cambridge, Mass. and London: Harvard University Press.

Smith, M.J., Glass, G.V., and Miller, T.I. (1980) *The Benefits of Psychotherapy*, Baltimore: Johns Hopkins University Press.

Speck, R. and Attneave, C. (1973) *Family Networks*, New York: Pantheon.

Springmann, R.R. (1970) 'The application of interpretations in a large group', *International Journal of Group Psychotherapy* 20: 333–41.

Stanton, A.H. and Schwartz, M.S. (1954) *The Mental Hospital: A Study of Institutional Participation in Psychiatric Illness and Treatment*, New York: Basic Books.

Stern, D.N. (1985) *The Interpersonal World of the Infant*, New York: Basic Books.

Stewart, H. (1972) 'Six months, fixed-term, once weekly psychotherapy: a report on twenty cases with follow-up', *British Journal of Psychiatry* 121: 425–35.

Storr, A. (1976) *The Dynamics of Creation*, Harmondsworth: Penguin Books.

—— (1979) *The Art of Psychotherapy*, London: Secker & Warburg.

Strachey, J. (1934) 'The nature of the therapeutic action of psychoanalysis', *International Journal of Psychoanalysis* 15: 127–59.

Sutherland, J.D. (1968) 'The consultant psychotherapist in the National Health Service: his role and training', *British Journal of Psychiatry* 114: 509–15.

—— (1976) 'Training in psychotherapy: some observations from the standpoint of analytical psychotherapy', pre-circulated paper, Association of University Teachers of Psychiatry Conference on Teaching of Psychotherapy, 24 September.

Symington, N. (1986) *The Analytic Experience: Lectures from the Tavistock*, London: Free Association Books.

Taylor, G.J. (1987) *Psychosomatic Medicine and Contemporary Psychoanalysis*, Madison, Wis.: International Universities Press.

Temperley, J. (1978) 'Psychotherapy in the setting of general medical practice', *British Journal of Medical Psychology* 51: 139–45.

Tuckman, B.W. (1965) 'Developmental sequences in small groups', *Psychological Bulletin* 63: 384–99.

Vernon, P.E. (1970) *Creativity*, Harmondsworth: Penguin Books.

REFERENCES

Wallerstein, R. (1969) 'Introduction to panel on psychoanalysis and psychotherapy', *International Journal of Psychoanalysis* 50: 117–26.

—— (1989) 'Psychoanalysis and psychotherapy: an historical perspective', *International Journal of Psychoanalysis* 70: 563–91.

Walrond-Skinner, S. (1976) *Family Therapy. The Treatment of Natural Systems*, London: Routledge & Kegan Paul.

Walton, H. (ed.) (1971) *Small Group Psychotherapy*, Harmondsworth: Penguin Books.

Watzlawick, P., Beavin, J.H., and Jackson, D.D. (1968) *Pragmatics of Human Communication*, London: Faber.

Whitaker, C. (1975) 'Psychotherapy of the Absurd', *Family Process* 14: 1–16.

Whitaker, D.S. (1985) *Using Groups to Help People*, London: Routledge & Kegan Paul.

Whitaker, D.S. and Lieberman, M. (1964) *Psychotherapy through the Group Process*, New York: Atherton.

Whiteley, J.S. and Gordon, J. (1979) *Group Approaches in Psychiatry*, London: Routledge & Kegan Paul, pp.77–83.

Whyte, L.L. (1962) *The Unconscious before Freud*, London: Tavistock Publications.

Winnicott, D.W. (1947) 'Hate in the countertransference', in D.W. Winnicott *Through Paediatrics to Psycho-Analysis*, London: Hogarth Press (1975).

—— (1960) 'Ego distortion in terms of true and false self', in D.W. Winnicott *The Maturational Processes and the Facilitating Environment*, London: Hogarth Press, 1965.

—— (1963) 'The development of the capacity for concern', in D.W. Winnicott *The Maturational Processes and the Facilitating Environment*, London: Hogarth Press, 1965.

—— (1965) *The Maturational Processes and the Facilitating Environment*, London: Hogarth Press.

—— (1971) *Playing and Reality*, London: Tavistock Publications.

—— (1975) *Through Paediatrics to Psycho-Analysis*, London: Hogarth Press.

Wolf, A. and Schwartz, E.K. (1962) *Psychoanalysis in Groups*, New York: Grune & Stratton.

Wynne, L.C., Ryckoff, L., Day, J., and Hirsch, S. (1958) 'Pseudomutuality in the family relations of schizophrenics', *Psychiatry* 21: 205–23.

Yalom, I.D. (1985) *The Theory and Practice of Group Psychotherapy*, 3rd edn, New York: Basic Books.

Yerkes, R.M. and Dodson, J.D. (1908) 'The relation of strength of stimulus to rapidity of habit-formation', *Journal of Comparative Neurology and Psychology* 18: 459–82.

Zinkin, L. (1983) 'Malignant mirroring', *Group Analysis* 16: 113–29.

NAME INDEX

SUBJECT INDEX

action techniques 166, 183
adolescence 39, 45, 84, 148, 186
Adult part of mind 6, 49, 50,
    55–9, 124
aggression 13, 33, 34–5, 104, 105,
    185
aggressor, identification with 25
agoraphobia 28–9, 54, 90, 119
alexithymic persons 28, 79
alienation 5, 69, 149
altruism 133–4
amnesia 26
amputation 25
anal phase 38, 41
analytic psychotherapy 5, 58–9,
    69, 101, 102, 109, 185; brief or
    focal 112, 114, 117–18, 204;
    definition 112; journals 69–70;
    patient's role 112–13; selection
    of 189; setting 110–12;
    supportive psychotherapy
    comparison 99–100;
    therapeutic process 103,
    114–18; therapist's role 62–3,
    103, 113–14; working
    alliance 58–9
animal behaviour:
    aggression 34–5;
    attachment 35; conflict 13;
    mothering 35; sexual
    roles 42–3; territorial 13, 34
Animus and Anima 102
anomie 150
anorexia nervosa 30, 75, 147

anxiety 6, 20–4, 135, 154, 172–3;
    depression and 22–3, learning
    and 86; management 179;
    origins 21, 44; psychotherapy
    and 86
Archetypes 102, 124
art therapy 80, 156
assessment 135, 195
association, free 11, 102, 110–11
assumptions, basic 121–2
atonement 84
attachment behaviour 35–6, 42,
    73
attention, selective 19–20
Autogenic Training 80, 173
autonomy 42, 45
auto-suggestion 10, 18
avoidance, phobic 28–9
awareness, dual levels of 50–1

basic assumptions 121–2
basic fault 108
bed-wetting 30, 53
behavioural psychotherapy 4,
    89–90, 109, 121, 146, 179, 188,
    203
belief system 121
bereavement 13, 22–3, 25, 92,
    104, 186
Bioenergetics 5, 76, 164, 172–3
birth trauma 174–5
bisexuality 43
body language 165, 172; see also
    communication (non-verbal)